# jQuery for Designers Beginner's Guide
## Second Edition

Design interactive websites to improve user experience
by using the popular JavaScript library

**Natalie MacLees**

**[PACKT]** open source✱
PUBLISHING   community experience distilled

BIRMINGHAM - MUMBAI

# jQuery for Designers Beginner's Guide
## Second Edition

First published: April 2012

Second edition: July 2014

Production reference: 1220714

Published by Packt Publishing Ltd.
Livery Place
35 Livery Street
Birmingham B3 2PB, UK.

ISBN 978-1-78328-453-5

www.packtpub.com

Cover image by Suresh Mogre (suresh.mogre.99@gmail.com)

# Credits

**Author**

Natalie MacLees

**Reviewers**

Olivier Pons

M. Ali Qureshi

Dan Wellman

**Acquisition Editor**

Vinay Argekar

**Content Development Editor**

Neeshma Ramakrishnan

**Technical Editors**

Pramod Kumavat

Pooja Nair

Mukul Pawar

**Copy Editors**

Janbal Dharmaraj

Deepa Nambiar

Alfida Paiva

**Project Coordinators**

Priyanka Goel

Danuta Jones

**Proofreaders**

Simran Bhogal

Maria Gould

Ameesha Green

**Indexers**

Hemangini Bari

Mehreen Deshmukh

Rekha Nair

Tejal Soni

Priya Subramani

**Graphics**

Valentina D'silva

**Production Coordinators**

Pooja Chiplunkar

Manu Joseph

**Cover Work**

Pooja Chiplunkar

# About the Author

**Natalie MacLees** is a frontend web developer and UI designer, and the founder and principal of the interactive agency Purple Pen Productions. She founded and runs the jQuery LA users' group and together with Noel Saw, she heads the Southern California WordPress user's group, organizing WordPress meetups, help sessions, and workshops. She was the lead organizer for WordCamp Los Angeles 2013 and 2014 and organized the first annual Website Weekend LA. She's also the founder of the Los Angeles chapter of Girl Develop It, bringing affordable and accessible coding classes to the community.

She makes periodic appearances on the WPwatercooler podcast and co-hosts the WP Unicorn Project podcast with Suzette Franck. She makes her online home at `nataliemac.com`.

Her obsession with the Web began when she bought her first computer in 1996 and promptly used it to build her first website. She spends the few moments she manages to be offline each day watching baseball, crafting, reading, baking, belly dancing, collecting Hello Kitty items, and avoiding avocados and olives at all costs.

# Acknowledgments

Gracious thanks first and foremost to John Resig and the rest of the jQuery team for creating and sharing such a useful and elegant library with the rest of us.

A big thank you to Marlene Angel, Ninno DePatrick, Ed Doolittle, Crystal Ehrlich, Suzette Franck, Teresina Goheen, LeHang Huynh, Michelle Kempner, Mark Tapio Kines, Chloë Nguyễn, Mario Noble, Joss Rogers, Noel Saw, Kimberly Wilkinson, and Tammy Wilson for their support, advice, and cheerleading—I couldn't ask for better friends.

Thank you to Beebe Lee and Brittany Brooks, my Purple Pen support team.

Thank you to my sisters, Stefanie Elder and Bethany MacLees, for being properly impressed that somebody wanted me to write a book. Thank you to my mom, Patricia Demby, and stepfather, John Demby, for being proud of me no matter what.

Thank you to all members of our local WordPress and jQuery communities including Dre Armeda, Lucy Beer, Andrew Behla, Glenn Bennett, Stephen Carnam, Jason Cosper, Ryan Cowles, Joe Chellman, Gregory Dahl, Greg Douglas, Brandon Dove, Chris Ford, Gregg Franklin, Megan Gray, Lane Halley, John Hawkins, Susie Karasic, Chris Lema, Paul Lumsdaine, Kari Leigh Marucchi, Karim Marucchi, Karen McCamy, Andrei Mignea, Troy Miles, Konstantin Obenland, Joseph Karr O'Connor, David Oshima, Sé Reed, Andy Roberts, Mike Schroder, Adam Silver, Verious Smith, Jason Tucker, Nathan Tyler, Alex Vasquez, Sarah Wefald, Steve Zehngut, Jeffery Zinn, and too many others to count or mention.

And finally, thank you to Diane Colella Jones for believing in me, even before I did.

# About the Reviewers

**Olivier Pons** is a developer who's been building websites since 1997. He's a teacher at IngeSup (École Supérieure d'Ingénierie Informatique; for more information visit `http://www.ingesup.com/` and `http://www.y-nov.com`), at the University of Sciences (IUT) in Aix-en-Provence/France, and École d'Ingénieurs des Mines de Gardanne, where he teaches HTML, CSS, jQuery/jQuery Mobile, PHP, MVC fundamentals, WordPress, Symfony, Linux basics, and advanced VIM techniques. He has already done some technical reviews, including the books *Ext JS 4 First Look, Packt Publishing* and *jQuery Mobile Web Development Essentials Second Edition, Packt Publishing,* among others. In 2011, he left a full-time job as a Delphi and PHP developer to concentrate on his own company, HQF Development (`http://hqf.fr`). He currently runs a number of websites, including `http://www.benativo.fr`, `http://www.inesushi.com`, `http://www.papdevis.fr`, and `http://olivierpons.fr`, his own web development blog. He works as a consultant, teacher, project manager, and sometimes a developer.

**M. Ali Qureshi**, who is a web developer based in Lahore, Pakistan, has been involved in web development in 2001. Having worked in a number of companies in different capacities, he is aware of how project goals are achieved efficiently. Ali founded PI Media (`http://parorrey.com`) in 2002 and has developed creative, interactive, and usable web solutions, making them a successful technology investment for clients. He has also worked on a number of successful products and authored WordPress plugins and themes and osCommerce and PrestaShop add-ons.

Apart from PI Media, Ali currently works as a software architect for E2ESP (`http://e2esp.com`)and ConvoSpark (`http://convospark.com`). He regularly makes contributions to the latest tips and trends in web design, PHP, WordPress and CMS development, Flash ActionScript, and Facebook App Development on his blog `http://parorrey.com/blog/`.

Ali has previously reviewed *jQuery Mobile Web Development Essentials, Packt Publishing*. When not working, he spends his time blogging and exploring new technologies. He is an avid sports fan and especially likes watching cricket. Pakistan and Australia are his favorite teams.

**Dan Wellman** is an author and software engineer based in the south coast of the UK. By day, he works for the Skype division at Microsoft bringing web-based audio and video calling to the world. By night, he writes books and tutorials for many online digital media outlets including Nettuts, Infinite Skills, and many others. He has written seven books so far, mostly centered on jQuery and jQuery UI.

# www.PacktPub.com

## Support files, eBooks, discount offers, and more

You might want to visit www.PacktPub.com for support files and downloads related to your book.

Did you know that Packt offers eBook versions of every book published, with PDF and ePub files available? You can upgrade to the eBook version at www.PacktPub.com and as a print book customer, you are entitled to a discount on the eBook copy. Get in touch with us at service@packtpub.com for more details.

At www.PacktPub.com, you can also read a collection of free technical articles, sign up for a range of free newsletters and receive exclusive discounts and offers on Packt books and eBooks.

http://PacktLib.PacktPub.com

Do you need instant solutions to your IT questions? PacktLib is Packt's online digital book library. Here, you can access, read and search across Packt's entire library of books.

### Why subscribe?

- Fully searchable across every book published by Packt
- Copy and paste, print and bookmark content
- On demand and accessible via web browser

### Free access for Packt account holders

If you have an account with Packt at www.PacktPub.com, you can use this to access PacktLib today and view nine entirely free books. Simply use your login credentials for immediate access.

# Table of Contents

# Preface

This book is intended for designers who have a basic understanding of HTML and CSS, but want to advance their skill set by learning basic JavaScript. It's not necessary that you understand JavaScript well. Even if you've never attempted to write JavaScript before, this book will guide you through the process of setting up basic JavaScript and accomplishing common tasks such as collapsing content, drop-down menus, and slideshows; all thanks to the jQuery library.

## What this book covers

*Chapter 1*, *Designer, Meet jQuery*, is an introduction to the jQuery library and JavaScript. You'll learn about jQuery's rise to fame, why it's so great for designers, and how it can help you create some fancy special effects without having to learn a lot of code. This chapter also includes a gentle and small introduction to JavaScript, progressive enhancement, and graceful degradation, and guides you through writing your first JavaScript code.

*Chapter 2*, *Enhancing Links*, walks you through some basic enhancements to links. You'll learn how to use jQuery to turn a list of links into a tabbed interface. Then, we'll take our first look at jQuery plugins where you'll learn to add custom tooltips to your links using the jQuery PowerTip plugin.

*Chapter 3*, *Making a Better FAQ Page*, will introduce you to collapsing and showing content, as well as creating simple animations and traversing an HTML document to move from one element to another. In this chapter, we'll set up a basic FAQ list, then work to progressively enhance it to make it easier for our site visitors to use.

*Chapter 4, Building an Interactive Navigation Menu*, guides you through setting up fully functioning and visually stunning drop-down and fly-out menus. We'll walk through the complex CSS required to get these types of menus working, use the Superfish plugin to fill in features missing from pure CSS solutions, and then take a look at customizing the appearance of the menus.

*Chapter 5, Showing Content in Lightboxes*, will walk you through showing photos and slideshows in a lightbox using the Colorbox jQuery plugin. Once we get the basics down, we'll also take a look at using the Colorbox plugin to create a fancy login, play a collection of videos, and even set up a single-page website gallery.

*Chapter 6, Creating Slideshows and Sliders*, walks you through setting up a simple crossfade slideshow without a plugin. Then, we'll take a look at the Basic Slider plugin to create a simple slideshow with controls. Finally, we'll take a look at the Cycle2 plugin, a flexible and customizable option that can be used to create sliders, slideshows, and carousels.

*Chapter 7, Working with Responsive Designs*, will dive deep into jQuery techniques for responsive designs. This includes fitting videos to the viewport, turning a drop-down menu into a responsive menu, and building a tiled layout for displaying image galleries.

*Chapter 8, Getting the Most from Images*, walks you through a few techniques to work with images in a more effective way. We'll take a look at lazy-loading images so that images are only loaded if our site visitor scrolls to them. We'll add an image zoom capability and finally, we'll take a look at creating fullscreen background images and slideshows for our pages.

*Chapter 9, Improving Typography*, shows you techniques to deal with typography effectively in responsive designs. We'll take a look at the FitText plugin to fit headlines to the width of the browser window, the SlabText plugin to create multiline headlines, the Lettering.js plugin to fine-tune kerning and to apply special effects, and finally, the ArcText plugin to set a text on a curve.

*Chapter 10, Displaying Data Beautifully*, takes a look at the important task of displaying data in an easy-to-understand way for your site visitors. First of all, we'll take a look at turning an ordinary HTML table into an interactive data grid with the DataTables plugin. Then, we'll look at turning HTML tables into charts and graphs that communicate our data clearly to our site visitors in an accessible and progressively enhanced way.

*Chapter 11, Reacting to Scrolling*, dives into the fun task of scrolling animations and parallax effects. We'll use the Scrollorama plugin to create a parallax effect, trigger animations on scroll, and activate a navigation bar that reacts to us scrolling down the page.

*Chapter 12, Improving Forms*, takes a look at how forms can be improved. This chapter walks you through setting up an HTML form properly using some of the latest HTML5 form elements. Then, we enhance the form by placing the cursor in the first field and validating the site visitor's form entries. Finally, we take a look at the FancyForm jQuery plugin, which allows us to style even the most stubborn and challenging form elements to achieve a consistent look for our forms across browsers.

# What you need for this book

You'll need a text editor to create HTML, CSS, and JavaScript files. Some great free options available are TextWrangler for Mac or Notepad++ for Windows. There are many other options available, and you are free to use your favorite text editor for any of the examples in this book. My personal favorite is Sublime Text, which is easy to work with and has a very nice feature set. If you haven't tried it before, I encourage you to download an evaluation copy for free to give it a try.

You'll also need a browser. My personal favorite is Google Chrome, which includes some really helpful built-in debugging tools for both CSS and JavaScript. Again, you are free to use your favorite browser for the examples in the book.

If you want to create images for your own designs, then Adobe Photoshop and Adobe Illustrator will be helpful, though they are not strictly necessary. All images needed to set up the examples used in this book are included in the sample code.

jQuery and jQuery plugins are being updated all the time. As new browsers are released with new support and capabilities, and as JavaScript, HTML, and CSS are further developed, new versions of jQuery and plugins are released to keep pace with the change. On one hand, this is a great news—jQuery and accompanying plugins get faster and more powerful all the time. On the other hand, it can be tough to keep up with all the changes. All versions of the plugins referenced were current at the time of writing the book, but you might find some differences when you work through the exercises. Plugin developers are usually very good at documenting the changes and updates, so don't be afraid to read through the documentation so you can understand what's changed and what adjustments you might need to make.

# Who this book is for

This book is for designers who know the basics of HTML and CSS, but want to extend their knowledge by learning how to use JavaScript and jQuery.

# Conventions

In this book, you will find several headings that appear frequently.

To give clear instructions of how to complete a procedure or task, we use:

## Time for action – heading

1. Action 1
2. Action 2
3. Action 3

Instructions often need some extra explanation so that they make sense, so they are followed with:

## What just happened?

This heading explains the working of tasks or instructions that you have just completed.

You will also find some other learning aids in the book, including:

## Pop quiz – heading

These are short multiple-choice questions intended to help you test your own understanding.

## Have a go hero – heading

These are practical challenges that give you ideas for experimenting with what you have learned.

You will also find a number of styles of text that distinguish between different kinds of information. Here are some examples of these styles and an explanation of their meaning.

Code words in text, database table names, folder names, filenames, file extensions, pathnames, dummy URLs, user input, and Twitter handles are shown as follows: "This returns the `<body>` tag wrapped in a `jQuery` object."

A block of code is set as follows:

```
var x = 5;
var y = 2;
var z = x + y;
```

When we wish to draw your attention to a particular part of a code block, the relevant lines or items are set in bold:

```
<head>
  <title>Practice Page</title>
  <link rel="stylesheet" href="styles/styles.css"/>
</head>
```

**New terms** and **important words** are shown in bold. Words that you see on the screen, in menus or dialog boxes for example, appear in the text like this: "Just go to your browser's **File** menu and choose **Save Page As...** or right-click on the page and select **Save As....**"

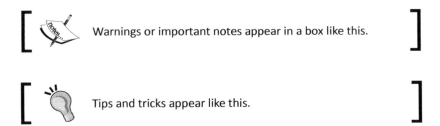

Warnings or important notes appear in a box like this.

Tips and tricks appear like this.

# Reader feedback

Feedback from our readers is always welcome. Let us know what you think about this book—what you liked or may have disliked. Reader feedback is important for us to develop titles that you really get the most out of.

To send us general feedback, simply send an e-mail to feedback@packtpub.com, and mention the book title through the subject of your message.

If there is a topic that you have expertise in and you are interested in either writing or contributing to a book, see our author guide on www.packtpub.com/authors.

# Customer support

Now that you are the proud owner of a Packt book, we have a number of things to help you to get the most from your purchase.

## Downloading the example code

You can download the example code files for all Packt books you have purchased from your account at http://www.packtpub.com. If you purchased this book elsewhere, you can visit http://www.packtpub.com/support and register to have the files e-mailed directly to you.

## Downloading the color images of this book

We also provide you a PDF file that has color images of the screenshots/diagrams used in this book. The color images will help you better understand the changes in the output. You can download this file from the following link:

```
https://www.packtpub.com/sites/default/files/downloads/4535OS_
ColoredImages.pdf
```

## Errata

Although we have taken every care to ensure the accuracy of our content, mistakes do happen. If you find a mistake in one of our books—maybe a mistake in the text or the code—we would be grateful if you would report this to us. By doing so, you can save other readers from frustration and help us improve subsequent versions of this book. If you find any errata, please report them by visiting http://www.packtpub.com/submit-errata, selecting your book, clicking on the **errata submission form** link, and entering the details of your errata. Once your errata are verified, your submission will be accepted and the errata will be uploaded to our website, or added to any list of existing errata, under the Errata section of that title.

## Piracy

Piracy of copyright material on the Internet is an ongoing problem across all media. At Packt, we take the protection of our copyright and licenses very seriously. If you come across any illegal copies of our works, in any form, on the Internet, please provide us with the location address or website name immediately so that we can pursue a remedy.

Please contact us at copyright@packtpub.com with a link to the suspected pirated material.

We appreciate your help in protecting our authors, and our ability to bring you valuable content.

## Questions

You can contact us at questions@packtpub.com if you are having a problem with any aspect of the book, and we will do our best to address it.

# 1

# Designer, Meet jQuery

*You might have heard quite a lot about jQuery over the past couple of years. It has quickly become one of the most popular code packages in use on the Web today. And you might have wondered what all the fuss was about.*

*Whether you've tried to figure out JavaScript before and have thrown up your hands in frustration or have been too intimidated to even give it a go, you'll find that jQuery is a wonderfully approachable and easy-to-understand way to get started with JavaScript.*

In this chapter, we will cover the following topics:

- What jQuery is and why it's ideal for designers
- Progressive enhancement and graceful degradation
- JavaScript basics
- Downloading jQuery
- Your first jQuery script

## What is jQuery?

jQuery is a JavaScript library. This means that it's a collection of reusable JavaScript code that accomplishes common tasks. Since web developers often find themselves solving the same problems over and over again, it makes sense to collect useful bits of code into a single package that can be included and used in any project. The creators of jQuery have written code to smoothly and easily handle the most common and most tedious tasks we want to accomplish with JavaScript, and they've ironed out all the little differences that need to be worked out to get the code working in different browsers.

It's important to remember that jQuery is JavaScript, not a language of its own. It has all the same rules and is written the same way as JavaScript. Don't let this frighten you away—jQuery really does make writing JavaScript much easier.

jQuery's official tagline is "write less, do more." This is an excellent and accurate description of the jQuery library—you can really accomplish amazing things in just a few lines of code. My own unofficial tagline for jQuery is "find stuff and do stuff to it", because finding and manipulating different parts of an HTML document is extremely tedious with raw JavaScript and requires lines and lines of code, while jQuery makes that same task painless and quick. Thanks to jQuery, you can not only quickly create a drop-down menu but you can also create one that's animated and works smoothly in many different browsers.

# Why is jQuery awesome for designers?

So what is it about jQuery that makes it so easy to learn, even if you have limited or no experience with JavaScript?

## It uses CSS selectors you already know

The first thing you'll often do in a jQuery script is select the elements you'd like to work with. For example, if you're adding some effects to a navigation menu, you'll start by selecting the items in the navigation menu. The tools you use for this job are selectors—ways to select certain elements on the page you want to work with.

jQuery borrowed selectors from CSS all the way up through CSS3, and they work even in browsers that don't support CSS3 selectors just yet.

Even though CSS offers a pretty robust set of selectors, jQuery adds a few more of its own to make accessing just the elements you need easy.

If you already know how to do things with CSS, such as make all the first-level headings blue or make all the links green and underlined, you'll easily learn how to select the elements you'd like to modify with jQuery.

## It uses HTML markup you already know

If you want to create new elements or modify existing elements with raw JavaScript, you better crack your knuckles and get ready to write lots and lots of code—and it won't make much sense either.

For example, if we wanted to append a paragraph to our page that says **This page is powered by JavaScript**, we need to first create the paragraph element, then assign the text that should be inside the paragraph to a variable as a string, and finally append the string to the newly created paragraph as a text node. And after all this, we'd still have to append the paragraph to the document. Phew! (Don't worry if you didn't understand all of that—it was just to illustrate how much work and code it requires to do something simple.)

With jQuery, adding a paragraph to the bottom of our page is as simple as the following line of code:

```
$('body').append('<p>This page is powered by jQuery.</p>');
```

That's right! You just append a bit of HTML directly to the body, and you're all set. I bet that without understanding JavaScript at all, you can read the line of code and grasp what it's doing. This code is appending a paragraph that reads This page is powered by jQuery. to the body of the HTML document.

# Impressive effects in just a few lines of code

You've got better things to do than sit and write lines and lines of code to add fade-in and fade-out effects. jQuery provides you with a few basic animations and the power to create your own custom animations right out of the box. Let's say, we wanted to make an image fade into the page; we will use the following code line for this:

```
$('img').fadeIn();
```

Yep, that's it! We use one little line of code in which I select the image and then tell it to fade in. Later in the chapter, you'll see exactly where this line of code will go in your HTML page.

# Huge plugin library available

As I said earlier, web developers often find themselves solving the same problems over and over again. You're most likely not the first person who wants to build a rotating image slideshow, an animated drop-down menu, or a news ticker.

jQuery has an impressively large library of scripts available freely—scripts to create tooltips, slideshows, news tickers, drop-down menus, date pickers, character counters, and on and on. You don't need to learn how to build all these things from scratch; you just have to learn how to harness the power of plugins. We'll be covering some of the most popular jQuery plugins in this book, and you'll be able to apply what you've learned to use any plugin in the jQuery plugin library.

# Great community support

jQuery is an open source project, which means that it's being collectively built by a team of super-smart JavaScript coders and is freely available for anyone to use. The success or failure of an open source project often depends on the community behind the project, and jQuery has a large and active community that supports it.

This means that jQuery itself is being constantly improved and updated. And on top of that, there are thousands of developers out there who are creating new plugins, adding features to existing plugins, and offering support and advice to newcomers. You'll find new tutorials, blog posts, and podcasts on a daily basis for just about anything you want to learn.

# JavaScript basics

In this section, we're going to cover a few basics of JavaScript that will make things go more smoothly. We're going to look at a little bit of code and step through how it works. Don't be intimidated; this will be quick and painless, and then we'll be ready to get on with actually doing something with jQuery.

## Progressive enhancement and graceful degradation

There are a few different schools of thought when it comes to enhancing your HTML pages with JavaScript. Let's talk about some of the things we should consider before we dive into the cool stuff.

Progressive enhancement and graceful degradation are essentially two sides of the same coin. They both mean that our page with its impressive JavaScript animations and special effects will still work for users who have less capable browsers or devices. Graceful degradation means that we create our special effect and then make sure it fails gracefully if JavaScript is not enabled. If we take the progressive enhancement approach, we'll first build out a bare bones version of our page that works for everyone, and then enhance it by adding our JavaScript special effects. I tend to favor the progressive enhancement approach.

Why should we care about users who don't have JavaScript enabled? Well, some of the Web's biggest users and search engines have either no JavaScript capabilities or very limited JavaScript capabilities. When search engines are crawling and indexing your pages, they will not have access to all of the content and features that are being added to your pages by JavaScript. This is often referred to as dynamic content, and it can't be reliably indexed or found by search engines if it can't be reached with JavaScript disabled.

We're also in an era where we can no longer count on users who access the web pages we build with a conventional desktop or laptop computer. We're quick to think of smartphones and tablets as the next candidates, and while they are very popular, they still account for a tiny fraction of Internet access. People are accessing the Web from gaming consoles, feature phones, e-book readers, internet-enabled televisions, a huge variety of mobile devices, and dozens of other ways. Not all of these devices are capable of executing JavaScript, and some of them don't even have color screens! Your number one priority should be making sure that your content is available to anyone who asks for it, no matter what device they happen to be using.

# Gotta keep 'em separated

To accomplish this task of making our content available to as wide an audience as possible, we have to think of our web pages in three separate and distinct layers: content, presentation, and behavior.

## Content

Content is the meat of our web page. It's the text or audio or video content that we're most interested in presenting on our page; so this is where we start.

Mark up your content with clean and simple HTML code. Use HTML elements the way they were intended to be used. Mark up headings with heading tags, paragraphs with paragraph tags, lists with list tags, and save tables for tabular data.

Browsers have built-in styles for these basic HTML tags—headings will be of a larger type and will probably look bold. Lists will have bullets or numbers. It might not look very fancy, but it's readable and accessible to anyone.

## Presentation

The presentation layer is where we start to get fancy. This is where we introduce CSS and start applying our own styles to the content we've created. As we style our page, we might find that we have to go back into our HTML code and add some new containers and markup to make things such as multicolumn layouts possible, but we should still strive to keep our markup as simple and as straightforward as we can.

## Behavior

Once our page has all of our content properly marked up and is styled to look the way we like, we can think about adding in some interactive behavior. This is where JavaScript and jQuery come in. This layer includes animations, special effects, AJAX, and so on.

# Designer, Meet JavaScript

JavaScript is a powerful and complex language. You can work with it for 10 years and still have more to learn. However, don't let that frighten you away. You don't have to know everything about it to be able to take advantage of what it has to offer. In fact, you just have to get down to a few basics.

This section introduces some JavaScript basics and JavaScript syntax. Don't be scared away by that developer word, syntax. Syntax just means the rules for writing a language, much like we have rules of grammar to write English.

## Variables

Let's start with something simple:

```
var x = 5;
```

This is a "sentence" in JavaScript. In English, we end a sentence with a period or maybe a question mark or an exclamation mark. In JavaScript, we end our sentences with a semicolon.

In this sentence, we're creating a variable (var), x. A variable is just a container for holding something. In this case, x holds the number 5.

We can do math with JavaScript as shown in the following code snippet:

```
var x = 5;
var y = 2;
var z = x + y;
```

Just like algebra, our variable z now holds the value of the number 7 for us.

However, variables can also hold things other than numbers. For example:

```
var text = 'A short phrase';
```

Here, we've named our variable text and it's holding some alphabetical characters for us. This is called a **string**. A string is a set of alphanumeric characters.

## Objects

Objects might be the hardest thing for a newcomer in JavaScript to grasp, but that's often because we overthink it, convinced it has to be more complicated than it actually is.

An object is just what it sounds like—a thing, anything, just as a car, a dog, and a coffee maker are objects..

Objects have properties and methods. A property is a characteristic of an object. For example, a dog could be tall or short, have pointy ears or floppy ears, and could be brown or black or white. All of these are properties of a dog. A method is something an object can do. For example, a dog can run, bark, walk, and eat.

Let's take my dog, Magdelena von Barkington, as an example to see how we'd deal with objects, properties, and methods in JavaScript:

```
var dog;
```

Here, I've created a variable `dog` that I'm using as a container to hold my dog, mostly because I don't want to have to type out her full name each time I refer to her in my code. Now, let's say I wanted to get my dog's color:

```
var color = dog.color;
```

I created a container called `color` and I'm using it to hold my dog's color property—`color` is now equal to my dog's color.

Now, I've trained my dog very well and I'd like her to roll over. The following line of code shows how I'd tell her to roll over with JavaScript:

```
dog.rollOver();
```

The `rollOver()` method is something that my dog can do. After my dog rolls over, I might like to reward her with a treat. The following line of code shows how my dog eats a treat with JavaScript:

```
dog.eat('bacon');
```

Wait, what's going on here? Let's take it one step at a time. We have `dog`, which we know is a container for my dog, Magdelena von Barkington. We have the `eat` method, which we know is something that my dog can do. However, my dog can't just eat—she has to eat "something". We can use some extra code inside the parentheses to say what it is that she is eating. In JavaScript, we call the code inside the parentheses an **argument**. In this case, my lucky dog is eating bacon. So in JavaScript, we'd describe this bit of code by saying we are passing `bacon` to the `eat()` method of the `dog` object.

So you see, objects aren't so difficult—they're just things. Properties are like adjectives—they describe traits or characteristics of an object. Methods are like verbs—they describe actions that an object can do.

# Functions

A function is a bit of reusable code that tells JavaScript to do something. For example, have a look at the following code:

```
function saySomething() {
  alert('Something!');
}
```

This function tells JavaScript to pop up an alert box that says `Something!`. We always start a function with the word `function` and then we name our function. This is followed by a set of parentheses and a set of curly brackets. The lines of instruction go inside the curly brackets.

Now, my `saySomething()` function won't actually do anything until it's called, so I need to add a line of code to call my function, as follows:

```
function saySomething() {
  alert('Something!');
}
saySomething();
```

You might wonder what those parentheses are for. Do you remember how we could pass arguments to a method by including them in parentheses? We used the following line of code:

```
dog.eat('bacon');
```

In this case, we passed bacon to say what the dog was eating. We can do the same thing for functions. In fact, methods actually are functions; they're just functions that are specialized to describe what an object can do. Let's look at how we modify our `saySomething()` function so that we can pass text to it, as follows:

```
function saySomething(text) {
  alert(text);
}
saySomething('Hello there!');
```

In this case, when I wrote the `saySomething()` function, I just left a generic container in place. This is called a **parameter**. In JavaScript, we'd say the `saySomething()` function takes a text parameter, as I've called my parameter `text`. I chose the name `text` because it's a short and handy descriptor of what we're passing in. We can pass in any bit of text to this function, so `text` is an appropriate name. You can name your parameter anything you'd like, but you'll make your code easier to read and understand if you apply some sensible rules when you're selecting names for your parameters. A parameter behaves very much like a variable—it's just a container for something.

# Downloading jQuery and getting set up

We're ready to include the magic of jQuery into a project, but first, we need to download it and figure out how to get it attached to an HTML page. Here, we'll walk through getting a sample HTML file started and all the associated files and folders we'll need to work through a sample project. Once we're finished, you can use these files as a template for all the future exercises in the book.

## Time for action – downloading and attaching jQuery

Earlier, I described the three layers of an HTML document: content, presentation, and behavior. Let's take a look at how to set up our files in these three layers, as follows:

1. First, let's set up a folder on your hard drive to hold all of your work as you work through the lessons in this book. Find a good place on your hard drive and create a folder called jQueryForDesigners.

2. Create a folder called images in the jQueryForDesigners folder to hold any images we'll use.

3. Next, create a folder called styles. We'll use this folder to hold any CSS files we create. Inside the styles folder, create an empty CSS file called styles.css.

   The styles represent our presentation layer. We'll keep all of our styles in this file to keep them separate.

 There is a standard CSS style sheet that we'll start with for each exercise in this book, which applies some basic colors and typography. You'll find the CSS code that should be included with all examples in the sample code for the book.

4. Next, create a folder called scripts to hold our JavaScript and jQuery code. Inside the scripts folder, create an empty JavaScript file called scripts.js.

   The JavaScript we write here represents our behavior layer. We'll keep all of our JavaScript in this folder to keep it separate from the other layers.

5. Now, inside the jQueryForDesigners folder, create a new HTML page—very basic with the following code:

```
<!DOCTYPE html>
<html>
  <head>
    <title>Practice Page</title>
  </head>
  <body>
```

```
    <!-- Our content will go here -->
  </body>
</html>
```

Save this file as `index.html`. The HTML file is our content layer and is arguably the most important layer, as it's likely to be the reason site visitors are coming to our website at all.

**6.** Next, we'll attach the CSS and JavaScript files that we created to our HTML page. In the head section, add a line of code to include the CSS file, as follows:

```
<head>
  <title>Practice Page</title>
  <link rel="stylesheet" href="styles/styles.css"/>
</head>
```

Then, head down to the bottom of the HTML file, just before the closing `</body>` tag, and include the JavaScript file as follows:

```
  <script src="scripts/scripts.js"></script>
  </body>
</html>
```

As these files are just empty placeholders, attaching them to your HTML page won't have any effect. However, now, we have a place to write our CSS code and JavaScript that will come handy when we're ready to dive into an exercise.

It's perfectly fine to self-close a `<link>` element, but a `<script>` element always needs a separate closing `</script>` tag. Without it, your JavaScript won't work.

The following screenshot is what my folder looks like at this point:

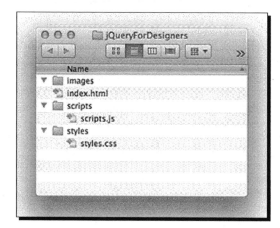

**7.** Now, we have to include jQuery in our page. Head over to `http://jquery.com` and hit the **Download jQuery** button.

This will take you to the **Download** page where you'll see that you've got quite a few options to download jQuery these days.

As of April 2013, you officially have two versions of jQuery to choose from. In developer speak, these versions are called **branches**. To easily understand which branch you should use, keep this rule in mind. The 2.x branch of jQuery no longer has support for **Internet Explorer (IE)** 6, 7, or 8. If you're working on a project that will need to work in these older versions of IE, then you'll need to work with the 1.x branch of jQuery. If you don't need to support these older versions of IE, then you can choose to work with the 2.x branch. All the code files in this book will use the 2.x branch, since my philosophy with web development is to look forward, not back. However, all of the code samples will work fine with either the 1.x branch or the 2.x branch of jQuery.

Note that the jQuery team will be discontinuing support for IE6 and IE7, even in the 1.x branch, with the jQuery 1.12 release in 2014.

On the **Download** page, in the section for your selected branch, you'll see several files available for download: a compressed version and an uncompressed version, a map file, and release notes. The only file we need to be concerned with is the compressed, production version.

**Downloading the example code**

You can download the example code files for all Packt books you have purchased from your account at `http://www.packtpub.com`. If you purchased this book elsewhere, you can visit `http://www.packtpub.com/support` and register to have the files e-mailed directly to you.

8. Clicking on the link for the compressed, production version of your selected branch of jQuery will open the production jQuery file in your browser window, and it looks a bit scary, as shown in the following screenshot:

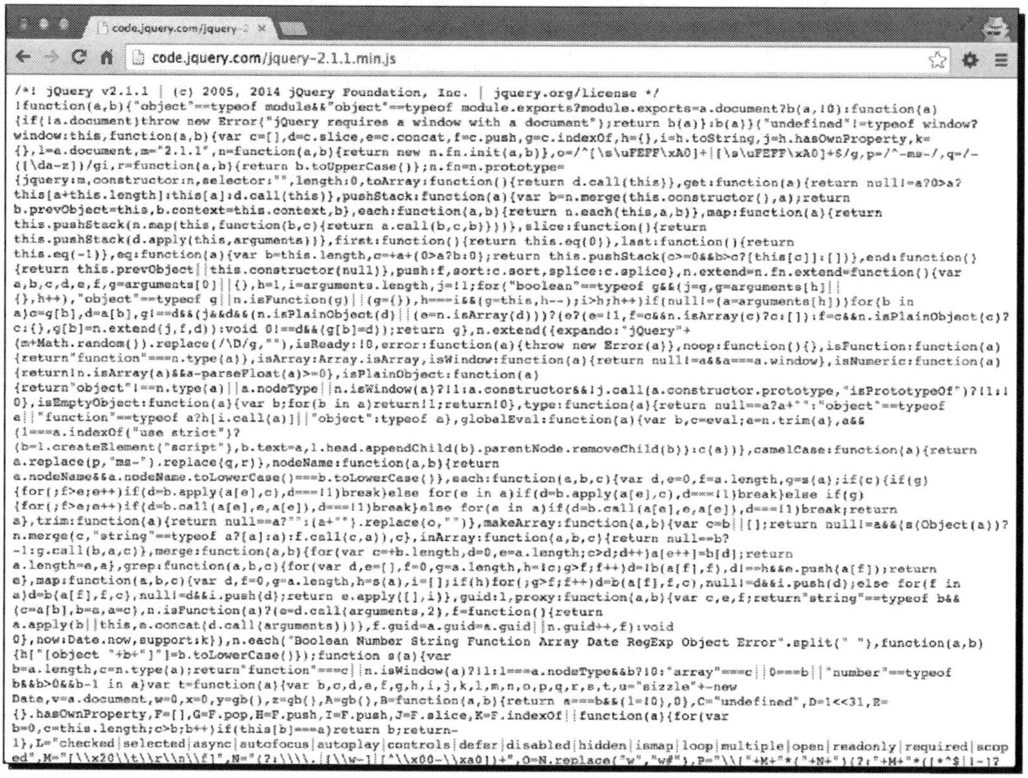

9. Don't worry, you don't have to read it and you definitely don't have to understand it. Just go to your browser's **File** menu and choose **Save Page As...** or right-click on the page and select **Save As...**. Then, save the file to your hard drive, inside the `scripts` folder we created. By default, the script will have the version number in the filename. I'm going to go ahead and rename the file to `jquery.js` to keep things simple.

10. Now, we just have to include our jQuery script in our page—just like we included our empty JavaScript file. Go to the bottom of your practice HTML file, just before the `<script>` tag we created earlier, and add a line to include jQuery, as follows:

```
<script src="scripts/jquery.js"></script>
<script type="text/javascript"
  src="scripts/scripts.js"></script>
</body>
</html>
```

You won't notice any changes to your HTML page; jQuery doesn't do anything on its own. It just makes its magic available for you to use.

## What just happened?

We learned how to set up our files and folders to work through the practice exercises in this book. We also learned how to select and download the correction version of jQuery and get it attached to our HTML page. Now we're all set to start coding pages and adding jQuery magic to them.

## Pop quiz – setting up a new project

Q1. Which of the following is the content layer of a project?

1. HTML
2. CSS
3. JavaScript

# Another option for using jQuery

There is nothing wrong with downloading and using your own copy of jQuery, but you do have another option available that can help to improve the performance of your websites. That's to use a CDN-hosted copy of jQuery.

In case you don't know, a **CDN** is a **Content Delivery Network**. The premise behind a CDN is that files download faster from servers that are physically closer to a site visitor's location. So, for example, if you're in Los Angeles, California, a copy of jQuery that's on a server in Phoenix, Arizona will download faster than a copy that's on a server in New York City. To help this along, a CDN has a copy of the same file on lots of different servers all around the world. Each time a site visitor requests a file, the CDN smartly routes their request to the closest available server, helping to improve response times and overall site performance.

It won't make much of a difference for the relatively simple examples and pages that we'll build in this book, but for a public-facing website, using a CDN-hosted copy of jQuery can make a noticeable difference. There are a few options out there, but the most popular by far is Google's Ajax API CDN. You can get the information on the latest version available and the correct URL at `http://code.google.com/apis/libraries/devguide.html#jquery`.

There are several CDN-hosted copies of jQuery available. You can find out about these on jQuery's **Download** page (http://jquery.com/download/). Just scroll down to the section titled *Using jQuery with a CDN* to find all your current options.

If you'd like to use the Google CDN-hosted version of jQuery in your files, it's as simple as adding the following line of code to your HTML file, instead of the line we used in the previous section to include jQuery:

```
<script src
 ="http://ajax.googleapis.com/ajax/libs/jquery/2.1.1/jquery.min.js">
 </script>
```

No downloading the file, no saving your own copy; you can just point your `<script>` tag directly at the copy of jQuery stored on Google's servers. Google will then take care of sending jQuery to your site visitors from the closest available server. Not only that, but as Google's CDN is so popular, there's a good chance that your site visitor has already visited another site that's also using a Google CDN-hosted copy of jQuery and that they'll have jQuery cached in their browser. This means that your site visitor won't have to download jQuery at all—it's already saved in their browser and available to be used. How's that for improving performance?

# Your first jQuery script

Alright, now that you understand a few basic things about JavaScript and know how to get your files and folders set up to build a sample exercise, let's build our first simple example page and make it do something fancy with jQuery.

## Time for action – getting ready for jQuery

Perform the following steps to start with your first jQuery script:

*1.* Set up your files and folders just like we did in the previous exercise. Inside the `<body>` tags of the HTML document, add a heading and a paragraph, as follows:

```
<body>
<div class="content">
  <h1>My First jQuery</h1>
  <p>Thanks to jQuery doing fancy JavaScript stuff is easy.</p>
</div>
</body>
```

Feel free to add some CSS code to the `styles.css` file in the `styles` folder. Style this however you'd like.

**2.** Next, open up that empty `scripts.js` file we created earlier and add this bit of script to the file:

```
$(document).ready();
```

## What just happened?

Let's take this statement one thing at a time—first, the dollar sign. Really? What's this doing in JavaScript?

The `$` here is just a variable—that's all. It's a container for the jQuery function. Remember how I said we might use a variable to save ourselves a few keystrokes? The clever writers of jQuery have provided the `$` variable to save us from having to write out jQuery every time we want to use it. The following code does the same thing that the preceding script did:

```
jQuery(document).ready();
```

Except that it takes longer to type. jQuery uses the `$` sign as its short name because it's unlikely that you'd call a variable `$` on your own as it's an uncommon character. Using an uncommon character reduces the chance that there will be some sort of conflict between some other JavaScript being used on a page and the jQuery library.

So, in this case, we're passing `document` to the `jQuery` (or `$`) function because we want to select our HTML document as the target of our code. When we call the `jQuery` function, we get a `jQuery` object. In JavaScript, we'd say that the `jQuery` function returns a `jQuery` object. The `jQuery` object is what gives the `jQuery` library its power. The entire `jQuery` library exists to give the `jQuery` object lots of properties and methods that make our lives easier. We don't have to deal with lots of different sorts of objects; we just have to deal with the `jQuery` object.

The `jQuery` object has a method called `ready`. In this case, the `ready` method will be called when the document is loaded into the browser and is ready for us to work with. We can pass a function to the `ready` method to say what should happen. So `$(document).ready()` just indicates when the document is ready.

# Adding a paragraph

Now, we're all set to do something when the document is ready, but what is it that we'll do? Let's add a new paragraph to our page.

# Time for action – adding a new paragraph

Perform the following steps to add a new paragraph to our page:

1. We need to tell jQuery what to do when the document is ready. Since we want something to happen, we'll pass in a function like this:

```
$(document).ready(function(){
  // Our code will go here
});
```

We'll write what's going to happen inside this function.

What about the line that starts with //? That's one way of writing a comment in JavaScript. The // sign tells JavaScript to ignore everything else on that line because it's a comment. Adding comments to your JavaScript is a great way to help yourself keep track of what's happening on what line. It's also great for helping along other developers who might need to work on your code. It can even be great for helping yourself if you haven't looked at your own code in a few months.

2. Next, we'll add what we want the function to do as soon as the document is ready:

```
$(document).ready(function(){
  $('body').
    append('<p>This paragraph was added with jQuery!</p>');
});
```

## What just happened?

Our new function is using the jQuery function again, as follows:

```
$('body')
```

Remember I said that jQuery uses CSS selectors to find stuff? This is how we use those CSS selectors. In this case, we want the `<body>` tag, so we'll going to pass body to the jQuery function. This returns the `<body>` tag wrapped in a jQuery object. Handily, the jQuery object has an append method that lets us add something new to the page, as follows:

```
$('body').append();
```

All we have to do is call the append method and pass in the paragraph we want to add to the page. In quotes, pass a line of HTML:

```
$('body').append('<p>This paragraph was added with jQuery!</p>');
```

That's it! Now, when you load the page in a browser, you'll see the heading followed by two paragraphs—jQuery will add the second paragraph as soon as the document is loaded in the browser. The following screenshot shows the page loaded in the browser:

## Have a go hero – adding more content

Try adding the following bit of HTML to the bottom of the document with jQuery:

```
<div><p>This was added with jQuery too!</p></div>
```

Style it with CSS so that it stands out.

# Summary

In this chapter, you have been introduced to the jQuery library and have learned a few things about it. We covered a bit of JavaScript basics and then we learned how to set up our files and folders for the exercises in this book. Finally, we set up a simple HTML page that took advantage of jQuery to add some dynamic content. Now, let's take a look at how we can make links more powerful with jQuery by creating tabs and custom tooltips.

# 2
# Enhancing Links

*We take links for granted these days, but the truth of the matter is that the humble link revolutionized documents and made the Web as we know it today possible. Being able to link a reader directly to another document or to another place within a document was not possible before.*

*For this reason, you can say that hyperlinks are the backbone of the Internet—without them, search engines wouldn't be possible, nor would most websites. Let's take a look at some of the ways we can make links work even harder for us.*

In this chapter, we will cover the following topics:

◆ How to turn a list of links into simple tabs

◆ How to customize tooltips

## Simple tabs

If we have a large amount of information to present that might not be relevant to all site visitors, we can compress the amount of space the information takes by hiding selected bits of information until the user requests it. One of the most common ways of making all the information available but hidden until requested is **tabs**. Tabs echo the real-world example of a tabbed notebook or labeled folders in a filing cabinet, and are easy for site visitors to understand. Believe it or not, they're also easy to implement with jQuery.

The following screenshot gives us an idea of what our page will look like after we've created our tabs:

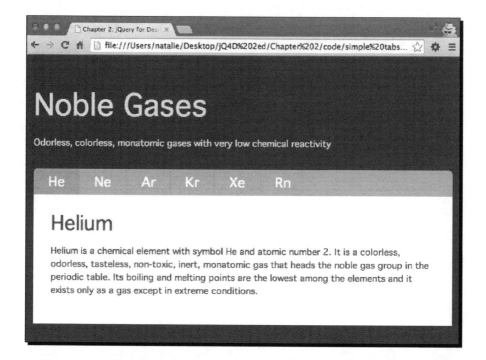

# Time for action – creating simple tabs

Perform the following steps to turn a list of links into tabs:

*1.*   We'll get started with our basic HTML file and associated folders, like we created in *Chapter 1, Designer, Meet jQuery*. Inside the `<body>` tag, we'll start by setting up a simple example that will work even for users with JavaScript disabled. We'll put a list of anchor links to different areas of the page at the top and then wrap each of our content sections in a `div` block with an ID, as shown in the following code:

```
<header class="content">
  <h1>Noble Gases</h1>
  <p>Odorless, colorless, monatomic gases with
    very low chemical reactivity</p>
</header>

<ul id="tabs">
  <li><a href="#he">He</a></li>
  <li><a href="#ne">Ne</a></li>
  <li><a href="#ar">Ar</a></li>
```

```
    <li><a href="#kr">Kr</a></li>
    <li><a href="#xe">Xe</a></li>
    <li><a href="#rn">Rn</a></li>
</ul>

<div id="he">
  <h2>Helium</h2>
  <p>Info about helium here.</p>
</div>

<div id="ne">
  <h2>Neon</h2>
  <p>Info about neon here.</p>
</div>

<div id="ar">
  <h2>Argon</h2>
  <p>Info about argon here.</p>
</div>

<div id="kr">
  <h2>Krypton</h2>
  <p>Info about krypton here.</p>
</div>

<div id="xe">
  <h2>Xenon</h2>
  <p>Info about xenon here.</p>
</div>

<div id="rn">
  <h2>Radon</h2>
  <p>Info about radon here.</p>
</div>
```

Note that we added an id value of tabs to the list of links. This will make it easy to select the list with CSS for styling and with JavaScript to create the tab behavior.

If you view this HTML in a browser, you'll see a list of links at the top of the page, which when clicked on the ID, jumps down to the appropriate section of the page so that the site visitor can easily find each section without scrolling on their own. We've basically created a clickable table of contents for our page.

2. Next, we want to style our page a bit so that it looks nice for those site visitors who have JavaScript disabled. We only want these styles to apply to the page if JavaScript is disabled, so let's learn a handy technique. Add a class of jsOff to the <body> tag, as follows:

```
<body class="jsOff">
```

Now, you can reference this class in your CSS file to write styles for site visitors who have JavaScript disabled, using the following code:

```
.jsOff ul#tabs {
  line-height: 1.5;
  margin: 1.125em 0;
}
```

Feel free to experiment with your CSS file and style the table of contents the way you want like for the no-JavaScript case.

3. Now, we want to enhance this for our site visitors that have JavaScript enabled. We'll start by adding a class name to each of the <div> blocks that contain our sections of content—this will make it easier for us to select just the pieces of the page we want with jQuery and will also make it easier for us to further style our tabs with CSS. Have a look at the following code:

```
<ul id="tabs">
  <li><a href="#he">He</a></li>
  <li><a href="#ne">Ne</a></li>
  <li><a href="#ar">Ar</a></li>
  <li><a href="#kr">Kr</a></li>
  <li><a href="#xe">Xe</a></li>
  <li><a href="#rn">Rn</a></li>
</ul>

<div id="he" class="content tab-section">
  <h2>Helium</h2>
  <p>Info about helium here.</p>
</div>

<div id="ne" class="content tab-section">
  <h2>Neon</h2>
  <p>Info about neon here.</p>
</div>

<div id="ar" class="content tab-section">
  <h2>Argon</h2>
  <p>Info about argon here.</p>
</div>
```

```
<div id="kr" class="content tab-section">
  <h2>Krypton</h2>
  <p>Info about krypton here.</p>
</div>

<div id="xe" class="content tab-section">
  <h2>Xenon</h2>
  <p>Info about xenon here.</p>
</div>

<div id="rn" class="content tab-section">
  <h2>Radon</h2>
  <p>Info about radon here.</p>
</div>
```

Here, we used the class of `content` to apply document-wide styles to the tabbed sections. We also added the `tab-section` class for styles specific to just the tabbed sections. The following screenshot shows what we've got so far:

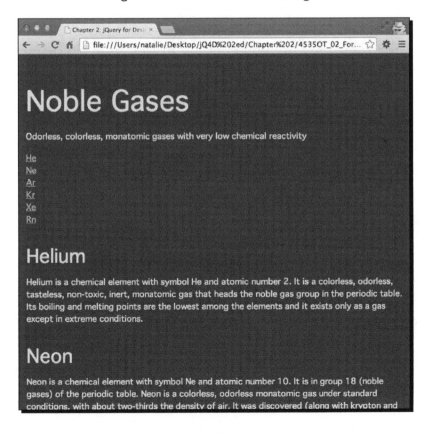

4. Now, we'll go back to the `jsOff` class we added to the `<body>` tag. Remember how we wrote some CSS styles that applied only when our site visitor has JavaScript disabled? Now, we can use some jQuery magic to change this class for site visitors who have JavaScript enabled.

   jQuery makes it easy for us to add or remove classes from elements. In this case, we want to remove the `jsOff` class from the `<body>` section. To do this, we'll use jQuery's `removeClass()` method. Then, we will add a new class called `jsOn` to the `<body>` section. To do this, we'll use jQuery's `addClass` method.

   Open the `scripts.js` file inside your `scripts` folder and write a document ready statement, as shown in the following code, just like we did in *Chapter 1, Designer, Meet jQuery*:

   ```
   $(document).ready(function(){
      // Our code will go here
   });
   ```

   Inside the document ready statement, write the following code to remove the `jsOff` class:

   ```
   $(document).ready(function(){
      $('body').removeClass('jsOff');
   });
   ```

   Next, we need to write the following code to add the new `jsOn` class:

   ```
   $(document).ready(function(){
      $('body').removeClass('jsOff');
      $('body').addClass('jsOn');
   });
   ```

   This code will work, but jQuery actually makes it a little bit easier for us. We can write less code! As we're working with the `<body>` element both times, we can actually write both of these methods on one line, as follows:

   ```
   $(document).ready(function(){
      $('body').removeClass('jsOff').addClass('jsOn');
   });
   ```

   Now we can use the `jsOn` class to write CSS just for those site visitors who have JavaScript enabled.

5. We'll make use of the new `jsOn` class to hide all of our `tab-section` `<div>` elements. Inside the `styles.css` file, add the following CSS code to hide all the sections as soon as our page loads:

   ```
   .jsOn .tab-section {
      display: none;
   }
   ```

Now, when we reload the page, we'll only see our table of contents as shown in the following screenshot:

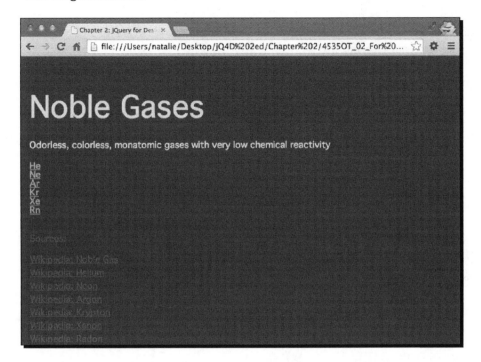

6.   Now, let's write some CSS styles to get the list of links to look like tabs. Open the
     `styles.css` file that's inside your `styles` folder and add some CSS styles.
     As we want these styles to be applied only for site visitors with JavaScript enabled,
     we'll use the `jsOn` class in our selectors. Feel free to customize the CSS code to suit
     your own taste. I have customized it as follows:

```css
.jsOn ul#tabs {
  background: #a0d468;
  border-top-left-radius: 7px;
  border-top-right-radius: 7px;
  font-size: 1.5em;
  margin: 1.5em 0 0 0;
}

.jsOn ul#tabs:after {
  clear: both;
  content: '';
  display: table;
}
```

```
.jsOn ul#tabs li {
  display: block;
  float: left;
}

.jsOn ul#tabs a {
  border-right: 1px solid #8cc152;
  color: white;
  display: block;
  padding: 0.5em 1.125em;
  text-decoration: none;
}

.jsOn ul#tabs li:first-child a {
  border-top-left-radius: 7px;
}

.jsOn ul#tabs a:hover {
  background: #8cc152;
}

.jsOn .tab-section {
  background: white;
  color: #444;
  padding: 2em;
}

.jsOn .tab-section h2 {
  margin-top: 0;
}
```

Note that this sample CSS uses several CSS3 properties that, at the time of publication, are not supported by all browsers. Feel free to add in vendor prefixes to get these styles working in more current browsers if you wish. Have a look at the following screenshot:

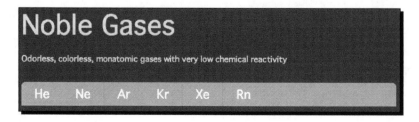

**Browser support for new features**

If you're curious to know what browser support is available for different new CSS3 properties you might like to use in your CSS, a great resource to check out is http://caniuse.com. It's kept up to date and will give you detailed information about which browsers support each new property.

**7.** Next, let's get our tabs working. When a site visitor clicks on a tab, we want to show the appropriate section of content. First, we have to select the element or elements that we want to work with. In this case, we want to do something when our site visitor clicks on a link inside the `<ul>` element with the `id` value of `tabs`. We can select these links as follows:

```
$(document).ready(function(){
  $('body').removeClass('jsOff').addClass('jsOn');

  $('#tabs a')
});
```

**8.** Now, we've got the links and we want to do something when these links are clicked. jQuery makes this easy for us with the `on()` method, which looks like the following code snippet:

```
$(document).ready(function(){
  $('body').removeClass('jsOff').addClass('jsOn');

  $('#tabs a').on();
});
```

In this case, we want to do something when our site visitor clicks on one of the tab links. In JavaScript, the click is called an **event**. There are all sorts of events: clicking on an element, moving the mouse over an element, changing the text in a form field, submitting a form, and so on. We just have to tell jQuery which event we're working with. In this case, it's `click`:

```
$('#tabs a').on('click');
```

Now, jQuery knows that we want to do something when the user clicks on a tab link, but we haven't said what we want to do. We can say what should happen with a function, as follows:

```
$('#tabs a').on('click', function(){
  // Event code will go here
});
```

In JavaScript, this function is called an **event handler**. That makes sense, right? It's the code that handles an event.

**9.** Remember how the page worked when JavaScript was disabled? The list of links appeared at the top of the page, and clicking on one of them would jump to the corresponding section of the page. As we're going to hide and show those bits of content depending on which link was clicked, we need to make sure that we cancel the default action—we don't want the page to jump. The following code is how we cancel the browser's default reaction to an event:

```
$('#tabs a').on('click', function(e){
  e.preventDefault();
});
```

We have to pass our event inside the parentheses of the function shown in the preceding code. You may call this what you want. Sometimes, developers will name it e, event, or evt. Then, inside our function, we call the preventDefault method for the event. If you load the page in a browser at this point, you'll see that clicking on the links does nothing—the default action has been cancelled. Now, we have to write a function to specify what should happen instead.

**10.** When a site visitor clicks on a table of contents link, we want to select the appropriate section and show it. To do this, we'll use hash, or the part of the href attribute that includes the # symbol:

```
$('#tabs a').on ('click', function(e){
  $(this.hash).show();
  e.preventDefault();
});
```

When we pass this.hash to the jQuery function, the this keyword we're dealing with is the link that was just clicked on and this.hash is the value of the href attribute starting with the # symbol and continuing to the end. For example, if a site visitor were to click on the **He** tab, passing this.hash to the jQuery function is the same as writing the following line of code:

```
$('#he');
```

Of course, we've done it in a much more flexible way and our code will work for any tab linked to any section of the site. So, for example, if I wanted to remove the **Rn** tab or expand my list to include the halogens in addition to the noble gases, I wouldn't have to update JavaScript, only the HTML markup itself—JavaScript is flexible enough to adjust to changes.

**11.** If you reload the page in the browser at this point, you'll see that when you click on one of the tab links, the associated section becomes visible. We're making progress! However, if you keep clicking on links, the sections just keep showing up, and after clicking on all the links, all the sections are visible—this not what we want. We'll have to hide the visible section and show only the section we want. Let's add a line to our code, as follows, to select the visible `<div>` with the class of `tab-section` and hide it before we show the new section:

```
$('#tabs a').on('click', function(e){
  $('.tab-section:visible').hide();
  $(this.hash).show();
  e.preventDefault();
});
```

You're probably familiar with **pseudoclass** selectors in CSS—they're often used to select the hover, visited, and active states of links (`a:hover`, `a:visited`, and `a:active`). jQuery makes a few additional pseudoclass selectors available to us. There are pseudoclass selectors for buttons, empty elements, disabled form fields, checkboxes, and so on. You can check out all the available selectors for jQuery in the jQuery documentation at `http://api.jquery.com/category/selectors/`. Here, we're using the `:visible` pseudoclass to select the `.tab-section` that's currently visible. Once we've selected the visible `.tab-section`, we hide it and then find the correct `tab-section` and show it.

**12.** Now, if you load this in a browser, you'll see that there's something missing; we should highlight the currently selected tab to make it obvious which one is selected. We can do that by adding a CSS class to the current tab. Go back to your `scripts.js` file and add a bit of code to add a class to the current tab and remove the class from any non-current tabs as follows:

```
$('#tabs a').on ('click', function(e){
  $('#tabs a.current').removeClass('current');
  $('.tab-section:visible').hide();
  $(this.hash).show();
  $(this).addClass('current');
  e.preventDefault();
});
```

First, we'll find the tab that has the `current` class and remove this class. Then, we'll get the tab that was just clicked and add the `current` class to it. In this way, we make sure that only one tab will be marked as the current tab at any given time.

The $(this) element is the jQuery way of referring to the jQuery object that we're currently working with. In this case, we're selecting all the tab links and we've attached this function to be called whenever our site visitor clicks on a link. When a site visitor clicks on a link, we want to work with the link that was clicked. A simple and quick way of referring to the current link is to use $(this).

13. Next, we'll add some styles in our CSS file for our new class. Open styles.css and add a bit of CSS to distinguish the currently selected tab. I'm styling mine as follows, but feel free to customize the style to suit your own tastes:

```
.jsOn ul#tabs a.current {
  background: #4fc1e9;
}
```

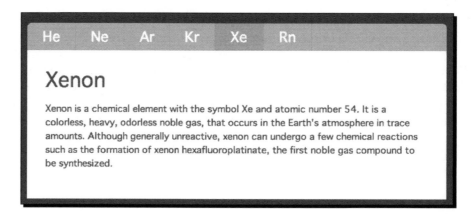

14. Now our tabs are working the way we expect, and the only thing left to do is to make the first tab active and show the first content section when the page is first loaded instead of leaving them all hidden. We've already written the function to do this, so now all we have to do is call it for our first tab, as shown in the following code snippet:

```
$('#tabs a').on ('click', function(e){
  $('#tabs a.current').removeClass('current');
  $('.tab-section:visible').hide();
  $(this.hash).show();
  $(this).addClass('current');
  e.preventDefault;
}).filter(':first').click();
```

The jQuery object's `filter` method will allow us to filter a previously selected set of elements. In this case, we're dealing with all of the `<a>` tags inside the `<ul>` tags with the `#tabs` ID. We bind a `click` function to all of these links, then we'll filter out just the first link using the `:first` pseudoclass made available to us in jQuery, and tell jQuery to click on the first tab for us. This will run our function, adding the `current` class to the first link and showing the first `.tab-section`—just the way we'd expect the page to look when we load it, as seen in the following screenshot:

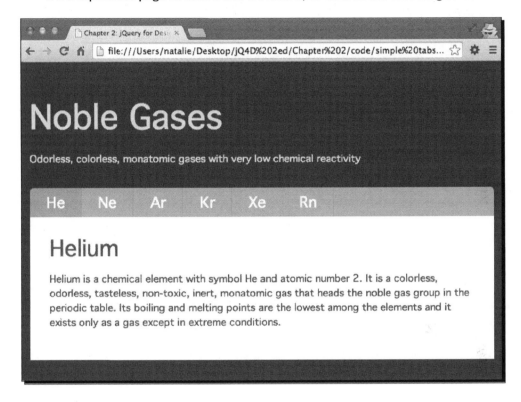

## What just happened?

We set up a set of simple tabs with jQuery. For site visitors with JavaScript disabled, the tabs will function like a table of contents at the top of the document, jumping them to the various sections of content when they're clicked. For site visitors with JavaScript enabled, the sections of content will be completely hidden until needed. Clicking on each tab reveals the content associated with that tab. This is a great way to save space in a UI, making all the content available on demand in a small space.

We used our `jsOn` class name to hide the tab contents to be sure that users without JavaScript enabled would still be able to access all of our content.

## Pop quiz – working with events

Q1. Which of the following are the examples of events in JavaScript?

1. Clicking on a link

2. Entering a value in a form input

3. Moving the mouse over an image

4. Pressing a key on the keyboard

5. All of the above

Q2. What is an event handler?

1. The site visitor that decides which button to click

2. A bit of code that is run in response to an event

3. The site visitor submitting a form

# Designer, meet plugins

We've already talked about how programmers solve the same problems over and over again. It's these common tasks that jQuery simplifies so that we can accomplish these tasks with a minimum amount of code. What about the tasks that are only somewhat common, like the ability to customize the appearance of tooltips?

That's where the jQuery community becomes important. Developers in the jQuery community write code that extends the functionality of jQuery to simplify tasks that are only somewhat common. These bits of code are called **plugins**, and they are used in conjunction with the jQuery library to make coding complex interactions, widgets, and effects as simple as using the features already built into jQuery.

You'll find a library of hundreds of jQuery plugins on the official jQuery site at `http://plugins.jquery.com`. In addition to this, there are literally thousands more available from sites across the Web for just about any task you want to accomplish.

To create custom-designed tooltips, we'll be using Steven Benner's jQuery PowerTip plugin. You'll learn how to install the plugin on your page and how to configure the CSS code and options to make your tooltips look and work the way you want.

# Choosing a plugin

Recently, the jQuery team has started supporting a small number of official jQuery plugins, and you can use them confidently, knowing that they have the same level of expertise, documentation, and support behind them that jQuery itself has. All other jQuery plugins are provided by various members of the jQuery community, and those authors are solely responsible for the documentation and for their own plugins. Writing and providing jQuery plugins is a bit of a free-for-all, and sadly, you will come across a fair number of jQuery plugins that are poorly documented, poorly supported, and even worse, poorly written. What kinds of things should you, as a newcomer to jQuery, look for when choosing a plugin?

- **A recent update to the plugin**: Frequent updates mean that a plugin is well supported and that the author is keeping the plugin up to date as jQuery and browsers evolve. You'll even sometimes find other community members making contributions and updates to a plugin, as is the case with the jQuery PowerTip plugin.

- **Thorough and easy-to-understand documentation**: Before attempting to download and use a plugin, take a look through the plugin's documentation and make sure that you understand how to implement the plugin and how to use the options that the plugin makes available to you.

- **Browser support**: Great plugins generally have the same browser support as the jQuery library.

- **Working demo**: Most plugins will offer one or more working demos of their plugin in action. Check out the demo(s) in as many different browsers as possible to make sure that the plugin works as advertised.

- **Reviews and ratings**: You won't find reviews and ratings for all plugins, but if you can find some, they can be helpful indicators of the quality and reliability of the plugin.

# Simple custom tooltips

Browsers automatically create tooltips when you include the `title` attribute on your HTML element. Titles are usually used on links and images, but they can be added to nearly every type of HTML element. When your site visitors hover their mouse cursor over an element with a `title` attribute or move focus to the item by tabbing to it using the keyboard, the tooltip will appear—usually as a small yellow box that appears to be floating over the page.

Tooltips are a great way to add a little additional information to your page. Screen reader software reads out tooltip text for site visitors with disabilities who are using assistive technology, making them useful for enhancing accessibility. Furthermore, the `title` attributes on images and links can help search engines index your content more effectively.

I hope I've convinced you that the `title` attributes are great for enhancing both the usability and the accessibility of your site. The only problem with tooltips is that they can't be customized in any way. Each browser has its own style of tooltip and that style is not accessible via CSS. This is fine, but sometimes, it's nice to have more control over the appearance of tooltips.

# Time for action – simple custom tooltips

We'll start off by creating a simple replacement for the browser's default tooltips that we can style any way we'd like. Perform the following steps:

**1.** Set up a basic HTML file and associated files and folders like we did in *Chapter 1, Designer, Meet jQuery*. Our HTML file should contain a list of images with the `title` attributes as follows:

```
<div class="content">
  <h2 id="pb-gallery">Photo Gallery</h2>
  <ul class="gallery">
    <li><img src="images/bridge.jpg" title
      ="One of many bridges in Pittsburgh"/></li>
    <li><img src="images/downtown.jpg" title
      ="Downtown Pittsburgh with bridges"/></li>
    <li><img src="images/icecream.jpg" title
      ="A great way to beat the summer heat"/></li>
  </ul>
</div>
```

Feel free to use CSS to style this list in the way like. If you open the page in a browser and move your mouse over the images, you'll see the text that's contained in the `title` attributes displayed as tooltips. Where the tooltip appears and what it looks like will depend on your browser, but here's how it looks in mine (Google Chrome on Mac OS):

**2.** Now, let's spruce that up a bit by replacing the default browser tooltip with our own styled one, at least for our site visitors that have JavaScript enabled. First, we'll need a copy of Steven Benner's jQuery PowerTip plugin. It's available on GitHub at `http://stevenbenner.github.io/jquery-powertip/`. The GitHub page has a list of features, some sample demos, the documentation you'll need to learn to use the plugin, and a link to the files available for download. Click on the green **Download** button to download a ZIP file that consists all the files you'll need. For this, have a look at the following screenshot:

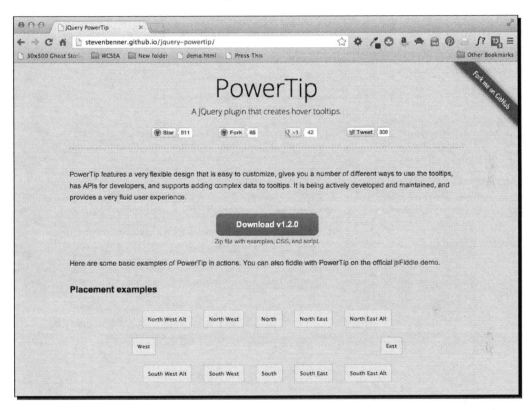

3. Unzip the file you downloaded and examine its contents. Inside, you'll find a css folder with several .css files, an examples folder with a few working examples for you to look at, two JavaScript files, and a LICENSE.txt file. Have a look at the following screenshot:

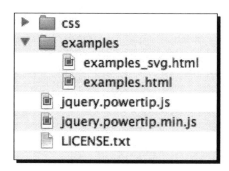

Let's start with all the CSS files. You'll find two files named jquery.powertip.css and jquery.powertip.min.css. These two files are the default tooltip styles for this plugin and have exactly the same content. The difference between them is that the second file is minified, making it smaller and ideal for use in production. The other file is a development version that we could easily edit ourselves or use as an example if we wanted to write our own custom styles for our tooltips.

The rest of the CSS files are assorted styles and color schemes for the tooltips. If you look closely, you'll see the names of colors in the filenames, for example, jquery. powertip-purple.css or jquery.powertip-blue.css. Each of these files also have a minified production version and a development version. All of these styles are prewritten and available to you to use in your project.

You can select one of these CSS files and attach it to your page. Copy jquery. powertip.css to your own styles folder and then attach the file to your HTML document in the <head> section, as follows:

```
<head>
  <title>Chapter 2: jQuery for Designers</title>
  <link rel="stylesheet" href="styles/styles.css">
  <link rel="stylesheet" href="styles/jquery.powertip.css">
</head>
```

**4.** Next, let's look at the JavaScript files. We have `jquery.powertip.js` and `jquery.powertip.min.js`. Just like the CSS files, these are two different versions of the same file, and we simply have to choose one and attach it to our HTML document. The first file, `jquery.powertip.js`, is the development version of the file and the largest at 35 KB. The second file is minified and is just 9 KB. As we don't need to edit the plugin itself and are going to use it as it is, let's select the smaller minified version. Copy `jquery.powertip.min.js` to your own `scripts` folder and attach it at the bottom of your HTML file, between jQuery and your own `scripts.js` file. This is shown in the following code:

```html
<script src="scripts/jquery.js"></script>
<script src="scripts/jquery.powertip.min.js"></script>
<script src="scripts/scripts.js"></script>
</body>
</html>
```

**5.** The last thing we need to do is call the plugin code. Open your `scripts.js` file and add the following document ready statement and function:

```javascript
$(document).ready(function(){

});
```

**6.** Inside the function, select the images inside the list and call the `powerTip` method on these links, as shown in the following code:

```javascript
$(document).ready(function(){
  $('.gallery img').powerTip();
});
```

Now, when you view the page in the browser and move your mouse over the images with the `title` attributes, you'll see the PowerTip-styled tooltips instead of the browser's default tooltips, as seen in the following screenshot:

The default style for PowerTip tooltips is a slightly transparent black tooltip that appears directly above the item you're hovering your mouse over. These tooltips will appear with this same style, no matter which browser and operating system we're using, except that the tooltip will be opaque in browsers that don't support RGBA colors for transparency.

## What just happened?

We downloaded the jQuery PowerTip plugin and attached one CSS file and one JavaScript file to our HTML document. Then, we added just a couple lines of jQuery code to activate the custom tooltips.

We selected all the images in the gallery list. We did this by taking advantage of jQuery's CSS selectors:

```
$('.gallery img')
```

Once we've selected all the images, all that was left to do was call the `powerTip` method that the PowerTip plugin provided for us. The `powerTip` method takes care of all the actions that need to be performed to replace the default tooltip with a custom one. But what if we want to alter the style or placement of the tooltips? Let's take a look at how we can customize the tooltips.

# Customizing PowerTip's appearance

The default PowerTip style displays the tooltip centered above the item that we're hovering our mouse over. The PowerTip plugin offers lots of options to customize where the tooltip appears and what it looks like. It does so in a straightforward and easy-to-understand way.

## Time for action – customizing PowerTip

Let's take a look at some of the options we have to customize PowerTip and how we can use them. We'll keep working with the files we set up in the preceding example:

1. Let's say that we want to change the position of the tooltip. PowerTip gives us plenty of options to position tooltips on our page, as follows:

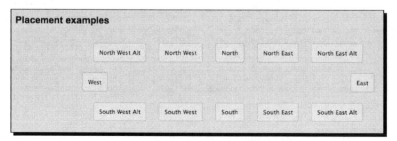

How do we tell PowerTip where we want our tooltips to appear? Let's go back to that line of code in our `scripts.js` file where we called the `powerTip` method to create the custom tooltips:

```
$('.gallery img').powerTip();
```

Remember in *Chapter 1, Designer, Meet jQuery*, we talked about how we can pass things to methods and functions by putting them inside the parentheses? We had the example `dog.eat('bacon');`, where we wanted to say that the dog was eating bacon. So, in JavaScript, we passed bacon to the `eat` method of the dog.

Well, in this case, we can pass a set of options to the `powerTip` method to define where our tooltips are placed, among other things. To define the position of our tooltips, we'll set the placement option to the direction we want (n, ne, ne-alt, e, se, se-alt, s, sw, sw-alt, w, nw, or nw-alt). We just have to make the following simple modification to our code:

```
$('.gallery img').powerTip({placement: 'sw-alt'});
```

In this example, we'll place the tooltips underneath the image we're hovering over and anchor them to the bottom-left (or south-west) corner.

You'll notice that each of the four corner options for PowerTip have an additional `alt` placement option. The default corner option will display the tooltip anchored to your chosen corner and the tooltip itself to the side of the item you're hovering over.

The `alt` option for each corner also displays the tooltips anchored to your chosen corner, but shows the tooltip directly above or below the item you're hovering over rather than to the side, as shown in the following screenshot:

As our images are side-by-side in this example, the `alt` placement option makes more sense, so that's the one we'll use.

2.   Depending on the width of our browser window and the layout of our content, our chosen placement for the tooltips might sometimes result in the tooltip being displayed completely or partly out of view. Luckily, the developers of this plugin have anticipated this possibility and have provided us with an option to make sure that the tooltips are always visible. It's called **Smart Placement**, and we can enable this option by setting the `smartPlacement` option to `true`, as shown in the following code:

```
$('.gallery img').powerTip({smartPlacement: true});
```

What if you need to pass more than one option to the `powerTip` method? To pass more than one option, you just have to separate the options with a comma. So, we can define our tooltip position and turn on **Smart Placement** as follows:

```
$('.gallery img').powerTip({placement:
  'sw-alt', smartPlacement: true});
```

Now, you can see that if I were setting a dozen or more options, this line of code would get long and hard to read. For this reason, it's a common practice to break options out on separate lines as follows:

```
$('.gallery img').powerTip({
  placement:      'sw-alt',
  smartPlacement: true
});
```

The content is the same, it's just that it's easier for us humans to read and understand the code when it's broken into lines this way. A computer doesn't care one way or the other.

> Be careful not to add an extra comma after the last option/value pair. Most browsers will handle this gracefully, but IE will throw a vague error and your JavaScript won't work at all. It can be a frustrating problem to try and track it down.

3. In addition to changing the position of the tooltip, we can use CSS to change the appearance of the tooltip itself. If you wanted to use one of the alternate color schemes that was included with PowerTip, you'd just have to swap the style sheet in your HTML document with the one you wanted to use. That's very simple and straightforward.

However, we can also write our own CSS styles for our tooltips. To get started, we'll examine the `jquery.powertip.css` file that was included with the PowerTip download. The following code is an example from this file that shows how the colors and styles are specified:

```
#powerTip {
  cursor: default;
  background-color: #333;
  background-color: rgba(0,0,0,.8);
  border-radius: 6px;
  color: #fff;
  display: none;
  padding: 10px;
  position: absolute;
  white-space: nowrap;
  z-index: 2147483647;
}

#powerTip:before {
  content: "";
  position: absolute;
}

#powerTip.n:before, #powerTip.s:before {
```

```css
  border-right: 5px solid transparent;
  border-left: 5px solid transparent;
  left: 50%;
  margin-left: -5px;
}

#powerTip.n:before {
  border-top: 10px solid #333;
  border-top: 10px solid rgba(0,0,0,.8);
  bottom: -10px;
}

#powerTip.s:before {
  border-bottom: 10px solid #333;
  border-bottom: 10px solid rgba(0,0,0,.8);
  top: -10px;
}
```

You'll notice that there's quite a lot of code using the `:before` and `:after` CSS pseudoclasses, and you might wonder what exactly is going on with that. This is a clever CSS technique to create triangle shapes without relying on images. This code creates the triangle-shaped connector between the tooltip and the item you're hovering your mouse over. If you'd like to learn more about this technique, there's an excellent tutorial with plenty of explanations at `http://konigi.com/tools/css-tooltips-and-speech-bubbles`.

**4.** By examining the CSS code, you can see that all we need to do to create our own color scheme is replace all the color definitions in this file with a color of our own choosing. I'm going to choose a melon orange shade, which is `#fc6e51` as a hex color and `252, 110, 81` as an RGB color. The RGB color is important because we can use it to create an RGBA color that is transparent.

To switch to a new color scheme, all we need to do is go through the `jquery.powertip.css` file and switch the color values to the newly selected values. An example from the new CSS is shown in the following code:

```css
#powerTip {
  cursor: default;
  background-color: #fc6e51;
  background-color: rgba(252, 110, 81, 0.8);
  border-radius: 6px;
  color: #fff;
  display: none;
  padding: 10px;
  position: absolute;
  white-space: nowrap;
  z-index: 2147483647;
}
```

```
#powerTip:before {
  content: "";
  position: absolute;
}

#powerTip.n:before, #powerTip.s:before {
  border-right: 5px solid transparent;
  border-left: 5px solid transparent;
  left: 50%;
  margin-left: -5px;
}

#powerTip.n:before {
  border-top: 10px solid #fc6e51;
  border-top: 10px solid rgba(252, 110, 81, 0.8);
  bottom: -10px;
}

#powerTip.s:before {
  border-bottom: 10px solid #fc6e51;
  border-bottom: 10px solid rgba(252, 110, 81, 0.8);
  top: -10px;
}
```

Similarly, go on replacing the color values throughout the entire file. Now, when you preview the tooltip in the browser, you'll see an orange tooltip, as shown in the following screenshot:

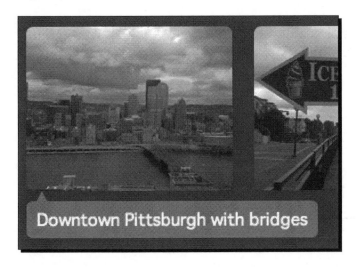

You can take the customization as far as you want. You can modify the border radius, add a gradient, add a text shadow and/or a box shadow, change the text color, add a border, and so on.

## *What just happened?*

We learned how we can adjust the positioning of our tooltips, how we can use other options provided by the PowerTip plugin, and we created our own custom style for the tooltips. You can use any CSS styles you like to customize the appearance of the tooltips; there's virtually no limit to the possibilities of styles for your tooltips.

# Enhancing navigation with tooltips

Once you know how to make custom tooltips, you'll find that there are many possible uses for them. Let's take a look at enhancing a standard navigation bar with custom tooltips using the PowerTip plugin.

## Time for action – building a fancy navigation bar

Let's take a look at how we can use custom-designed tooltips to add a little progressively enhanced punch to a basic navigation bar. We'll continue working with the files we've set up in the last two custom tooltips examples. Perform the following steps:

*1.* Let's get started by adding a navigation bar to the top of our HTML page. While we're at it, let's go ahead and also add a header to the top of the page:

```
<header class="content">
  <h1>Pittsburgh, Pennsylvania</h1>
  <p>City of Bridges, Steel City, City of Champions,
    The 'Burgh</p>
</header>

<nav>
  <ul>
    <li><a href="#pb-gallery" title
      ="View photos of Pittsburgh">Photo Gallery</a></li>
    <li><a href="#pb-about" title
      ="Read about Pittsburgh">About</a></li>
    <li><a href="#pb-geography" title
      ="Learn about Pittsburg's geography">Geography</a></li>
    <li><a href="#pb-moreinfo" title
      ="Get more info about Pittsburgh">More Information
      </a></li>
  </ul>
</nav>
```

We've made sure to include the `title` attributes on each link. For the purpose of this example, these are internal links that will jump to different sections within this HTML document.

**2.** Next, we'll add some CSS styles to our navigation bar. If you prefer a different style, feel free to customize the CSS code to suit your own taste. Have a look at the following code:

```css
nav {
  margin: 2em 0;
}

nav ul {
  background: #fff;
  border-radius: 7px;
  text-align: center;
}

nav li {
  display: inline-block;
}

nav a {
  display: block;
  color: #444;
  padding: 1.5em;
  text-decoration: none;
  text-transform: uppercase;
}

nav a:hover {
  color: #a0d468;
}
```

Now, we have a navigation bar horizontally across our page, as shown in the following screenshot:

When you move your mouse over the links in this navigation bar, the browser's default tooltips appear. We'll replace those boring browser tooltips with friendly looking conversation bubbles above the navigation bar.

**3.** Next, open your `scripts.js` file so that we can call the `powerTip` method and pass in our customizations. Hey, wait a minute—we're already calling the `powerTip` method in `scripts.js`. Yes, you're right, we are. However, we're going to learn how to call it again and have two different tooltip styles in one single document.

Let's get started by adding a comment for ourselves to help us keep track of what we're doing in our code, as follows:

```
$(document).ready(function(){
  /* Add text tooltips to photo gallery */
  $('.gallery img').powerTip({
    placement: 'sw-alt'
  });
});
```

**4.** Now that we can easily keep track of the code for our photo gallery tooltips, let's go ahead and add a comment and selector and call to `powerTip` for the navigation:

```
$(document).ready(function(){

  /* Add tooltips to navigation */
  $('nav a').powerTip();

  /* Add text tooltips to photos */
  $('.gallery img').powerTip({
    placement: 'sw-alt'
  });
});
```

Open up the HTML file in a browser to take a look and you'll see that we now have orange tooltips that appear directly above each of our navigation items, as seen in the following screenshot):

This is okay, but as the navigation items turn green when they are hovered over, it would be better if these tooltips were green. Let's see how we can change the style.

**5.** If you'll recall from `jquery.powertip.css`, all the styles we wrote for our tooltips were based on the `#powerTip` ID, which was assigned to our tooltips by the PowerTip plugin. We have a configuration option to change the ID, which will allow us to write some new CSS code to create a new tooltip style. Let's start by modifying the ID of the tooltips that are displayed on our navigation bar, as follows:

```
$('nav a').powerTip({
  popupId: 'navTip'
});
```

**6.** Next, we can open `jquery.powertip.css` and add some new styles for `navTip`.

```
#navTip {
  cursor: default;
  background-color: #a0d468;
  border-radius: 6px;
  color: #fff;
  display: none;
  padding: 10px;
  position: absolute;
  white-space: nowrap;
  z-index: 2147483647;
}
```

Similarly, go on styling those however you want. Now, when we move our mouse over the navigation, green tooltips will be displayed.

## What just happened?

We reviewed how to create and attach a custom-styled tooltip to our HTML document. We learned how to include two different tooltip styles in the same document. Now, we have orange tooltips that are displayed below the photos in our photo gallery and green tooltips that are displayed above our navigation bar. Let's find out what else we can do with PowerTip.

# Showing other content in tooltips

So far, we've seen how we can customize the appearance and position of the tooltips that the PowerTip plugin helps us create. However, we've only used these tooltips to display text, namely, the text we've placed inside an element's `title` attribute. We have a lot more powerful options though. We can load just about any content we want in our tooltips. Let's take a look at how we can load content from somewhere else in the HTML document into our tooltips.

## Time for action – showing custom content in tooltips

Perform the following steps to load custom content into your tooltips:

1. We'll keep working with the document that we've been building over the past few tooltip tutorials. The first thing we want to add is some new content. First, we'll create some blocks of helpful content at the bottom of our HTML page, as shown in the following code:

```
<h2 id="pb-moreinfo">More Information</h2>
<ul class="info-boxes">
  <li id="info-box-bridge">
    <div class="info-box-container">
      <img src="images/bridge.jpg"/>
      <div class="info-box-content">
        <p>One of many bridges in Pittsburgh</p>
      </div>
    </div>
  </li>
  <li id="info-box-downtown">
    <div class="info-box-container">
      <img src="images/downtown.jpg"/>
      <div class="info-box-content">
        <p>Downtown<br/>Pittsburgh</p>
      </div>
    </div>
  </li>
  <li id="info-box-icecream">
    <div class="info-box-container">
      <img src="images/icecream.jpg"/>
      <div class="info-box-content">
        <p>Ice cream beats the summer heat</p>
      </div>
    </div>
  </li>
</ul>
```

We're including some images and a bit of text about each one. Next, we'll style this with CSS as follows:

```
Ul.info-boxes li {
  display: inline-block;
  margin-right: 1em;
}
```

```
.info-box-container {
  width: 200px;
}

.info-box-container img {
  border-top-left-radius: 7px;
  border-top-right-radius: 7px;
}

.info-box-content {
  background: white;
  border-bottom-left-radius: 7px;
  border-bottom-right-radius: 7px;
  color: #444;
  line-height: 1.5;
  padding: 1em;
  text-align: center;
}

.info-box-content p {
  margin: 0;
}
```

Now, if we look at this page in a browser, we'll see the information boxes lined up and nicely styled at the bottom of the page, as shown in the following screenshot:

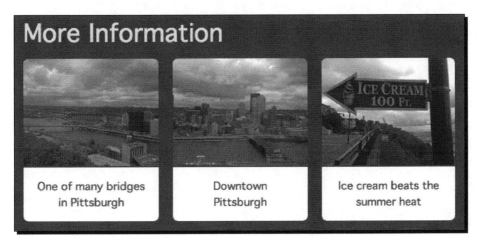

2. Next up, we'll add a couple of paragraphs of text that link to these information boxes. Add this text above the information boxes so that they are displayed between the photo gallery and the information boxes, using the following code:

```
<h2 id="pb-about">About Pittsburgh</h2>
<p>Pittsburgh is the second-largest city in the US Commonwealth
   of Pennsylvania and the county seat of Allegheny County.
   <a href="#info-box-downtown" class="info-box">
   Downtown Pittsburgh</a>
   retains substantial economic influence,
   ranking at 25th in the nation for jobs within
   the urban core and 6th in job density.</p>

<h2 id="pb-geography">Geography</h2>
<p>Pittsburgh is known colloquially as "The City of Bridges"
   and "The Steel City" for its
   <a href="#info-box-bridge" class="info-box" >many bridges</a>
   and former steel manufacturing base.</p>
<p>Conditions are often humid, and combined with the 90&deg;F
   (occurring on an average of 8.4 days per annum),
   a considerable
   <a href="info-box-icecream" class="info-box">heat index</a>
   arises.</p>
```

We need an easy way to select and interact with the links to the information boxes, so we've added a CSS class of `info-box` to each one.

3. Now, what we'll do is load the corresponding information box in the tooltip when each of these links is hovered over. Pretty cool, right?

First, we'll have to associate each of the links with the corresponding information box. We can do this by adding an HTML5 `data` attribute to each link, as shown in the following code snippet:

```
<a href="#info-box-downtown" class="info-box"
   data-powertiptarget="info-box-downtown">
   Downtown Pittsburgh</a>
```

The documentation on the PowerTip plugin explains that the plugin will look for a `data` attribute named `powertiptarget`. If the attribute exists, then PowerTip will pull in the content from the element with that ID and display it in the tooltip.

Let's talk about the `data` attributes. They can be used to attach all different sorts of hidden information to the HTML elements, which we can then use in JavaScript to achieve all sorts of special effects. You start a `data` attribute with `data-`. After this, you name the `data` attribute. In this case, we knew from the PowerTip documentation that the attribute should be named `powertiptarget`. In other cases, you'll be able to name your `data` attributes whatever you wish. Picking names that make logical sense will help you and others make sense of your code more easily—in much the same way that picking logical names for JavaScript variables helps your code make sense.

When we hover over this link, we want to display the information box that we've given the ID of `info-box-downtown`, so this is the value we'll assign to the `powertiptarget` `data` attribute.

4. Next up, we're ready to jump back into `scripts.js`. Add a new line inside your document ready statement and comment it so that you remember this is the code to add the information box tooltips, as shown in the following code:

```
$(document).ready(function() {
  /* Add tooltips to navigation */
  $('nav a').powerTip({
    popupId: 'navTip'
  });

  /* Add text tooltips to photos */
  $('.gallery img').powerTip({
    placement: 'sw-alt'
  });

  /* Add new content to text links */
  $('.info-box').powerTip();
});
```

If you view the page in a browser, you'll see that the data attributes we applied to our links are already working; if you hover over one of the links, you'll see the corresponding information box displayed in a tooltip, as shown in the following screenshot:

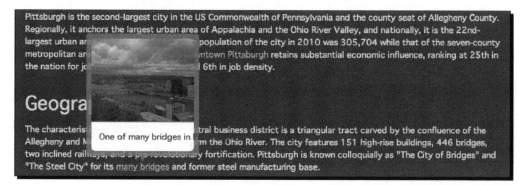

That's a good start, but we'll want to change some of the PowerTip configuration options and also the style of the tooltip.

**5.** We'll tackle the configuration options first. We'd like the information box tooltip to show to the right of the links unless they don't fit on the screen. We'd like to write some new CSS styles, and we'd like to allow our site visitors to move their mouse over the information boxes. The following code shows what we'll add as configuration options:

```
$('.info-box').powerTip({
    placement: 'e',
    mouseOnToPopup: true,
    smartPlacement: true,
    popupId: 'infoTip'
});
```

Setting the placement option to e will make the tooltips display on the right-hand (or east) side of the links. We can make sure the tooltips are visible even for links near the right-hand side of the screen by setting smartPlacement to true. We can use an option called mouseOnToPopup and set it to true to allow site visitors to move their mouse onto the tooltip—this feature is particularly useful for those cases where we might have links or other interactive content included in our tooltip content. Finally, as we want to write some new CSS styles for the tooltip, we're going to set a new ID for the tooltips, for which we've chosen the infoTip ID.

**6.** Now, the only thing left to do is to write some new CSS styles for the tooltips. We're going to change the background color to white and make sure the text can wrap. Feel free to style your tooltips the way you want. The following code is a sample from the example code included with the book:

```css
/* Info box tooltips */
#infoTip {
  cursor: default;
  background-color: #fff;
  border-radius: 7px;
  box-shadow: 0 0 15px rgba(0,0,0,0.5);
  color: #444;
  display: none;
  padding: 0;
  position: absolute;
  z-index: 2147483647;
}
#infoTip:before {
  content: "";
  position: absolute;
}
#infoTip.n:before, #infoTip.s:before {
  border-right: 5px solid transparent;
  border-left: 5px solid transparent;
  left: 50%;
  margin-left: -5px;
}
#infoTip.n:before {
  border-top: 10px solid #fff;
  bottom: -10px;
}
#infoTip.s:before {
  border-bottom: 10px solid #fff;
  top: -10px;
}
```

Now, if you view the page in a browser, you'll see that the tooltips have their own
style and are displayed where we specified, as seen in the following screenshot:

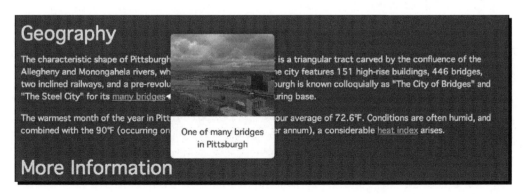

Also, if the link gets too close to the right, PowerTip will figure out how to adjust the placement of the tooltip to make sure it's visible, as seen in the following screenshot:

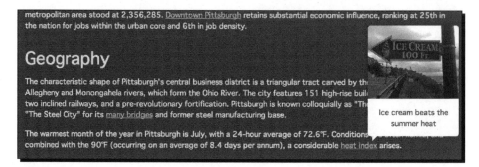

Also, if you move your mouse over the tooltip, you'll see it stays open to allow you to interact with any content that might be inside.

7. Now, there's just one issue with our page: for users with JavaScript disabled, we set up the links to jump down the page so that the relevant associated content was visible on the screen. Now that our tooltips are working, this behavior feels a little odd; if the content is already visible, why jump down the page to it?

   We can fix that by canceling the browser's default behavior when a link is clicked. Go back to scripts.js and adjust your JavaScript as follows:

```
$('.info-box')
  .on( 'click', function(e) {
    e.preventDefault();
  })
  .powerTip({
    placement: 'e',
    mouseOnToPopup: true,
    smartPlacement: true,
    popupId: 'infoTip'
  });
```

There are a few things going on here. Let's start by talking about how .on and .powerTip are divided in separate lines. For the most part, JavaScript doesn't care about white space, so we're free to format our code the way we want. Computers don't have any issues parsing or reading our code even if it's sloppy and the indentations don't line up. When our code is broken up onto separate lines, as shown in the preceding code snippets, it's easier for us humans, who might want to read or edit the code, to read and understand. We don't have to go searching through one long line of code for what we're looking for because, believe it or not, all this code is technically just one line of JavaScript.

It's easy for us to see that we're working with some HTML element that has a CSS class of `info-box`. We've got a function to tell the browser what to do when someone clicks on this HTML element, and we're setting up the `powerTip` method to display tooltips.

Next, let's talk about chaining. You can see in the preceding code that we're only referring to the HTML element with the class of `info-box` once, but we're writing two bits of code for it. jQuery allows us to do this with the feature called **chaining**. Most jQuery functions (but not all) can be chained. For example, consider the following line of code:

```
$('.foo').hide().addClass('bar').show();
```

This line of code will select an HTML element with a class of `foo`, hide it, add a new CSS class to it, and then show it again. You can see how this chaining feature would allow us to save quite a lot of typing.

## What just happened?

We learned how we can pull in content from elsewhere on the page to be displayed inside our tooltips. Being able to display the `title` attributes in a more attractive way is definitely a nice feature, but the PowerTip plugin is even more powerful than that. By adding HTML5 `data` attributes to our elements, we can specify any content to be displayed inside our tooltips: links, images, text, icons, and so on. We learned how to allow site visitors to move their mouse over the tooltips to interact with the content there. Also, we saw how we can stop the browser from jumping down the page when the links are clicked by preventing the default events from happening in response to actions.

## Have a go hero – create clickable tooltips for an image gallery

Set up an image gallery of a set of images of your choice. When each image is hovered over, show a tooltip that provides a short description and links to an article on Wikipedia for more information. Style the image gallery and tooltips the way you like.

# Summary

In this chapter, we learned how to take basic links—the backbone of the Internet—and enhance them to add some new behaviors and capabilities. We learned how to turn a list of links into a tabbed interface and how to create customized tooltips for links. We also learned how to load in any kind of content into those tooltips; we are no longer limited to displaying simple text in them. Next up, let's take a look at how we can combine link customization with some other behaviors to create an interactive FAQ page.

# 3
# Making a Better FAQ Page

*The **Frequently Asked Questions (FAQ)** page has been a mainstay of all types of websites since the dawn of the Web. It's used as a marketing page, as an attempt to reduce the number of calls or e-mails to a customer service department and as a helpful tool for site visitors to learn more about the company or organization they're dealing with or the products or services they're interested in purchasing.*

*Though we'll be building an FAQ page, for this example, the expand and collapse techniques will be useful in many different situations—a list of events with event details, a listing of staff or members with bios, a list of products with details—any situation where a listing of items should be quick and easy for site visitors to scan, but where more information should be readily and easily available upon demand when they find the thing they're looking for.*

In this chapter, you'll learn:

- ◆ How to traverse an HTML document with jQuery
- ◆ How to show and hide elements
- ◆ How to use simple jQuery animations
- ◆ How to easily toggle a class name for an element

## Marking up the FAQ page

We'll get started by taking some extra care and attention with the way we mark up our FAQ list. As with most things that deal with web development, there's no right way of doing anything, so don't assume this approach is the only correct one. Any markup that makes sense semantically and makes it easy to enhance your list with CSS and JavaScript is perfectly acceptable.

# Time for action – setting up the HTML file

Perform the following steps to get the HTML file set up for our FAQ page:

**1.** We'll get started with our sample HTML file and associated files and folders, like we set up in *Chapter 1, Designer, Meet jQuery*. In this case, our HTML page will contain a definition list with the questions inside the `<dt>` tags and the answers wrapped in the `<dd>` tags. By default, most browsers will indent the `<dd>` tags, which means the questions hang into the left margin, making them easy to scan. Inside the `<body>` tag of your HTML document, add a heading and a definition list as shown in the following code:

```
<h1>Frequently Asked Questions</h1>
<dl>
  <dt>What is jQuery?</dt>
  <dd>
    <p>jQuery is an awesome JavaScript library</p>
  </dd>

  <dt>Why should I use jQuery?</dt>
  <dd>
    <p>Because it's awesome and it makes writing
      JavaScript faster and easier</p>
  </dd>

  <dt>Why would I want to hide the answers to my
    questions?</dt>
  <dd>
    <p>To make it easier to peruse the list of available
      questions - then you simply click to see the answer
      you're interested in reading.</p>
  </dd>

  <dt>What if my answers were a lot longer and more
    complicated than these examples?</dt>
  <dd>
    <p>The great thing about the &lt;dd&gt;
      element is that it's a block level element
      that can contain lots of other elements.</p>
    <p>That means your answer could contain:</p>
    <ul>
```

```
      <li>Unordered</li>
      <li>Lists</li>
      <li>with lots</li>
      <li>of items</li>
      <li>(or ordered lists or even another
        definition list)</li>
    </ul>
    <p>Or it might contain text with lots of
      <strong>special</strong>
      <em>formatting</em>.</p>
    <h2>Other things</h2>
    <p>It can even contain headings.
      Your answers could take up an entire screen or
      more all on their own - it doesn't matter since
      the answer will be hidden until the user wants
      to see it.</p>
  </dd>


  <dt>What if a user doesn't have JavaScript enabled?</dt>
  <dd>
    <p>You have two options for users with JavaScript
      disabled - which you choose might depend on the
      content of your page.</p>
    <p>You might just leave the page as it is - and
      make sure the &lt;dt&gt; tags are styled in a
      way that makes them stand out and easy to pick
      up when you're scanning down through the page.
      This would be a great solution if your answers
      are relatively short.</p>
    <p>If your FAQ page has long answers,
      it might be helpful to put a table of contents
      list of links to individual questions at the top
      of the page so users can click it to jump directly
      to the question and answer they're interested in.
      This is similar to what we did in the tabbed example,
      but in this case, we'd use jQuery to hide the table
      of contents when the page loaded since users with
      JavaScript wouldn't need to see the table of
      contents.</p>
  </dd>
</dl>
```

**2.** You can adjust the style of the page however you'd like by adding in some CSS styles. The following screenshot shows how the page is styled in the example code included with the book:

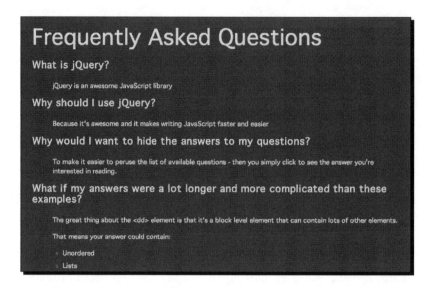

For users with JavaScript disabled, this page works fine as is. The questions hang into the left margin and are bolder and larger than the rest of the text on the page, making them easy to scan.

## What just happened?

We set up a basic definition list to hold our questions and answers. The default style of the definition list lends itself nicely to making the list of questions scannable for site visitors without JavaScript. We can enhance that further with our own custom CSS code to make the style of our list match our site.

 As this simple collapse-and-show (or accordion) action is such a common one, two new elements have been proposed for HTML5: `<summary>` and `<details>` that will enable us to build accordions in HTML without the need for JavaScript interactivity. However, at the time of writing this, the new elements are only supported in Webkit browsers, which require some finagling to get them styled with CSS, and are also not accessible. Do keep an eye on these new elements to see if more widespread support for them develops. You can read about the elements in the HTML5 specs (`http://www.whatwg.org/specs/web-apps/current-work/multipage/interactive-elements.html`). If you'd like to understand the elements better, the HTML5 Doctor has a great tutorial that explains their use and styling at `http://html5doctor.com/the-details-and-summary-elements/`.

# Time for action – moving around an HTML document

Perform the following steps to move from one element to another in JavaScript:

**1.** We're going to keep working with the files we set up in the previous section. Open up the `scripts.js` file that's inside your `scripts` folder. Add a document ready statement, then write a new empty function called `dynamicFAQ`, as follows:

```
$(document).ready(function(){
});

function dynamicFAQ() {
  // Our function will go here
}
```

**2.** Let's think through how we'd like this page to behave. We'd like to have all the answers to our questions hidden when the page is loaded. Then, when a user finds the question they're looking for, we'd like to show the associated answer when they click on the question.

This means the first thing we'll need to do is hide all the answers when the page loads. We can do this just like we did with the tab exercise in the *Chapter 2, Enhancing Links*. Get started by adding a class `jsOff` to the `<body>` tag, as follows:

```
<body class="jsOff">
```

Now, inside the document ready statement in `scripts.js`, add the line of code that removes the `jsOff` class and adds a `class` selector of `jsOn`:

```
$(document).ready(function(){
  $('body').removeClass('jsOff').addClass('jsOn');
});
```

Finally, in the `styles.css` file, add this bit of CSS to hide the answers for the site visitors who have JavaScript enabled:

```
.jsOn dd {
  display: none;
}
```

Now if you refresh the page in the browser, you'll see that the `<dd>` elements and the content they contain are no longer visible (see the following screenshot):

3. Now, we need to show the answer when the site visitor clicks on a question. To do that, we need to tell jQuery to do something whenever someone clicks on one of the questions or the `<dt>` tags. Inside the `dynamicFAQ` function, add a line of code to add a click event handler to the `<dt>` elements, as shown in the following code:

```
function dynamicFAQ() {
  $('dt').on('click', function(){
    //Show function will go here
  });
}
```

When the site visitor clicks on a question, we want to get the answer to that question and show it because our FAQ list is set up as follows:

```
<dl>
  <dt>Question 1</dt>
  <dd>Answer to Question 1</dd>
  <dt>Question 2</dt>
  <dd>Answer to Question 2</dd>
  ...
</dl>
```

We know that the answer is the next node or element in the DOM after our question. We'll start from the question. When a site visitor clicks on a question, we can get the current question by using jQuery's `$(this)` selector. The user has just clicked on a question, and we say `$(this)` to mean the question they just clicked on. Inside the new click function, add `$(this)` so that we can refer to the clicked question, as follows:

```
$('dt').on('click', function(){
  $(this);
});
```

**4.** Now that we have the question that was just clicked, we need to get the next thing, or the answer to that question so that we can show it. This is called **traversing the DOM** in JavaScript. It just means that we're moving to a different element in the document.

jQuery gives us the `next` method to move to the next node in the DOM. We'll select our answer by inserting the following code:

```
$('dt').on('click', function(){
  $(this).next();
});
```

**5.** Now, we've moved from the question to the answer. Now all that's left to do is show the answer. To do so, add a line of code as follows:

```
$('dt').on('click', function(){
  $(this).next().show();
});
```

**6.** If you refresh the page in the browser, you might be disappointed to see that nothing happens when we click the questions. Don't worry—that's easy to fix. We wrote a `dynamicFAQ()` function, but we didn't call it. Functions don't work until they're called. Inside the document ready statement, call the function as follows:

```
$(document).ready(function(){
$('body').removeClass('jsOff').addClass('jsOn');
dynamicFAQ();
});
```

**7.** Now, if we load the page in the browser, you can see that all of our answers are hidden until we click on the question. This is nice and useful, but it would be even nicer if the site visitor could hide the answer again when they're done reading it to get it out of their way. Luckily, this is such a common task, jQuery makes this very easy for us. All we have to do is replace our call to the `show` method with a call to the `toggle` method as follows:

```
$('dt').on('click', function(){
  $(this).next().toggle();
});
```

Now when you refresh the page in the browser, you'll see that clicking on the question once shows the answer and clicking on the question a second time hides the answer again.

## What just happened?

We learned how to traverse the DOM—how to get from one element to another. Toggling the display of elements on a page is a common JavaScript task, so jQuery already has built-in methods to handle it and make it simple and straightforward to get this up and running on our page. That was pretty easy—just a few lines of code.

# Sprucing up our FAQ page

That was so easy, in fact, that we have plenty of time left over to enhance our FAQ page to make it even better. This is where the power of jQuery becomes apparent—you can not only create a show/hide FAQ page, but you can make it a fancy one and still meet your deadline. How's that for impressing a client or your boss?

## Time for action – making it fancy

Perform the following steps to add some fancy new features to the FAQ page:

1. Let's start with a little CSS code to change the cursor to a pointer and add a little hover effect to our questions to make it obvious to site visitors that the questions are clickable. Open up the `styles.css` file that's inside the `styles` folder and add the following bit of CSS code:

```
.jsOn dt {
  cursor: pointer;
}

.jsOn dt:hover {
  color: #ac92ec;
}
```

We're only applying these styles for those site visitors that have JavaScript enabled. These styles definitely help to communicate to the site visitor that the questions are clickable. You might also choose to change something other than the font color for the hover effect. Feel free to style your FAQ list however you'd like. Have a look at the following screenshot:

## Frequently Asked Questions

What is jQuery?

Why should I use jQuery?

Why would I want to hide the answers to my questions?

What if my answers were a lot longer and more complicated than these examples?

What if a user doesn't have JavaScript enabled?

**2.** Now that we've made it clear that our `<dt>` elements can be interacted with, let's take a look at how to show the answers in a nicer way. When we click on a question to see the answer, the change isn't communicated to the site visitor very well; the jump in the page is a little disconcerting and it takes a moment to realize what just happened. It would be nicer and easier to understand if the questions were to slide into view. The site visitor could literally see the question appearing and would understand immediately what change just happened on the screen.

jQuery makes that easy for us. We just have to replace our call to the `toggle` method with a call to the `slideToggle` method:

```
$('dt').on('click', function(){
  $(this).next().slideToggle();
});
```

Now if you view the page in your browser, you can see that the questions slide smoothly in and out of view when the question is clicked. It's easy to understand what's happening when the page changes, and the animation is a nice touch.

**3.** Now, there's just one little detail we've still got to take care of. Depending on how you've styled your FAQ list, you might see a little jump in the answer at the end of the animation. This is caused by some extra margins around the `<p>` tags inside the `<dd>` element. They don't normally cause any issues in HTML, and browsers can figure how to display them correctly. However, when we start working with animation, sometimes this becomes a problem. It's easy to fix. Just remove the top margin from the `<p>` tags inside the FAQ list as follows:

```
.content dd p {
  margin-top: 0;
}
```

If you refresh the page in the browser, you'll see that the little jump is now gone and our animation smoothly shows and hides the answers to our questions.

## *What just happened?*

We replaced our `toggle` method with the `slideToggle` method to animate the showing and hiding of the answers. This makes it easier for the site visitor to understand the change that's taking place on the page. We also added some CSS to make the questions appear to be clickable to communicate the abilities of our page to our site visitors.

# We're almost there!

jQuery made animating that show and hide so easy that we've still got time left over to enhance our FAQ page even more. It would be nice to add some sort of indicator to our questions to show that they're collapsed and can be expanded, and to add some sort of special style to our questions once they're opened to show that they can be collapsed again.

## Time for action – adding some final touches

Perform the following steps to add some finishing touches to our FAQ list:

1. Let's start with some simple CSS code to add a small arrow icon to the left side of our questions. Head back into `style.css` and modify the styles a bit to add an arrow as follows:

```
.jsOn dt:before {
  border: 0.5em solid;
  border-color: transparent transparent transparent #f2eeef;
  content: '';
  display: inline-block;
  height: 0;
  margin-right: 0.5em;
  vertical-align: middle;
  width: 0;
}

.jsOn dt:hover:before {
  border-left-color: #ac92ec;
}
```

You might be wondering about this sort of odd bit of CSS. This is a technique to create triangles in pure CSS without having to use any images. If you're not familiar with this technique, I recommend checking out appendTo's blog post that explains pure CSS triangles at `http://appendto.com/2013/03/pure-css-triangles-explained/`.

We've also included a hover style so that the triangle will match the text color when the site visitor hovers his/her mouse over the question. Note that we're using the jsOn class so that arrows don't get added to the page unless the site visitors have JavaScript enabled. See the triangles created in the following screenshot:

## Frequently Asked Questions

▶ ·What is jQuery?

▶ Why should I use jQuery?

▶ Why would I want to hide the answers to my questions?

▶ What if my answers were a lot longer and more complicated than these examples?

▶ What if a user doesn't have JavaScript enabled?

2. Next, we'll change the arrow to a different orientation when the question is opened. We'll create a new CSS class open and use it to define some new styles for our CSS arrow using the following code:

```
.jsOn dt.open:before {
  border-color: #f2eeef transparent transparent transparent;
  border-bottom-width: 0;
}
.jsOn dt.open:hover:before {
  border-left-color: transparent;
  border-top-color: #ac92ec;
}
```

 Just make sure you add these new classes *after* the other CSS we're using to style our <dt> tags. This will ensure that the CSS cascades the way we intended.

3. So we have our CSS code to change the arrows and show our questions are open, but how do we actually use that new class? We'll use jQuery to add the class to our question when it is opened and to remove the class when it's closed.

jQuery provides some nice methods to work with CSS classes.

The addClass method will add a class to a jQuery object and the removeClass method will remove a class. However, we want to toggle our class just like we're toggling the show and hide phenomenon of our questions. jQuery's got us covered for that too. We want the class to change when we click on the question, so we'll add a line of code inside our dynamicFAQ function that we're calling each time a <dt> tag is clicked as follows:

```
$('dt').on('click', function(){
  $(this).toggleClass('open');
  $(this).next().slideToggle();
});
```

Now when you view the page, you'll see your open styles being applied to the <dt> tags when they're open and removed again when they're closed. To see this, have a look at the following screenshot:

4. However, we can actually crunch our code to be a little bit smaller. Remember how we chain methods in jQuery? We can take advantage of chaining again. We have a bit of redundancy in our code because we're starting two different lines with $(this). We can remove this extra $(this) and just add our toggleClass method to the chain we've already started as follows:

```
$(this).toggleClass('open').next().slideToggle();
```

This helps keep our code short and concise, and just look at what we're accomplishing in one line of code!

## *What just happened?*

We created the CSS styles to style the open and closed states of our questions, and then we added a bit of code to our JavaScript to change the CSS class of the question to use our new styles. jQuery provides a few different methods to update CSS classes, which is often a quick and easy way to update the display of our document in response to input from the site visitor. In this case, since we wanted to add and remove a class, we used the `toggleClass` method. It saved us from having to figure out on our own whether we needed to add or remove the open class.

We also took advantage of chaining to simply add this new functionality to our existing line of code, making the animated show and hide phenomenon of the answer and the change of CSS class of our question happen all in just one line of code. How's that for impressive power in a small amount of code?

# Summary

In this chapter, you learned how to set up a basic FAQ page that hides the answers to the questions until the site visitor needs to see them. Because jQuery made this so simple, we had plenty of time left over to enhance our FAQ page even more, adding animations to our show and hide phenomenon for the answers, and taking advantage of CSS to style our questions with special open and closed classes to communicate to our site visitors how our page works. And we did all of that with just a few lines of code!

Next, we'll learn how to build an interactive drop-down navigation menu.

# 4

# Building an Interactive
# Navigation Menu

In 2003, an article published on A List Apart (`http://alistapart.com`)
called Suckerfish Dropdowns showed how HTML and CSS alone (with just a little
JavaScript help for IE 6) can be used to build a complex multilevel drop-down
menu. The Suckerfish name derived from the gorgeously designed demo of the
technique, which featured illustrations of remoras and sharksuckers. While useful,
the original requires that the site visitors not move their mouse outside the menu
area while navigating or the menu disappears. Over the years, the Suckerfish
Dropdowns article has inspired a lot of spinoffs—Sons of Suckerfish, Improved
Suckerfish, and so on—that attempt to address the shortcomings of the original.
Because jQuery can make everything better, we'll build on this idea using the
Superfish jQuery plugin to make the menu easier to use.

The developer of the Superfish plugin, Joel Birch, says that most support issues
with the plugin come from people not understanding the CSS for the menu.
To be sure you have a firm grasp on the CSS, I highly recommend reading
the original Suckerfish Dropdowns article on A List Apart at `http://www.`
`alistapart.com/articles/dropdowns`.

To get started with this plugin, we'll be building on a basic Suckerfish menu—as
this menu only requires CSS, we still get an interactive menu if we have JavaScript
disabled. The menu is just improved for users with JavaScript enabled.

In this chapter, we'll learn:

◆ How to use the Superfish jQuery plugin to create a horizontal drop-down menu

◆ How to create a vertical fly-out menu with the Superfish plugin

◆ How to customize the drop-down and fly-out menus created with the Superfish plugin

# The horizontal drop-down menu

The horizontal drop-down menu was for a long time a common item in desktop software but challenging if not impossible to implement in websites until first CSS and, later, JavaScript finally arrived on the scene to make them possible.

## Time for action – creating a horizontal drop-down menu

Let's take a look at how we can use the Superfish plugin to enhance a CSS horizontal drop-down menu:

**1.** To get started, we'll create a simple HTML page and the associated folders and files like we created in *Chapter 1, Designer, Meet jQuery*. To get started, we won't attach the `styles.css` file to our page. We'll add that in later. The body of our HTML file will contain a heading and a navigation menu that consists of nested unordered lists, as follows:

```
<div class="content">
<h1>Butterflies</h1>
</div>

<ul id="sfNav" class="sf-menu">
  <li><a href="#">Papilionidae</a>
    <ul>
      <li><a href="#">Common Yellow Swallowtail</a></li>
      <li><a href="#">Spicebush Swallowtail</a></li>
      <li><a href="#">Lime Butterfly</a></li>
      <li><a href="#">Ornithoptera</a>
        <ul>
          <li><a href="#">Queen Victoria's Birdwing</a></li>
          <li><a href="#">Wallace's Golden Birdwing</a></li>
          <li><a href="#">Cape York Birdwing</a></li>
        </ul>
      </li>
    </ul>
  </li>
```

```html
<li><a href="#">Pieridae</a>
  <ul>
    <li><a href="#">Small White</a></li>
    <li><a href="#">Green-veined White</a></li>
    <li><a href="#">Common Jezebel</a></li>
  </ul>
</li>
<li><a href="#">Lycaenidae</a>
  <ul>
    <li><a href="#">Xerces Blue</a></li>
    <li><a href="#">Karner Blue</a></li>
    <li><a href="#">Red Pierrot</a></li>
  </ul>
</li>
<li><a href="#">Riodinidae</a>
  <ul>
    <li><a href="#">Duke of Burgundy</a></li>
    <li><a href="#">Plum Judy</a></li>
  </ul>
</li>
<li><a href="#">Nymphalidae</a>
  <ul>
    <li><a href="#">Painted Lady</a></li>
    <li><a href="#">Monarch</a></li>
    <li><a href="#">Morpho</a>
      <ul>
        <li><a href="#">Sunset Morpho</a></li>
        <li><a href="#">Godart's Morpho</a></li>
      </ul>
    </li>
    <li><a href="#">Speckled Wood</a></li>
  </ul>
</li>
<li><a href="#">Hesperiidae</a>
  <ul>
    <li><a href="#">Mallow Skipper</a></li>
    <li><a href="#">Zabulon Skipper</a></li>
  </ul>
</li>
</ul>
```

Note that we've added an `id` variable of `sfNav` and a `class` of `sf-menu` to the `<ul>` element that contains our menu. This will make it easy for us to select and style the menu the way we'd like. If you view your page in the browser, it will look something like the following screenshot:

# Butterflies

- Papilionidae
  - Common Yellow Swallowtail
  - Spicebush Swallowtail
  - Lime Butterfly
  - Ornithoptera
    - Queen Victoria's Birdwing
    - Wallace's Golden Birdwing
    - Cape York Birdwing
- Pieridae
  - Small White
  - Green-veined White
  - Common Jezebel
- Lycaenidae
  - Xerces Blue
  - Karner Blue
  - Red Pierrot
- Riodinidae
  - Duke of Burgundy
  - Plum Judy
- Nymphalidae
  - Painted Lady
  - Monarch
  - Morpho
    - Sunset Morpho
    - Godart's Morpho
  - Speckled Wood
- Hesperiidae
  - Mallow Skipper
  - Zabulon Skipper

As you can see, we've organized our links into a hierarchy. This is useful to find the information that we want, but it takes up quite a lot of space. This is where we can use a technique of hiding extra information until it's needed.

2. Next, we need a copy of the Superfish plugin. Head over to `http://plugins.jquery.com/superfish/`, where you'll find Joel Birch's Superfish plugin available for download along with links to documentation and examples. Superfish is available in the official jQuery plugin repository, as shown in the following screenshot:

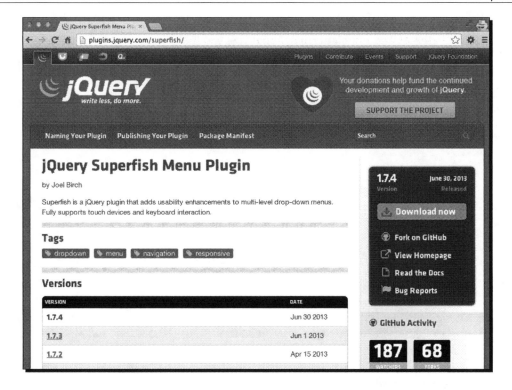

You can download a copy of the plugin by clicking on the orange **Download now** button in the black box on the right-hand side corner of the page. By clicking on this button, you will download a ZIP file to your computer. We'll open that up and take a look in a minute.

3. In the black box on the right-hand side corner, you'll also find links to more information about the plugin. If you follow the **Read the Docs** link, you'll find the documentation that explains how to use the Superfish plugin.

At the bottom of the **Getting Started** tab, you'll find the plugin's **Quick Start Guide**, where you can see that there are three simple steps to implement the Superfish plugin:

1. Write the CSS to create a Suckerfish-style drop-down menu.

2. Link to the `superfish.js` file.

3. Call the `superfish()` method on the element that contains your menu.

**4.** Now let's unzip that file we downloaded and take a look inside. There are a lot of files in there, and not all of them make sense.

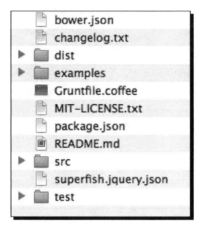

Don't be intimidated by those extra files that you don't quite understand. Files such as bower.json, Gruntfile.coffee, package.json, and superfish. jquery.json are all for more advanced developers—you don't have to give them a second thought at this point, but if you realize that you actually kind of like working with JavaScript, you might one day investigate things such as Grunt, CoffeeScript, and Bower.

In fact, the only folders we need to pay attention to here are dist and examples. In the examples folder, you'll find a couple of HTML files with working examples of Superfish. Go ahead and open those in the browser if you'd like to take a look.

Inside the dist folder, you'll find the JavaScript files required to get Superfish drop-down menus working along with some sample CSS files.

We'll use those sample CSS files to get started quickly. We'll look at customizing the appearance of our menu later, but for now, we'll go ahead and use the CSS included with the plugin.

**5.** Inside the dist folder, the first file we'll need is the superfish.css file from the css folder. Copy this file to your own styles folder.

**6.** Next, we'll edit our HTML file to include the `superfish.css` file in the head of the document:

```
<head>
  <title>Chapter 4: jQuery for Designers</title>
  <link rel="stylesheet" href="styles/superfish.css"/>
</head>
```

**7.** Now, if you refresh the page in a browser, you'll see that the long list of nested `<ul>` elements has become a working Suckerfish drop-down menu, as shown in the following screenshot:

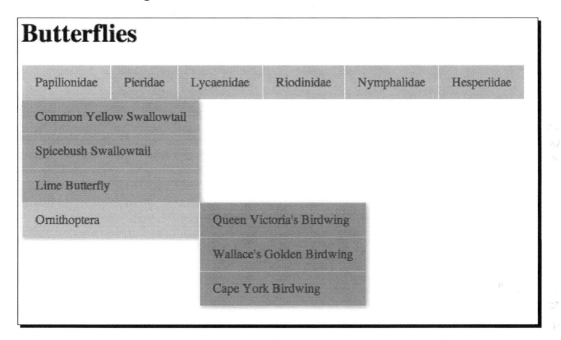

When you move your mouse over the first link, the nested `<ul>` element becomes visible. If you move your mouse down to the last link in the drop-down menu, the `<ul>` element nested at the third level becomes visible.

Keep in mind that all of this is accomplished without JavaScript—just CSS. If you spend a few moments using the menu, you'll probably quickly recognize some shortcomings. First, if you want to move your mouse from the Ornithoptera link to the Cape York Birdwing link, your natural inclination is to move your mouse diagonally. However, as soon as your mouse leaves the blue menu area, the menu closes and disappears. You have to adjust to move your mouse directly right onto the submenu, then down to the link you're interested in.

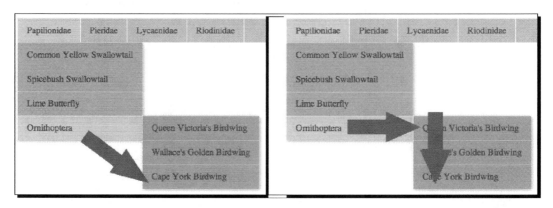

This is awkward and makes the menu feel fragile. If your mouse moves even 1 pixel outside the menu, the menu collapses and disappears. Another problem is that the menu opens as soon as the mouse hovers over it. If you are moving your mouse over the menu moving from one part of the page to another, the menu opens and closes quickly, which can be distracting and unexpected.

This is a great place for jQuery to step in to make things a bit better and more usable.

**8.** Go back to the files we downloaded, and find the `superfish.js` file inside the `js` folder. Copy it to your own `scripts` folder, and then attach the Superfish plugin to the HTML page at the bottom of the file, between jQuery and the `scripts.js` file:

```
    <script src="scripts/jquery.js"></script>
    <script src="scripts/superfish.js"></script>
    <script src="scripts/scripts.js"></script>
  </body>
</html>
```

**9.** Next, open your `scripts.js` file and we'll write the code to call the `superfish()` method. As usual, we'll get started with the document ready statement so that our script runs as soon as the page is loaded into the browser:

```
$(document).ready(function(){
  // Our code will go here.
});
```

**10.** Looking at the documentation for the Superfish plugin, we see that we only have to select the element that contains our menu and then call the `superfish()` method. Inside our `ready()` method, we'll add the following code:

```
$(document).ready(function(){
  $('#sfNav').superfish();
});
```

Now, if you refresh the page in the browser, you'll see the menu still looking very similar, but with much improved behavior. The Superfish JavaScript and CSS work together to add arrows to the menu items that have nested children. If you move your mouse away from the menu, it does not disappear immediately, making it possible to move the mouse diagonally to nested menu items. There's also a subtle fade in animation when the menu items appear. And a background color change to each menu item on hover, making it easy to see which item is currently active.

## What just happened?

We set up a navigation menu that consists of a set of nested lists, forming a hierarchy. Next, we attached a CSS file to add simple drop-down functionality to our menu. However, this CSS-only menu had a few shortcomings. So we attached the Superfish plugin to take care of those and make our menu more user friendly.

# The vertical fly-out menu

We saw how the addition of the Superfish plugin enhanced the user experience of our drop-down menu, but what if we wanted to create a vertical fly-out menu instead?

## Time for action – creating a vertical fly-out menu

Switching from a horizontal drop-down menu to a vertical fly-out menu couldn't be easier. We'll use the same HTML markup and our JavaScript code will stay the same. The only difference we'll need to make is to add some new CSS to make our menu display vertically instead of horizontally. We can keep working with the same files we used in the last example. Perform the following steps to create a fly-out menu:

**1.** In the `css` folder of the Superfish download, you'll find a file named `superfish-vertical.css`. Copy that file to your own `styles` folder. In the `head` section of the HTML file, we'll attach the new CSS file, after `superfish.css`, as shown in the following code:

```
<link rel="stylesheet" href="styles/superfish.css"/>
<link rel="stylesheet" href="styles/superfish-vertical.css"/>
```

**2.** Now, inside your `index.html` file, find the `<ul>` element that holds the entire menu and add a `class` of `sf-vertical`:

```
<nav>
  <ul id="sfNav" class="sf-menu sf-vertical">
    <li><a href="#">Papilionidae</a>
```

Now refresh the page in a browser; you'll see that the menu displays vertically with flyouts:

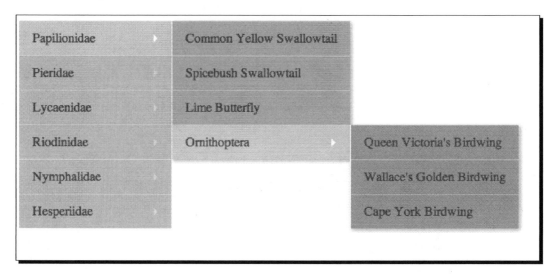

## *What just happened?*

The only difference between the horizontal drop-down menu and the vertical fly-out menu is the CSS file and a class name added to the menu container. By simply adding a new CSS file, it's possible to create a vertical fly-out menu instead of a horizontal drop-down menu.

# Customizing the navigation menu

The included CSS with the Superfish plugin makes creating an interactive navigation menu quick and simple, but a soft blue menu isn't going to fit into every design, so let's customize the menu.

We're going to take a look at how we can customize the look of the menu by writing our own CSS, customize the animation to show the nested menus, and enhance the hover behavior of the menu.

We're going to get started by writing some CSS code to create a custom look for our menus. We're going to use the *Suckerfish Dropdown* approach to create a menu that will work for our site visitors who don't have JavaScript enabled. We're going to create a simple white menu with drop-downs in green with rounded corners, as shown in the following screenshot:

Here are some things to keep in mind as you write custom CSS for a drop-down or fly-out menu.

## :hover and .sfHover

In the CSS file provided with the Superfish plugin, you'll see that the `:hover` pseudoclass is always used together with the `.sfHover` class. So you'll see the following lines in the `.css` file:

```
.sf-menu li:hover > ul,
.sf-menu li.sfHover > ul {
   display: block;
}
```

Prior to IE 7, the IE browsers did not support the `:hover` pseudoclass for elements other than links (`<a>`). The plugin dynamically added and removed this class from list items that were hovered over to enable the drop-down menus to work in all the versions of IE.

These days, usage of IE 6 has fallen off to tiny proportions for most websites and it's often not worth the extra effort required to make sure your pages look and work perfectly in this outdated browser.

Just in case you do find yourself in the unenviable position of having to write code that works in IE 6, you'll want to make sure that you include the `.sfHover` class in your CSS file. However, if you don't need to support IE 6, then you can safely skip including the extra lines in your CSS file.

## Cascading inherited styles

It's the very nature of CSS for styles to cascade down the DOM and be applied to all children of the selector as well as the selector itself. So, write code to style the list items of the first-level menu as follows:

```
ul.sf-menu li  {
   background: #cc0000; /* Dark red background */
}
```

All of the `<li>` elements in your menu are going to have a dark-red background, no matter which level of the menu they appear in. If you want to apply different styles to different menu levels, you'll have to override the cascade in other lines of code. For example, if I wanted to make the second-level menu have a dark-blue background, I'd add the following snippet of CSS *after* the preceding code:

```
ul.sf-menu li li  {
   background: #0000cc; /* Dark blue background */
}
```

This means for an `<li>` inside another `<li>`, the background will be blue. Keep in mind that now this style will in turn cascade down to other menu levels, so if you want a dark-green background for the third-level menu, you'll need to add another bit of CSS as follows:

```
ul.sf-menu li li li  {
   background: #00cc00; /* Dark green background */
}
```

In some cases, making use of direct descendent selectors in your CSS file can help to prevent you from having to write too many lines of CSS overriding styles written for elements higher up in the DOM. For example, consider the following code:

```
ul.sf-menu > li  {
   background: #cc0000; /* Dark red background */
}
```

This bit of CSS takes advantage of a direct descendent selector (>). The dark-red background, in this case, will only apply to `<li>` elements nested directly inside the `<ul>` element with a class of `.sf-menu`. It will *not* cascade down to the second- or third-level menus.

## Pop quiz – understanding the cascade in CSS

Go through the following CSS code for a nested list navigation menu:

```
ul { background: #3BAFDA; }

ul li { background: #4FC1E9; }

ul > li { background: #AC92EC }

ul li li {    background: #967ADC; }
```

Q1. What color will the background of the second level of links be?

1. #3BAFDA

2. #4FC1E9

3. #AC92EC

4. #967ADC

# Styling the :focus pseudoclass

You won't want to leave out anyone who chooses to navigate your page with their keyboard rather than their mouse, so you'll want to make sure that each time you style the `:hover` pseudoclass for links, that you also write styles for the `:focus` pseudoclass. This will make it possible for a site visitor to easily see what link is currently selected. Style both the `:hover` and `:focus` pseudoclasses as follows:

```
.sf-arrows > li > .sf-with-ul:focus:after,
.sf-arrows > li:hover > .sf-with-ul:after {
  border-top-color: white;
}
```

Note that it's not necessary to write the `:focus` styles for list items. List items don't receive focus by using the *Tab* key on the keyboard, so adding extra styles for them won't have any effect. You only have to worry about the `:focus` styles for links.

# Time for action – customizing Superfish menus

Customizing a Superfish menu mostly involves writing your own CSS code to style the menu the way you'd like. The following steps show how we'll create a custom look for the menu:

1. If you remember some web basics, you'll remember that **CSS** stands for **Cascading Style Sheets**. This cascading feature is what we'll focus on here. Any styles we write for the top level of our menu are going to cascade down to the other levels of the menu. We have to remember this and handle all the cases where we'd rather stop a style from cascading downward.

   We'll keep working with the same index.html file, but we won't need the `superfish.css` or `superfish-vertical.css` files any longer. We'll now attach our `styles.css` file to the `index.html` file to apply all of our default styles. Let's get started by writing some general styles for the menu container and other elements. Place the following code inside your `styles.css` file:

   ```
   /* General */

   nav {
     margin: 2em 0;
   }

   .sf-menu {
     background: white;
     border-radius: 7px;
   }

   .sf-menu:after {
     clear: both;
     content: '';
     display: table;
   }
   ```

   Here we're just giving our navigation menu some breathing room with a generous margin and giving the menu a white background and round corners. However, what's that last bit, with the `:after` pseudoclass in the selector?

   We're going to float our list items inside our navigation bar. We have to make sure we clear the floats so that the background color we've set is visible. This method of using the `:after` pseudoclass and setting the `clear`, `content`, and `display` attributes is clean and simple, which doesn't require any extra markup and works well across many browsers.

2. Next, let's style the top level of our menu. Add the following code to your `styles.css` file:

   ```
   /* Level 1 */

   .sf-menu li {
   ```

```
    position: relative;
    white-space: nowrap;
}

.sf-menu li:hover {
    background: #a0d468;
}

.sf-menu a {
    color: #444;
    display: block;
    padding: 1.5em 1em;
    position: relative;
    text-decoration: none;
}

.sf-menu a:hover {
    background: #a0d468;
    color: white;
}

.sf-menu > li:first-child,
.sf-menu > li:first-child a {
    border-top-left-radius: 7px;
}

.sf-menu > li {
    float: left;
}
```

We're adding a green background to the menu items on hover and changing the font color from a dark grey to white. We're also adding the corner radius to the first item to make sure the menu bar still has a top-left rounded corner when the first item is hovered over.

3. Next, let's take a look at how we'll style the second level of our menus. Add the following CSS code to your `styles.css` file to style the second level:

```
/* Level 2 */

.sf-menu ul {
    background: #a0d468;
    border-bottom-right-radius: 7px;
    border-bottom-left-radius: 7px;
```

```css
  display: none;
  left: 0;
  min-width: 12em;
  position: absolute;
  top: 100%;
  z-index: 99;
}

.sf-menu ul li:hover {
  background: #8cc152;
}

.sf-menu ul a:hover {
  background: #8cc152;
}

.sf-menu li:hover > ul {
  display: block;
}

.sf-menu ul > li:last-child,
.sf-menu ul > li:last-child a {
  border-bottom-left-radius: 7px;
  border-bottom-right-radius: 7px;
}
```

The items in this menu level have a green background and turns to a darker green on hover. We have also added rounded corners to the bottom, which requires us then to add rounded corners to the last item in each nested `<ul>` element.

**4.** Finally, we still have a third level of menu to style. Add these styles to your `styles.css` file:

```css
/* Level 3 */

.sf-menu ul ul {
  background: #8cc152;
  border-top-right-radius: 7px;
  top: 0;
  left: 100%;
}

.sf-menu ul ul li:hover {
  background: #7bb140;
}
```

```css
.sf-menu ul ul a:hover {
  background: #7bb140;
}

.sf-menu ul ul > li:first-child,
.sf-menu ul ul > li:first-child a {
  border-top-right-radius: 7px;
}

.sf-menu ul ul > li:last-child,
.sf-menu ul ul > li:last-child a {
  border-bottom-right-radius: 7px;
}
```

This third level has a background color that's just a shade darker than the level before, and when hovered, turns another shade darker. The progression to darker shades of green helps to communicate the relationships between the items in our menu.

**5.** The last thing we need to do is write some styles to add arrows to our menu items if they have submenu items hiding underneath them. These styles are only used if JavaScript is enabled, but they're one more little thing Superfish does to make our menus more user-friendly. We'll use the same CSS triangle technique that we've seen a couple of times already. Add the following CSS code to your `styles.css` file:

```css
/* Extras */

.sf-arrows .sf-with-ul {
  padding-right: 2.5em;
}

.sf-arrows .sf-with-ul:after {
  border: 5px solid transparent;
  border-top-color: #444;
  content: '';
  height: 0;
  margin-top: -3px;
  position: absolute;
  right: 1em;
  top: 50%;
  width: 0;
}

.sf-arrows > li > .sf-with-ul:focus:after,
.sf-arrows > li:hover > .sf-with-ul:after {
```

```
  border-top-color: white;
}

.sf-arrows ul .sf-with-ul:after {
  margin-top: -5px;
  margin-right: -3px;
  border-color: transparent;
  border-left-color: #e7f2dc;
}

.sf-arrows ul li > .sf-with-ul:focus:after,
.sf-arrows ul li:hover > .sf-with-ul:after {
  border-left-color: white;
}
```

And take a deep breath, because we've finally reached the end of the CSS code to create a custom style for the menu. The bonus of this CSS code is that it will work even without JavaScript enabled. The Superfish plugin just enhances the menu and makes it more usable.

## What just happened?

We wrote custom CSS to style our menu to match a design that we created. We had to dig into the cascading feature of CSS and decide which styles should cascade down through all levels of the menu and which should not. Just be patient and keep the cascade in mind as you work down through the levels of the menu.

# The hoverIntent plugin

Earlier, I pointed out that one problem with our menu was how quickly the menu reacted to the mouseover event. Any time the mouse is moved over the menu, the nested menus open. While that might seem like a good thing at first, it might be disconcerting or surprising to site visitors if they are simply moving their mouse on the screen and aren't intending to use the drop-down or fly-out menus.

The Superfish plugin has built-in support for the hoverIntent plugin. The hoverIntent plugin sort of pauses the mouseover event and makes the page wait to see if the mouse slows down or stops on an item to make sure it's what the site visitor intended to do. That way if the site visitor just happens to roll their mouse over the drop-down menu on their way to something else on the page, the submenus won't start appearing, throwing them into confusion.

If you'll recall, the hoverIntent plugin was actually included in the ZIP file when we downloaded the Superfish plugin. To take advantage of the hoverIntent plugin, perform the following steps:

1. In the Superfish download, locate the `hoverIntent.js` file inside the `js` folder and copy the file to your own `scripts` folder.

2. Next, we need to attach the hoverIntent plugin to our HTML page.

 Don't forget to keep dependencies in mind when attaching multiple JavaScript files to a page. All jQuery plugins depend on jQuery to operate, so jQuery needs to be attached to your page before any plugins. In this case, the Superfish plugin depends on the hoverIntent plugin, so we need to make sure hoverIntent is added to our page before the Superfish plugin.

Add the new `<script>` tag to the bottom of your page with the other scripts as follows:

```
<script src="scripts/jquery.js"></script>
<script src="scripts/hoverIntent.js"></script>
<script src="scripts/superfish.js"></script>
<script src="scripts/scripts.js">
</script>
</body>
</html>
```

Now if you refresh the page in a browser, you'll see that there's a short pause when your mouse moves over the menu before the nested submenu appears. And if you run your mouse across the page quickly, crossing the menu, no unwanted submenus appear on the page.

# Time for action – incorporating custom animations

Next, a sliding animation would be better suited to our menu style. The default animation is to fade the submenus in. We can override this default behavior and replace it with a sliding animation.

*1.* Fading the menu in means that the menu opacity is animating from 0 percent to 100 percent. We'd rather animate the height of the submenu, so that the submenu slides into view. To do that, open up your `scripts.js` file and customize the animation value inside the `superfish()` method as follows:

```
$(document).ready(function(){
  $('#sfNav').superfish({
    animation:  {height:'show'}
  });
});
```

Just adding a value here will override the default behavior of the plugin and replace it with the animation we choose instead.

Now when you refresh the page in a browser, you'll see the submenus slide into view instead of fade in, which is a much more fitting animation for the CSS We've used to style the menus.

## What just happened?

We took advantage of one of the customization options for the Superfish plugin to change the show animation of the nested subnavigation links. There are more customization options covered in the documentation of the Superfish menu.

## Have a go hero – further customizing the Superfish menu

Review the styles that make a CSS-only drop-down menu work and look through the documentation for the Superfish plugin. Design and build your own custom drop-down or fly-out menu. Try using the different customization options for the Superfish plugin that are outlined in the documentation.

# Summary

Whew! That was a lot of work we just did, but I have to say we have a pretty impressive navigation menu to show for our efforts. We learned how to use the Superfish jQuery plugin to produce horizontal drop-down menus or vertical fly-out menus. Also, we learned how to fully customize the look and feel of our menu to fit our site design perfectly. Being able to hide subsections of the site until they're needed makes a complex navigation structure less overwhelming for your site visitors. It's simple and clear to see what the main sections of the site are, and they can easily drill down to just the content they want.

Next, we'll take a look at displaying content in lightboxes.

# 5

# Showing Content in Lightboxes

*It's become common to see galleries of photos displayed in lightboxes on the Web. Lightboxes can be useful for other things too—playing videos, showing additional information, displaying important information to site visitors, or even showing other websites. In this chapter, we'll see how to use the flexible and adaptable Colorbox plugin to create lightboxes for a variety of purposes.*

An example of an image shown in a lightbox is depicted in the following screenshot:

In this chapter, we'll take a look at how to use the Colorbox plugin to do the following:

◆ Create a simple photo gallery

◆ Customize photo gallery settings

◆ Build a fancy login box

◆ Play a collection of videos

◆ Create a one-page website portfolio

# A simple photo gallery

A simple photo gallery is probably the most common use for lightboxes. We'll set up a page that shows thumbnails of each photo and displays the full-size image in a lightbox when the thumbnail is clicked. To get started, you'll need a series of photographs with smaller-sized thumbnails of each.

## Time for action – setting up a simple photo gallery

We'll walk through the creation of a simple photo gallery with the Colorbox plugin:

***1.*** We'll get started by setting up a basic HTML page and associated files and folders just like we did in *Chapter 1, Designer, Meet jQuery*. The body of the HTML document will contain a heading and a list of thumbnails as shown in the following code:

```
<div class="content">
  <h1>Ireland</h1>
</div>
<ul class="thumb-list">
  <li><a href="images/cemetary.jpg" title="Celtic Cemetary with
Celtic Crosses" rel="ireland"><img src="images/thumbs/cemetary.
jpg" alt="Celtic Cemetary"/></a></li>
  <li><a href="images/cliffs-of-moher.jpg" title="Cliffs of
Moher" rel="ireland"><img src="images/thumbs/cliffs-of-moher.jpg"
alt="Cliffs of Moher"/></a></li>

  ...
</ul>
```

Note that we've wrapped each thumbnail in a link to the full-size version of the image. If you load the page in a browser, you'll see that the page works for users with JavaScript disabled. Clicking on a thumbnail opens the full-sized image in the browser. The back button takes you back to the gallery.

Note that we've also included a `title` attribute on each link. This is helpful for our site visitors as it will show a short description of the image in a tooltip when they hover over the thumbnail with their mouse, but it will also be used later on for the Colorbox plugin. We've also included a `rel` attribute on each link and set its value to `ireland`. This will make selecting our group of links to Ireland's images easy when we're ready to add the Colorbox plugin's magic.

2. Next, we'll add a bit of CSS to lay our images out in a grid. Open `styles.css` and add the following styles:

```css
.thumb-list {
  margin: 2em 0;
  text-align: center;
}

.thumb-list li {
  display: inline-block;
  padding: 0.5em;
}
```

Refresh the page and you will see something like the following screenshot:

Feel free to play around a bit with the CSS to create a different layout for your image thumbnails if you'd like.

**3.** Now, let's add the jQuery magic. We're going to use Jack Moore's Colorbox plugin. Head over to `http://jacklmoore.com/colorbox` to find the downloads, documentation, and demos. You'll find the download link near the top of the page. Just click on the big blue **Download** link to download a ZIP file.

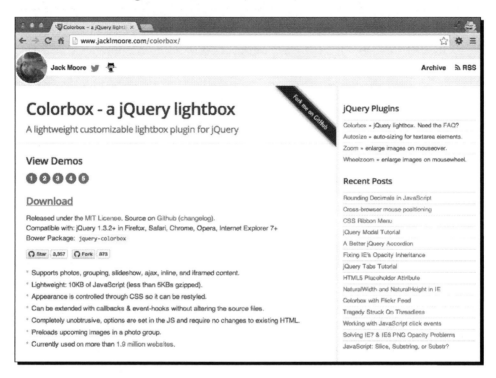

**4.** Unzip the folder and take a look inside it. You'll not only find the plugin script file but a lot of other goodies as well.

The plugin code itself is contained in the two JavaScript files—you'll find both the development and minified versions. Each of the five example folders contains an example file (index.html) that shows the plugin in action. Why five different folders you might ask? Each folder contains the same basic example but with five different styles for Colorbox. These same examples can be viewed on the Colorbox website by clicking the numbers in the **View Demos** section on the website.

Right out of the box, the plugin's developers provide us with five different possibilities for our Colorbox's look and feel. And if that's not enough choice, they've also included a colorbox.ai (Adobe Illustrator) file that contains all the image assets used to create these five different looks. You can customize them to your heart's content and then export your new fully customized look from Illustrator to create your own appearance. Changing colors and special effects is straightforward enough, but remember that if you change the size and shape of the image assets, you'll have to touch up the accompanying CSS file to accommodate the new sizes.

The content folder contains the image assets that make the examples work. We again see the .json files for Bower—you can safely ignore those for now. If you find that you really like working with jQuery and want to move on to more advanced techniques, you can explore Bower. We've also got a README file and an i18n folder—this is for internationalization or translating the plugin so that it can be used on sites written in languages other than English.

5. Try out each of the different examples, either on the website or using the example files included in the ZIP download file. Note that the appearance, size, and placement of the back and forward buttons, the close button, the caption, and the pagination indicator (**Image 1 of 3**), among others, are all controlled via CSS—not the plugin code itself. This makes it very easy to customize the look and feel; it's all done via CSS rather than in JavaScript.

6. Copy jquery.colorbox-min.js from the Colorbox download to your own scripts folder.

**7.** We'll get started by choosing one of the provided CSS styles. Pick your favorite, then copy and paste its CSS file to your own `styles` folder. Open up the images folder for that CSS skin and copy and paste the images from that folder to your own `images` folder. Once you've chosen a style, your own setup should look like the one shown in the following screenshot:

The `index.html` file contains the HTML with thumbnail images that link to full-sized versions. The `images` folder contains the images provided with your chosen Colorbox skin, along with your own images for the slideshow, both the thumbnail and full-sized versions. The `scripts` folder contains jQuery (`jquery.js`) and the Colorbox plugin script (`jquery.colorbox-min.js`). The `styles` folder contains the CSS file for the Colorbox skin you chose.

**8.** We do have to open up `colorbox.css` to make a minor set of edits. In the example files, the CSS file is not in a `styles` or `css` folder, but rather sits at the top level alongside the `index.html` file. We've chosen to follow our preferred convention and store our CSS in our `styles` folder. This means that we'll have to open the `colorbox.css` file and update the references to the images in the CSS. We'll have to modify file paths that look like this:

```
#cboxTopLeft{
  width: 21px;
  height: 21px;
  background: url(images/controls.png) no-repeat -100px 0;
}
```

The new file paths should look like this:

```
#cboxTopLeft{
  width: 21px;
  height: 21px;
  background:url(../images/controls.png) no-repeat -100px 0;
}
```

We're just telling the CSS to go up one level and then look for the images folder. You should be able to replace all of these quickly by using the **Find and Replace** functionality of your text editor.

**9.** Next, open up your index.html file and attach the colorbox.css file in the head section, before your own styles.css:

```
<head>
  <title>Chapter 8: Showing Content in Lightboxes</title>
  <link rel="stylesheet" href="styles/colorbox.css"/>
  <link rel="stylesheet" href="styles/styles.css"/>
</head>
```

**10.** Then, head down to the bottom of the file, just before the closing </body> tag and attach the Colorbox plugin, after jQuery and before your own scripts.js file:

```
<script src="scripts/jquery.js"></script>
<script src="scripts/jquery.colorbox-min.js"></script>
<script src="scripts/scripts.js"></script>
```

**11.** Now, remember the rel="ireland" attribute we included on each of our links? We're going to use that in our JavaScript to select all of our Ireland image links for the Colorbox plugin. Open your scripts.js file and write the attribute selector to select all links with a rel attribute equal to ireland inside the document's ready statement:

```
$(document).ready(function(){
  $('a[rel="ireland"]')
});
```

**12.** The only thing left to do is call the `colorbox()` method on those links—the Colorbox plugin will take care of everything else for us.

```
$('a[rel="ireland"]').colorbox();
```

Now, if you open the page in the browser and click on one of the thumbnail images, you'll see the full-size image open up in a Colorbox. You can navigate through all of the full-size images without having to close the lightbox, thanks to the back and forward buttons. You can also move between the images by pressing the left and right arrow keys on your keyboard. The pagination indicator helps you to see where you are in the collection of photos. You'll also notice that the `title` attribute included on each link gets reused as an image caption for each image. The Colorbox can be closed by clicking on the close button, clicking outside the Colorbox, or by hitting the *Esc* key on your keyboard. All in all, it's a pretty nice experience right out of the box.

## What just happened?

We used the Colorbox jQuery plugin to turn a list of links to images into a lightbox that allows site visitors to navigate through the full-size images without leaving the page. We used the `title` attribute of the links to provide captions for the images. We used one of the five Colorbox styles provided with the plugin to create a nicely designed lightbox.

# Customizing Colorbox's behavior

If you take a look through the **Settings** section of the Colorbox website, you'll see that you have plenty of options to customize how Colorbox behaves. Let's take a look at how we can put some of these options to use. For this section, we'll keep working with the files we set up in the previous section.

# Transition

First up, we'll try out the different transition effects that are available. The default transition is `elastic`. If your full-size images are all different sizes, you'll see that Colorbox uses a nice resizing animation to transition between them. The other options for transitions are `fade` and `none`. Let's take a look at how we can modify the transition.

# Time for action – using a custom transition

Follow these steps to change the default transition between images:

1. For this example, we'll take a look at how to use the `fade` transition. Open your `scripts.js` file. All we have to do is pass the `fade` value for `transition` to the `colorbox()` method as follows:

```
$(document).ready(function(){
  $('a[rel="ireland"]').colorbox({transition:'fade'});
});
```

   Note that we've added some curly braces inside the parentheses. Inside these curly braces, we can pass in key/value pairs to customize different aspects of the Colorbox. In this case, the key is `transition` and the value is `'fade'`.

   If you reload the page in the browser, click one of the thumbnails, and then click the next and previous buttons to flip through the images; you'll see that the Colorbox fades out and then back in between each image.

2. What if we decided that we'd rather get rid of the transitions altogether? We'd simply have to change the value for the `transition` key to `'none'`.

```
$(document).ready(function(){
  $('a[rel="ireland"]').colorbox({transition:'none'});
});
```

   Now, if you refresh the page in the browser, you'll see that the images change without any transition effect between them.

## What just happened?

We saw how to take advantage of one of the available settings with the Colorbox plugin and modified the transition between images as our site visitor moves through them.

## Fixed size

In a case where the photos you're loading into the Colorbox are of widely varying sizes, you might decide that all the resizing is distracting to the site visitors and that you want to set a fixed size for the Colorbox. That's easy to do as well, by passing in a couple more key/value pairs. Looking through the documentation, you'll see that there are many settings to control the width and height of the Colorbox. To keep things simple, we're going to use `width` and `height`.

## Time for action – setting a fixed size

Follow these steps to set a fixed width and height for the Colorbox:

1. Open up your `scripts.js` file. We're going to make a few changes to our code to set a fixed width and height for the Colorbox:

```
$('a[rel="ireland"]').colorbox({
  transition: 'none',
  width: '90%',
  height: '70%'
});
```

2. Now, if you refresh the page in the browser window, you'll see that the Colorbox remains the same size. No matter what size the images or the browser window is, Colorbox will always fill 90 percent of the width and 70 percent of the height of the browser window. The images inside resize proportionally to fit into the available space if they are too large.

3. You can set a fixed width and height in pixels or percentages. Percentage height and width are useful in responsive designs. You can be sure that your site visitor will see the entire image, no matter what size their screen happens to be.

## What just happened?

We set the `width` and `height` settings to percentage values. This is a really helpful option if you have large photos that could potentially be larger than your site visitor's browser window. Setting the `width` and `height` values to percentage values ensures that in this case, the Colorbox will be 90 percent of the width and 70 percent of the height of your site visitor's browser window, no matter what size the browser window happens to be. This way, if the browser window is small, your site visitor will be able to see the complete photo.

Colorbox also provides some other settings for the width and height:

◆ **innerWidth/innerHeight**: These keys provide the width and height values for the content *inside* the Colorbox instead of for the Colorbox itself. This can be helpful in cases where you know the exact width and height of the actual content, for example, a video player.

- **initialWidth/initialHeight**: Colorbox is very flexible and can be used for a variety of different content (as we'll see shortly). Setting an `initialWidth` and `initialHeight` set of values allows you to control the size of the Colorbox before any content is loaded in. If you load in content via AJAX, it can take a few moments to load into the Colorbox. Setting `initialWidth` and `initialHeight` allows you to specify how large the Colorbox should be while you wait for the content to be loaded in.

- **maxWidth/maxHeight**: These keys allow you to set a maximum width and maximum height for the Colorbox. If the content is smaller, then the box will appear smaller on the screen. However, when you're loading larger content, it won't exceed the `maxWidth` and `maxHeight` values you specify. For example, if you want to set up a Colorbox for images in a variety of sizes, you can allow Colorbox to be resized with fade or elastic transitions between images, but set `maxWidth` and `maxHeight` to be sure that larger images won't exceed the visitor's browser window.

## Creating a slideshow

Colorbox also provides us with an option to automatically cycle through all the images so that the visitor doesn't have to continually click on the next button to see them all.

## Time for action – creating a slideshow

We'll keep working with the files we created in the previous section. Here's how we can turn our lightbox image gallery into a slideshow:

1. Open `scripts.js`. We're going to add another key/value pair to our settings. To create a slideshow inside our Colorbox, set the `slideshow` key to `true`:

```
$('a[rel="ireland"]').colorbox({
  transition: 'none',
  width: '90%',
  height: '70%',
  slideshow: true
});
```

Now, if you refresh the page in the browser, you'll see that after you open the Colorbox, it automatically cycles through the images, using whichever transition effect you've chosen. A link is provided so that site visitors can stop the slideshow at any time. You will see your Colorbox similar to the one shown in the following screenshot:

2. Colorbox provides a few more keys that we can use to control the slideshow. We can provide a value for `slideshowSpeed` to set the number of milliseconds for which each photo will be displayed. If we don't want the slideshow to automatically play, we can set `slideshowAuto` to `false`. We can change the text that appears in the link to start and stop the slideshow by passing in values for the `slideshowStart` and `slideshowStop` keys respectively. This would all look like the following code:

```
$('a[rel="ireland"]').colorbox({
  transition: 'none',
  width: '90%',
  height: '60%',
  slideshow: true,
  slideshowSpeed: 2000,
  slideshowAuto: false,
  slideshowStart: 'Let\'s get started!',
  slideshowStop: 'Ok, that\'s enough.'
});
```

With this code, we've set up our slideshow to show each photo for 2 seconds (2000 milliseconds), to not start the slideshow automatically, and to customize the text on the links that start and stop the slideshow.

Note that each key/value pair is separated by a comma, but that there's no comma after the last key/value pair. No comma after the last one is only important for Internet Explorer—if you accidentally put a comma after the last key/value pair in Internet Explorer, it will throw an error and none of your JavaScript will work. Other browsers will ignore that last comma and continue to work gracefully.

 Always test your work in Internet Explorer before you make it available to the public.

Let's talk for a minute about the \ ' set of characters that appear in the text we're using for the link to start and stop the slideshow. Since these are strings, we have to wrap them in quote marks; either `'single'` quotes or `"double"` quotes will work, and which one you choose is a matter of personal preference. We have to tell JavaScript that these are part of my string and not characters that JavaScript should pay attention to. In JavaScript-speak this is called **escaping** those characters.

Consider the following line:

```
slideshowStart: 'Let's get started!'
```

When JavaScript got to the `'` character in `Let's`, it would get confused because it would think that it had reached the end of the string and wouldn't know what to make of the rest of that line of text. It would throw an error.

In this case, if our personal preference were for using double quotes to write strings, we wouldn't have to do anything at all. The following line of code would be perfectly acceptable:

```
slideshowStart: "Let's get started!"
```

Since we're using double quotes around our string, there's no chance that JavaScript will accidentally read it as the end of our string. Once JavaScript sees an opening `"` character, it will automatically look for the matching ending `"` character.

Now that we've got our slideshow customized, refresh the page in the browser and click on one of the image thumbnails to open the Colorbox. The only visible difference is the addition of the **Let's get started** link. Clicking on it kicks off the slideshow and switches the link to say **Ok, that's enough** so that we can stop the slideshow.

## What just happened?

We saw how to create and customize a slideshow. We did this by taking the simple lightbox photo gallery we created and customizing it by passing a series of key/value pairs to the `colorbox()` method.

# Fancy login

It's nice enough to be able to use a lightbox to display images, galleries, and slideshows, but Colorbox is more capable and flexible than that. In this section, we'll take a look at how to show a login form in a Colorbox. Note that our login form isn't hooked up to anything and won't actually function in the sample case. However, this same technique can be applied to a dynamic site to allow your site visitors to view the login form in a lightbox.

## Time for action – creating a fancy login form

Follow these steps to create a login form in a lightbox:

1. We'll get started by setting up an HTML page and the associated files and folders, like we did in *Chapter 1, Designer, Meet jQuery*. Our HTML page will contain a header that displays a login form as shown in the following code. It's common for sites to allow people to log in from any page on the site.

```
<header id="page-header">
  <h1>Ireland: The Emerald Isle</h1>
  <form action="#" id="login-form">
    <div><label for="username">Username:</label> <input
type="text" id="username"/></div>
    <div><label for="password">Password:</label> <input
type="password" id="password"/></div>
    <div><input type="submit" value="Log In"/></div>
  </form>
</header>
```

2. Next, we'll open `styles.css` and add some CSS so that the header is displayed with the title on the left and the form on the right:

```
#page-header {
  background: white;
  color: #444;
  border-radius: 7px;
  overflow: hidden;
}

#page-header h1 {
  background: #fc6e51;
  color: white;
```

```
    float: left;
    font-size: 1.5em;
    padding: 0.5em 0 0.5em 1em;
    width: 35%;
}

#login-form {
    float: right;
    line-height: 2.75em;
    padding: 0 1em 0 0;
}

#page-header #login-form div {
    display: inline;
}

#login-form input[type='text'],
#login-form input[type='password'] {
    width: 8em;
}

#login-form input[type='submit'] {
    background: #333;
    border: 0 none;
    border-radius: 7px;
    color: white;
    cursor: pointer;
    padding: 0.25em 1em;
}

#login-form input[type='submit']:hover {
    background: #fc6e51;
}

#login-link {
    display: block;
    float: right;
    line-height: 2.75em;
    padding-right: 1em;
}

input {
    font-family: inherit;
    font-size: inherit;
}
```

If you view the page in a browser, you'll see this:

This is perfectly acceptable for users without JavaScript enabled—they'll be able to log in to the site from any page. However, it is a bit cluttered, so if our site visitor has JavaScript enabled, we'll want to hide the login form and show it in a Colorbox when the site visitor is ready to log in.

3. Next, we'll get ready to use the Colorbox plugin the same way we did in the previous section. Choose one of the provided styles for Colorbox and attach its style sheet to the head section of our document, move all the required images to your image directory and update the path to the images in the CSS, and attach the Colorbox plugin at the foot of the document, between jQuery and our `scripts.js` tag.

4. Once all that's out of the way, we're ready to write our JavaScript. Open up `scripts.js` and write your document ready statement:

```
$(document).ready(function(){
  //Our code goes here
});
```

5. The first thing we need to do is hide the login form. We're going to do that using JavaScript rather than CSS because we do want the login form to be visible for the site visitors who don't have JavaScript enabled. We want to hide the form immediately as soon as the page is loaded, so we'll write our hidden code inside the `ready()` method for the document:

```
$(document).ready(function(){
  var form = $('#login-form');
  form.hide()
});
```

You'll notice that we created a variable called `form` and used it to store the jQuery selector for the form. We're going to have to refer to the login form several times in our code. We could write `$('#login-form')` each time we want to select the login form, but each time, jQuery would have to look through the DOM of the page to find it again. If we store it in a variable, our code will run faster and be more efficient since jQuery will not have to find the login form each time we refer to it. In JavaScript-speak, we'd call this *caching a selector*.

If you refresh the page in the browser, you'll see that the login form has disappeared.

6. However, now, we need a way to show it to the site visitors so they can log in to the site. We'll use jQuery to add a login link to the page, which will appear right where the form was:

```
$(document).ready(function(){
  var form = $('#login-form');
  form.hide()
  form.before('<a href="#login-form" id="login-link">Login</a>');
});
```

We're already referring to the form again by inserting the login link before the form. We already included some styles in the CSS to style the link and display it where we'd like. If you refresh the page in the browser, you'll see that the login form has been replaced with a login link.

| Ireland: The Emerald Isle | | Login |

**7.** However, clicking on the login link doesn't do anything. Let's fix this by adding in some Colorbox magic. We'll select our login link and call the `colorbox()` method as shown in the following code:

```
$(document).ready(function(){
  var form = $('#login-form');
  form.hide()
  form.before('<a href="#login-form" id="login-link">Login</a>');
  $('#login-link').colorbox();
});
```

Refresh the page in the browser and try clicking the link. We just get an empty Colorbox without any content inside. Hmmm. This is not really what we had in mind, right? We have to tell Colorbox that we want to load up some content that's already on the page.

**8.** We already put the reference to the login form in the `href` attribute of the link, so we'll use that to our advantage. We'll pass a couple of key/value pairs to the `colorbox()` method to tell Colorbox that we want to load some content that's already on the page, and we'll also tell Colorbox exactly which content we want to show:

```
$(document).ready(function(){
  var form = $('#login-form');
  form.hide();
  form.before('<a href="#login-form" id="login-link">Login</a>');
  $('#login-link').colorbox({
    inline: true,
    content: $(this).attr('href')
  });
});
```

Refresh the page in the browser and you'll see that the Colorbox opens, but it appears to be empty. This is because we hid our form. It's been loaded into the Colorbox, but it's hidden from view.

**9.** We'll use another key/value pair to tell Colorbox to show the form when the Colorbox opens:

```
$(document).ready(function(){
  var form = $('#login-form');
  form.hide()
  form.before('<a href="#login-form" id="login-link">Login</a>');
  $('#login-link').colorbox({
    inline: true,
    content: $(this).attr('href'),
    onOpen: function() { form.show(); }
  });
});
```

The onOpen tag is one of the keys provided by the Colorbox plugin. It allows us to write a function that will be run when the Colorbox opens. In this case, we're searching the form and showing it. Now, if you refresh the page in the browser, you'll be able to see the form in the Colorbox as shown in the following screenshot:

**10.** This looks good enough, and we'll touch this up with a bit of CSS in a moment to make it look even better. But what happens when you close the Colorbox? That pesky login form is visible again in the header. So we'll pass another key/value pair to our colorbox() method to hide the form when the Colorbox closes:

```
$(document).ready(function(){
  var form = $('#login-form');
  form.hide()
  form.before('<a href="#login-form" id="login-link">Login</a>');
  $('#login-link').colorbox({
```

```
    inline: true,
    content: $(this).attr('href'),
    onOpen: function() { form.show(); },
    onCleanup: function() { form.hide(); }
  });
});
```

This new function will hide our form when we close the Colorbox. This will ensure the form doesn't show up in the header again.

**11.** Now, let's make our login form look a bit friendlier. Open up `styles.css` and add some CSS that will style the login form only when it appears inside the lightbox:

```css
#cboxContent #login-form {
  line-height: 1.25;
  padding: 0.5em 1em;
}


#cboxContent #login-form div {
  padding: 0.25em 0;
}


#cboxContent #login-form div:after {
  clear: both;
  content: '';
  display: table;
}


#cboxContent input[type='text'],
#cboxContent input[type='password'],
#cboxContent input[type='submit'] {
  font-size: 1.25em;
  padding: 0.25em;
  width: 90%;
}
```

**12.** We also want to make the login form box a bit wider, so we're going to pass a `width` key to the `colorbox()` method:

```javascript
$(document).ready(function(){
  var form = $('#login-form');
  form.hide()
  form.before('<a href="#login-form" id="login-link">Login</a>');
  $('#login-link').colorbox({
    width: '400px',
```

```
      inline: true,
      content: $(this).attr('href'),
      onOpen: function() { form.show(); },
      onCleanup: function() { form.hide(); }
    });
});
```

Now, if you refresh the page in the browser, you'll see that the Colorbox is indeed 400 pixels wide, and our login form has taken on the nice chunky appearance we wanted with our CSS, but there's still a bit of a problem. Our form is too tall for the Colorbox, as shown in the following screenshot:

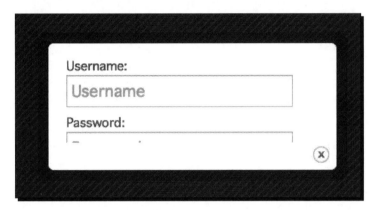

The Colorbox script hasn't realized that our form has a different set of CSS once it's displayed inside the Colorbox—it's still expecting the form to be of the same height it was when it was displayed in the header. However, that form is much smaller. If you take your mouse over the login form and scroll down, you'll see the rest of the login form is there—we just can't see it.

**13.** We don't want any scrolling in our Colorbox, so we'll turn that off and we'll tell the Colorbox to resize itself to its content instead by passing a couple more key/value pairs to the `colorbox()` method:

```
$(document).ready(function(){
  var form = $('#login-form');
  form.hide()
  form.before('<a href="#login-form" id="login-link">Login</a>');
  $('#login-link').colorbox({
    width: '400px',
    inline: true,
    scrolling: false,
```

```
        content: $(this).attr('href'),
        onOpen: function() { form.show(); },
        onComplete: function() { $.colorbox.resize(); },
        onCleanup: function() { form.hide(); }
    });
});
```

The `scrolling` key allows us to turn off any scrolling inside the Colorbox, and the `onComplete` key is a callback function that's called as soon as the content loads into the Colorbox. As soon as the content loads into the Colorbox, we're going to call a method that the Colorbox plugin has made available to us in order to resize the Colorbox to accommodate its content.

Now, if you refresh the page in the browser, you'll see the Colorbox slide open to a larger height to accommodate the new CSS for our form. Perfect!

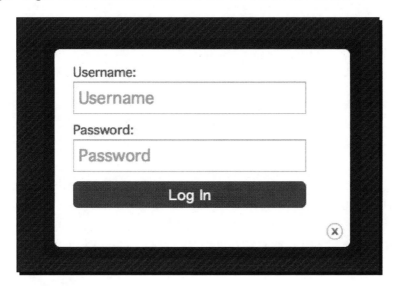

## What just happened?

We learned how to take a simple header login form and change it to a login link that opens a login form in a Colorbox when clicked. We worked through any potential problems caused by this approach by passing in callback functions as values for keys specified in the Colorbox plugin documentation. We learned how to call functions to run when the Colorbox opens, when the content is loaded into the Colorbox, and when the Colorbox closes. We learned that we can force the Colorbox to resize to accommodate its current contents by calling the `$.colorbox.resize()` method.

# Video player

Colorbox is flexible enough to be used to display a video player as content. We'll link out to a YouTube video, then add some Colorbox magic to display the video in a Colorbox.

In this section, we'll dive into using AJAX for the first time. In case you aren't familiar, AJAX is a method that is used to fetch some new content from the server and displays it to the site visitor without having to completely refresh the page. As the browser only gets and displays just the bit of information the site visitor needs, it's often much faster and snappier than loading a whole new page.

Just a quick note before we dive into AJAX for the first time. Modern browsers have several security rules for AJAX requests. You won't be able to simply view your ajaxified HTML files in a browser as we've been doing up until this point. In order to view AJAX in action, you'll either have to upload your files to a server before viewing them, or you'll have to set up a server on your own computer. For an easy and hassle-free way to set up a server on your own computer, I highly recommend DesktopServer from ServerPress. You can learn more and download DesktopServer from `http://serverpress.com/products/desktopserver/`. DesktopServer works for both Windows and Mac users.

## Time for action – showing a video in a lightbox

Follow these steps to set up Colorbox to play a set of videos:

1.  We'll get started as we usually do, by setting up a basic HTML file and the associated files and folders, just like we did in *Chapter 1, Designer, Meet jQuery*. In the body of our HTML document, we're going to include a link to a YouTube video:

    ```
    <p>
      <a href="http://www.youtube.com/embed/wsRk0TXYXuA?autoplay=1"
    id="video-link">Watch the video</a>
    </p>
    ```

    Note a couple of things about my video link. First, I'm using the embed URL for the video rather than the link to YouTube's video page. For users without JavaScript enabled, this will take them to a standalone video player page on YouTube's site. For users with JavaScript enabled, it will ensure that only the video player is loaded into the Colorbox rather than the full YouTube video page. Second, I'm adding a parameter to the URL for the video, setting `autoplay` to 1. This is how you can make embedded YouTube videos play automatically when the site visitor views your page. It's generally a bad idea to have a video autoplay, but in this case, the user will have already clicked a link that says **Watch the video**, so it seems like a safe bet that they'll be expecting a video to play once they've clicked that link.

**2.** Next, just as with the other Colorbox examples so far, you'll need to attach your chosen Colorbox skin's CSS file in the head of your document; make sure the images are available, update the path to the images in the CSS if necessary, and finally attach the Colorbox plugin in the foot of the document.

**3.** Now, we'll open up our `scripts.js` file and get set to write our custom JavaScript. We'll get started with the document ready statement:

```
$(document).ready(function(){});
```

**4.** Next, we'll select the video link and call the `colorbox()` method:

```
$(document).ready(function(){
  $('#video-link').colorbox();
});
```

However, if we refresh the page in a browser and attempt to view the video, we get an error. This is because we're attempting to load in the video via AJAX, and because of browser-security restrictions, we can't make asynchronous requests to a different server. In this case, we're trying to make a call to `http://youtube.com`, but that's not where our Colorbox page is hosted, so the browser blocks our request.

**5.** Luckily, we can create an iframe and load our external content into the iframe. Also, luckily, Colorbox provides a way for us to do this very easily. We'll just pass a key/value pair to the `colorbox()` method, setting `iframe` to `true` as shown in the following code:

```
$('#video-link').colorbox({
  iframe: true
});
```

Now, our video loads into the Colorbox, but the Colorbox has no idea how large our video might be, so we can't see it.

**6.** We'll have to tell Colorbox how big we expect our video player to be. We'll do this by passing in key/value pairs for the `innerWidth` and `innerHeight` properties. We're using `innerWidth` and `innerHeight` rather than `width` and `height` in this case because we're passing in values that specify how large we want the video player (or content) to be, rather than how large we want the Colorbox to be.

```
$('#video-link').colorbox({
  iframe: true,
  innerWidth: 640,
  innerHeight: 390
});
```

Since we didn't specify a unit of measurement for our width and height, Colorbox will assume we meant pixels. The video player will be 640 pixels wide and 390 pixels tall.

7. We can also use Colorbox to create a way for users to easily view several
videos. Let's go back into `index.html` and add a list of favorite videos to our
page instead of just one link to a video. We'll use a `rel` attribute that is set to
`favorites` for each one and provide a `title` attribute so our videos will display
a caption underneath:

```
<h3>Favorite Videos</h3>
<ul>
  <li>
    <a href="http://www.youtube.com/embed/wsRk0TXYXuA?autoplay=1"
title="Kid Snippets: Salesman" rel="favorites">Salesman</a>
  </li>
  <li>
    <a href="http://www.youtube.com/embed/IhK5lY1Phm8?autoplay=1"
title="Kid Snippets: Basketball Class" rel="favorites">Basketball
Class</a>
  </li>
  <li>
    <a href="http://www.youtube.com/embed/zG6NbAd8r2Q?autoplay=1"
title="Kid Snippets: Blind Date" rel="favorites">Blind Date</a>
  </li>
</ul>
```

8. The only update we have to make to our JavaScript in `scripts.js` is to update the
selector. Instead of selecting one single link by ID, we're going to select our set of
favorite links by their `rel` attribute:

```
$('a[rel="favorites"]').colorbox({
  iframe: true,
  innerWidth: 640,
  innerHeight: 390
});
```

If you view the page in the browser, you'll see that you have a caption under the
video and next and previous buttons that allow you to navigate between the videos
without closing the Colorbox.

9. The only thing that's a bit awkward is that our pagination indicator says **Image 1 of
3** when we're showing videos, not images. Luckily, Colorbox provides a way for us to
customize this text with the `current` key:

```
$('a[rel="favorites"]').colorbox({
  iframe: true,
  innerWidth: 640,
  innerHeight: 390,
  current: 'Video {current} of {total}'
});
```

Now, our pagination indicator correctly reads **Video 1 of 3**. Our site visitors can easily move from video to video without having to close the Colorbox, and each video displays a caption.

## What just happened?

We learned how to create both a standalone video player and a multiple video player inside a Colorbox. We learned how to pass in key/value pairs to tell Colorbox to load in external content in an iframe, working around cross-domain AJAX restrictions. We also learned how to modify the pagination indicator text to fit our current content type. We used the `innerWidth` and `innerHeight` keys to set the video player's size.

## Pop quiz – loading content into Colorbox

Which content type loads in an external link into a Colorbox?

1. iframe
2. Inline
3. HTML
4. Photo

# A one-page web gallery

Next up, we'll take a look at how we can create a single-page web gallery to show off your favorite sites or all the incredible sites you've designed yourself. Note that this example makes use of AJAX, so you'll either have to load your pages on a web server or create a web server on your own computer to see it in action.

## Time for action – creating a one-page web gallery

Follow these steps to create a one-page web gallery:

1. We'll get started by setting up a basic HTML file and the associated files and folders, just like we did in *Chapter 1, Designer, Meet jQuery*. Inside the body of our HTML document, we'll create a list of links to the sites we want to include in our design gallery, as shown in the following code:

```
<h3>One-Page Web Design Gallery</h3>
<ul>
  <li><a href="http://packtpub.com" rel="gallery">Packt
Publishing</a></li>
  <li><a href="http://nataliemac.com" rel="gallery">NatalieMac</
a></li>
  <li><a href="http://google.com" rel="gallery">Google</a></li>
</ul>
```

   Note that we've added a `rel` attribute equal to `gallery` to each link.

2. Now, just as with the other Colorbox examples, choose a style and attach the style sheet in the header of the document, make all the necessary images available to your page, update the path to the images in the CSS if necessary, and attach the Colorbox plugin at the bottom of the page.

3. Next, we'll open our `scripts.js` file and add our document ready statement:

```
$(document).ready(function(){});
```

4. Next, we'll select all links with the `rel` attribute equal to `gallery` and call the `colorbox()` method:

```
$(document).ready(function(){
  $('a[rel="gallery"]').colorbox();
});
```

**5.** Just as we did with the video example, we'll set the `iframe` key to `true` since we're loading in content from other domains. We'll also set the `width` and `height` attributes of the Colorbox to `90%` so that it takes up nearly the entire browser window. Finally, we'll adjust the pagination indicator text to read **Website** instead of **Image**:

```
$('a[rel="gallery"]').colorbox({
  iframe: true,
  width: '90%',
  height: '90%',
  current: 'Website {current} of {total}'
});
```

Now, if you refresh the page in the browser, you can see that clicking one of the links opens a Colorbox and loads that website into the Colorbox. A site visitor can interact with the loaded website just as they would if they had loaded it into a separate browser window, browsing through pages, and so on. When finished with one site, they can click the next arrow to visit the next website in the list and then hit the *Esc* key on the keyboard, or click the close button or click anywhere outside the Colorbox to close the Colorbox when they're finished. The Colorbox output will be as shown in the following screenshot:

Note that it is possible for website owners to block your ability to load their sites into an iframe. If you have set up a local server using Desktop Server, MAMP, or WAMP, then you might notice that the Google example won't load into your page. It will, however, load if you upload your code to an external server. Be sure to test all the sites you want to use in your web gallery to ensure that they work as expected.

## What just happened?

We used most of what we learned to create a Colorbox video player to display external websites inside a Colorbox. This allows our site visitor to browse through a collection of websites without ever leaving our page. We once again told Colorbox to load our content into an iframe to work around cross-domain AJAX restrictions. We customized the pagination indicator text and set the width and height for our Colorbox.

## Have a go hero – create a custom Colorbox

Create your own custom style and layout for Colorbox, including your own custom overlay pattern. Try moving the next and previous buttons, the caption, and the close button to different areas in the Colorbox.

# Summary

We've seen several uses for the adaptable and flexible Colorbox plugin, which can be used to display any kind of content in a lightbox. It can be used to create browsable image galleries, give access to forms and video players without cluttering up the page with clunky UI elements, and even to create a browsable website gallery. The Colorbox plugin is completely styled with CSS, making it possible for the lightbox to have any appearance you can dream of. The plugin even includes vector image assets that can be used as a starting point to create your own lightbox design. The behavior of the lightbox can be modified by passing a series of key/value pairs to the `colorbox()` method, making the Colorbox plugin suitable for any possible lightbox use.

Next up, we'll take a look at another common website task, that is, creating slideshows.

# 6

# Creating Slideshows and Sliders

*Traditionally created in Flash, slideshows and sliders are a great way to show off photos, products, illustrations, portfolios, and more. Hands-down, creating slideshows is one of the most common tasks for jQuery developers. In this chapter, we'll take a look at how to create a simple slideshow from scratch and then we'll take a look at the Basic Slider plugin to add some more features to a slideshow. Finally, we'll take a look at the powerful and flexible Cycle2 plugin, which can be used to create many different types of slideshows and sliders.*

In this chapter, we'll cover:

- ◆ How to plan a slideshow
- ◆ How to write a simple crossfading slideshow from scratch
- ◆ How to create a simple slideshow with controls using the Basic Slider plugin
- ◆ How to use the Cycle2 plugin to create animated slideshows
- ◆ How to create carousels with the Cycle2 plugin
- ◆ How to use the Cycle2 plugin to create a combination carousel/slideshow

# Planning a slideshow or slider

There are a few things to consider when you're preparing to build a jQuery slideshow or slider.

1. First, you have to decide what the experience will be for users who have JavaScript disabled. The priority of the various pieces of content in the slideshow should be your guide. If the slideshow is simply featuring bits of content available elsewhere on the site, then it should be sufficient to simply show one featured photo or slide. If the slideshow is the only way to access the content, then you'll have to be sure to make that content available for users without JavaScript enabled. We'll take a look at both strategies in the various examples in this chapter.

2. Second, you have to determine the ideal size for your slideshow. The size and aspect ratio of the slideshow could be determined by the content, by the page layout, or even by the browser window's size. If your slideshow or slider contains only images, cropping all images to a certain size is simple enough, but what if your slideshow or slider also contains video, text, buttons, or other elements? Plan how these elements will appear on the page.

3. Next, you need to consider whether your site visitors need to have any kind of control over the slideshow or slider. Sometimes, it's handy to simply have a set of images on automatic rotation. At other times, it's helpful to allow site visitors to pause the slideshow or manually move forward and backward through a slider.

# A simple crossfade slideshow

In this section, you'll learn how to build a simple crossfade slideshow. This type of slideshow is ideal for identically-sized images and can be displayed as a single image when JavaScript is disabled. Finally, this type of slideshow offers no control over the slideshow to your site visitors. They cannot pause the slideshow or manually move through the slides.

## Time for action – creating a simple crossfade slideshow

Follow these steps to create a simple crossfading slideshow from scratch:

1. We'll get started by creating a basic HTML document and the associated files and folders just like we did in *Chapter 1, Designer, Meet jQuery*. In the body of the HTML document, include a list of images. Each list item will contain an image, which can optionally be wrapped in a link. In the sample code for the book, the images are cropped to 800 pixels by 450 pixels. Here's what the HTML looks like:

```
<ul id="crossfade">
  <li><a href="http://en.wikipedia.org/wiki/Agua_Azul">
    <img src="images/AguaAzul.jpg"></a></li>
```

```
<li><a href="http://en.wikipedia.org/wiki/Burney_Falls">
  <img src="images/BurneyFalls.jpg"></a></li>
<li><a href="http://en.wikipedia.org/wiki/Deer_Leap_Falls">
  <img src="images/Deer_Leap_Falls.jpg"></a></li>
...
</ul>
```

2. Next, we'll write a few lines of CSS to style the slideshow. A slideshow shows just one image at a time, and the easiest way to show only one image is to stack the images on top of one another. If the site visitor has JavaScript disabled, they'll just see the last slide in the list. Add the following lines of code in the `styles.css` file:

```
#crossfade {
   height: 450px;
   overflow: hidden;
   position: relative;
   width: 800px;
}

#crossfade li {
   height: 450px;
   position: absolute;
   width: 800px;
}
```

If you view the page in a browser, you'll see that the last item in the slideshow is visible, but none of the other items are—they are all stacked beneath the last item. This is what our experience will be for site visitors with JavaScript disabled.

3. Next, open up `scripts.js` and we'll get started with writing our JavaScript code. This script will be a little bit different from the scripts that we've set up before. Instead of something happening just once when the document loads or when a site visitor clicks on a link, we actually want to set up a function that will happen on a timer. For example, if we want each slide of our slideshow to be visible for three seconds, we'll have to set up a function to switch slides, which gets called every three seconds.

   We've already got our slides stacked up on top of one another on the page with the last item on top. Think about how you handle a stack of photographs. You view the photograph on top, and then move it to the bottom of the stack to view the second photo. Then, you move the second photo to the bottom to view the third photo and so on. We're going to apply the same principle to our slideshow.

   Inside `scripts.js`, create a function called `slideshow`. This is the function that we'll call every three seconds when we want to switch photos.

```
function slideshow() {
}
```

**4.** The first thing we need to do inside our function is select the first photo in the stack:

```
function slideshow() {
  $('#crossfade li:first')
}
```

**5.** Now that we've got the first photo in the stack, we just need to move it to the bottom of the stack to make the next photo visible. We can do that by using jQuery's `appendTo()` method. This will remove the first photo from the beginning of the list and append it to the end of the list.

```
function slideshow() {
  $('#crossfade li:first').appendTo('#crossfade');
}
```

**6.** Our photo-flipping function is ready. Now, all we have to do is some initial setup as soon as our page loads. Then, we'll set up a call to our photo-flipping function every three seconds. We'll get that started by calling the `ready()` method on the document.

```
$(document).ready(function(){
  // Document setup code will go here
});

function slideshow() {
  $('#crossfade li:first').appendTo('#crossfade');
}
```

**7.** As soon as our document is ready, we want to prepare our slideshow. We'll start by selecting all the photos in the slideshow.

```
$(document).ready(function(){
  $('#crossfade li')
});
```

**8.** Next, we want to hide all the photos in the slideshow.

```
$(document).ready(function(){
  $('#crossfade li').hide();
});
```

**9.** Then, we'll filter that list of photos to get just the first one:

```
$(document).ready(function(){
  $('#crossfade li').hide().filter(':first');
});
```

**10.** Finally, we'll make that first photo visible. All other photos will remain hidden:

```
$(document).ready(function(){
  $('#crossfade li').hide().filter(':first').show();
});
```

**11.** At this point, if you refresh the page in the browser, you'll see that the last slide visible without JavaScript enabled is now hidden and the first slide in the list is now visible instead. Now, all that's left to do is to call our photo-flipping function every three seconds. To do this, we'll use a JavaScript method called `setInterval()`. This allows us to call a function at regular intervals. We pass two values to `setInterval`: the name of the function to be called and the number of milliseconds that should elapse between calls to the function. For example, to call the slideshow function every 3 seconds (or 3000 milliseconds), we'd write:

```
$(document).ready(function(){
  $('#crossfade li').hide().filter(':first').show();
  setInterval(slideshow, 3000);
});
```

**12.** Now, we're calling our photo-flipping function every three seconds, so you'd expect that if you refresh the page in the browser, you'd see the photos change every three seconds, but that doesn't appear to be the case. Reviewing the code, it's easy to see what's gone wrong; even though the actual order of the stack of photos is changing every three seconds, all the photos except the first one are invisible. Whether the first photo is on top or not, it's the only photo visible, so it appears that our slideshow isn't changing. We'll have to go back to our `slideshow` function and modify it to make the current photo invisible and make the next photo in the stack visible. Since we want the photos to switch with a nice, slow crossfading effect, we'll call the `fadeOut()` method to fade the first photo to be transparent, and we'll pass `'slow'` to that method to ensure it takes its time:

```
function slideshow() {
  $('#crossfade li:first').fadeOut('slow').appendTo('#crossfade');
}
```

**13.** Now, we need to move to the next photo in the list, which is currently invisible, and make it opaque. We're going to use the `next()` method to get the next item in the list and then call the `fadeIn()` method to make it appear. Once again, since we want a slow effect, we'll pass `'slow'` to the `fadeIn()` method:

```
function slideshow() {
  $('#crossfade li:first').fadeOut('slow').next().
    fadeIn('slow').appendTo('#crossfade');
}
```

**14.** We've gotten ourselves into a little bit of trouble with our chaining of jQuery methods. We started with the first photo in the stack, faded it out, then moved to the second photo in the stack and faded it in. Now, however, when we call the `appendTo()` method, we're appending the second photo in the stack to the end—we're moving the second photo in the stack to the bottom instead of the first one. Luckily, jQuery provides a method for us to return to our original selection—the `end()` method. We can call the `end()` method after fading in the second photo to make sure that it's the first photo that's getting appended to the bottom of the photo stack:

```
function slideshow() {
  $('#crossfade li:first').fadeOut('slow').next().
    fadeIn('slow').end().appendTo('#crossfade');
}
```

**15.** Finally, let's do a bit of cleaning up. If you take a look at the code we've written, you'll see that we've selected `#crossfade` several different times. Let's cache that selector in a variable so we don't have to keep re-querying the document to find it. The final bit of code after cleanup will look like this:

```
$(document).ready(function(){
  slides = $('#crossfade');

  slides.find('li').hide().filter(':first').show();
  setInterval(slideshow, 3000);
});

var slides;

function slideshow() {
  slides.find('li:first').fadeOut('slow').next().
    fadeIn('slow').end().appendTo(slides);
}
```

## What just happened?

If you refresh the page in the browser, you'll see that you've got a nice crossfading slideshow. As one photo fades out, the next photo fades in, smoothly transitioning between each photo. Since we're constantly moving the top photo in the stack to the bottom, we'll never reach the end of the slideshow, just as you can continuously flip through a stack of photos:

We set up a slideshow function that selected the first photo in the stack, faded it out, and moved it to the bottom of the stack. Simultaneously, we're finding the second photo in the stack and fading it in. We used the power of jQuery chaining to accomplish all of that in one line of code.

We set up a timer for 3 seconds and called our photo-flipping function at the end of each 3-second interval.

Finally, we did a bit of setup work as soon as the document is loaded, hiding all the photos and then making the first one visible. This will ensure that the photos are always displayed in order in our slideshow.

Next up, let's take a look at using a plugin that will give us some nice options for our slideshow.

## Pop quiz – working with jQuery chaining

Q1. In a long chain of jQuery methods, how do you return to the original selector after it's been filtered?

1.  Use the `original()` method.
2.  Start a new line of code that starts with the original selector.
3.  Use the `end()` method.
4.  Use the `prev()` method.

# Using the Basic Slider plugin

Our simple slideshow is nice and will be adequate for some situations, but we often want or need more features and flexibility out of our sliders and slideshows. There's no shortage of jQuery plugins out there to create sliders and slideshows. To avoid adding lots of unused code to projects, try to find the simplest slider that will do the job.

The Basic Slider, documented at and available for download at `http://www.basic-slider.com/`, is a relative newcomer to the scene. It's flexible, simple to use, and easy to style. It's a great fit for responsive designs. It can hold any kind of content, so we're not limited to images. We could use text, videos, images with text, or any other combination we can think up. The Basic Slider has got about a dozen options you can adjust, and for many projects, you'll find that's more than enough.

## Time for action – building a Basic Slider

Follow these steps to create a slider using the Basic Slider plugin:

1. We'll get started by writing our HTML markup. Looking at the documentation for the Basic Slider plugin, we see that the plugin requires an unordered list wrapped in a `<div>` element. Each of our slides is going to contain a photo with a headline overlay, and each slide is going to link to pages with more information about what's contained in that slide. Here's what our markup looks like:

```
<div id="slider">
  <ul class="bjqs">
    <li>
      <a href="http://en.wikipedia.org/wiki/Agua_Azul">
        <img src="images/AguaAzul.jpg">
        <div class="headline">
          <h2>Agua Azul</h2>
          <p>Tumbal&aacute;, Chiapas, Mexico</p>
        </div>
      </a>
    </li>
    <li>
      <a href="http://en.wikipedia.org/wiki/Burney_Falls">
        <img src="images/BurneyFalls.jpg">
        <div class="headline">
          <h2>Burney Falls</h2>
          <p>Shasta County, California, USA</p>
        </div>
      </a>
    </li>
    ...
  </ul>
</div>
```

It might surprise you to see that with the new HTML5 specification, we're allowed to wrap links (`<a>`) around block-level elements such as `<div>` and `<h2>`. This makes it easy to make the whole slide clickable.

2. Next up, we're going to write some CSS to style the slides, and we'll want to give some thought to site visitors with JavaScript disabled while we do so. In this particular case, we'll show all of the slides for customers who happen to have JavaScript disabled. First up, we'll place the headline on top of the photos with a few lines of CSS in `styles.css`:

```
ul.bjqs li {
  margin-bottom: 1em;
  position: relative;
}

ul.bjqs li .headline {
    background: rgba(0,0,0,0.5);
    left: 0;
    padding: 1em 2em 1em 3em;
    position: absolute;
    top: 2em;
    z-index: 9999;
}

.headline h2 {
    color: white;
    font-size: 2em;
    line-height: 1.125;
}

.headline p {
    line-height: 1.5;
}
```

Now, if you view the page in the browser, you'll see each of our slides in a single column down the page, each with a styled headline over the photo:

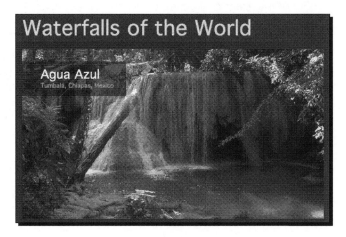

3. Now that we have our non-JavaScript case built, let's go ahead and progressively enhance it to build a more interactive experience for users who do have JavaScript. We'll get started by heading over to `http://basic-slider.com` and downloading the Basic Slider plugin ZIP file. Unzip the file and find the `bjqs-1.3.min.js` file inside the `js` folder. Copy this file to your own `scripts` folder, and then attach it to the HTML file in the footer between jQuery and the `scripts.js` file:

```
<script src="scripts/jquery.js"></script>
<script src="scripts/bjqs-1.3.min.js"></script>
<script src="scripts/scripts.js"></script>
</body>
</html>
```

4. The Basic Slider plugin comes with a small, simple CSS file of the styles that are required for the slider to work. Inside the plugin folder, you'll find a file named `bjqs.css`. Copy that file to your own `styles` folder and then attach it in the `<head>` section of your HTML document, before your own `styles.css` file:

```
<title>Chapter 6: jQuery for Designers</title>
<link rel="stylesheet" href="styles/bjqs.css">
<link rel="stylesheet" href="styles/styles.css">
```

5. If you head back to the browser now and refresh the page, you might see something you didn't expect; all the slides that will make up our slideshow have disappeared. A quick look in the `bjqs.css` file reveals that the `<ul>` list that holds our slideshow is being set to `display: none;`.

This is a necessary part of getting our slider to work, but what about our users without JavaScript? We can pull out the trick of adding a class to the `<body>` tag that we can use in CSS to write different styles for our page, depending on whether or not JavaScript is available. Add a class of `jsOff` to the `<body>` tag:

```
<body class="jsOff">
```

Then, open up your `scripts.js` file and add the necessary code to change this class if JavaScript is enabled:

```
$(document).ready(function(){
  $('body').removeClass('jsOff').addClass('.jsOn');
});
```

With all that out of the way, we can open up `styles.css` and write some code just for users without JavaScript to be sure they can see our slides:

```
.jsOff ul.bjqs {
  display: block;
}
```

Now, all of our slides are visible for site visitors who have JavaScript disabled, and we haven't interfered with the CSS that the Basic Slider plugin is relying on to work correctly.

**6.** Now we can jump into making the slideshow work for our site visitors who have JavaScript enabled. Open up `scripts.js`, select the `<div>` that wraps the slideshow `<ul>`, and call the `bjqs()` method

```
$(document).ready(function(){
  $('body').removeClass('jsOff').addClass('.jsOn');

  $('#slider').bjqs();
});
```

If you refresh the page in the browser now, you'll see that our slideshow is working, though it's not the right size, and the style isn't very attractive.

Let's see what we can do to get those details fixed.

**7.** First, let's set some options for the `bjqs()` method. We can tell the width and height of our slides to the Basic Slider:

```
$('#slider').bjqs({
  height: 450,
  width: 800
});
```

This set of pixel sizes works well as long as we're dealing with a design that's a fixed size. But many modern websites are responsive, meaning the design responds to the size of the browser window by adjusting element sizes and layout. If we want to use our slider inside a responsive design, the Basic Slider makes it really easy. We'll just add a responsive option and set it to true:

```
$('#slider').bjqs({
  height: 450,
  width: 800,
  responsive: true
});
```

Now if you refresh the page in the browser, you'll see the slides are now the correct size. If you make the window narrower, the slides resize to fit.

**8.** Now, let's jump into writing some CSS to make our slideshow even better. First up, while the slideshow itself shrinks to fit the size of the window as the browser window gets narrower, the slideshow is cropping the images. Instead, let's resize the images so that they're still fully visible inside the slideshow. Here's the code we can use to fit those images to the slideshow:

```css
.bjqs img {
  height: auto;
  max-width: 100%;
}
```

**9.** Next, those next and previous buttons are just link text laid directly over the photos, and they look a bit lost. Let's add a bit of CSS to style those nicely:

```css
.bjqs-prev a,
.bjqs-next a {
  background: rgba(0,0,0,0.5);
  color: white;
  padding: 1em;
  text-decoration: none;
}
```

**10.** The page numbers underneath the slider are handy to let site visitors get to any of the slides in the show, but let's replace them with dot indicators. Here's the CSS we can use to accomplish this:

```css
ol.bjqs-markers {
  margin: 1em 0;
}

ol.bjqs-markers li {
  border: 1px solid black;
  border-radius: 50%;
  display: inline-block;
  line-height: 1;
  margin: 0 2px;
  padding: 1px;
}

ol.bjqs-markers li a {
  background: rgba(0,0,0,0.5);
  border-radius: 50%;
  display: block;
  height: 0.6em;
  overflow: hidden;
  text-indent: -9999em;
  width: 0.6em;
}

ol.bjqs-markers li.active-marker a {
  background: #a0d468;
}
```

Now, if you refresh the page in the browser, you'll see a neat row of dots beneath the slideshow. Clicking on any dot will navigate you to that corresponding slide.

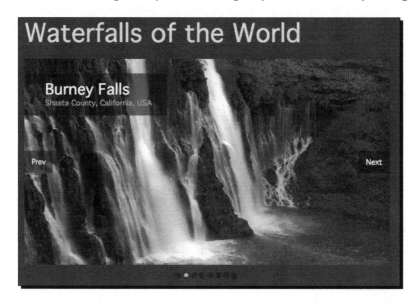

11. One final thing to touch up is that as the window gets narrower, the headline text stays huge and dominates the photo. Let's adjust this to reduce the text size on smaller screens so that more of the photo is visible. Here's what we'll add to the bottom of the CSS to accomplish this:

```
@media screen and (max-width: 650px) {
  .bjqs {
    font-size: 0.7em;
  }
}
```

This bit of code just shrinks the font size for the slider text when the window is narrower than 650 pixels wide. We'll use 650 pixels because it's around that width that the text starts to feel much too large for the images. Now, when you make the browser window narrower, you'll see that the text snaps to a smaller size and fits nicely on the smaller photos.

## *What just happened?*

We used the Basic Slider plugin to create a slideshow. Even though this plugin is lightweight and basic, we saw how we can use the available options combined with some fancy CSS work to customize the slider. Even though the Basic Slider is a pretty basic slider plugin, it has just the right options to make it a great choice for a variety of projects. It's also easy to customize and style with CSS.

But what about those cases where we need more options? Let's take a look at the flexible Cycle2 plugin, which gives us dozens of options.

### Have a go hero – customize the Basic Slider

Design and build your own custom version of the Basic Slider. Try a different size, different transition effects, and different layouts for the content inside each slide. Use numbered pagination and style the next and previous buttons as you like.

## Creating a Cycle2 slideshow

Let's take a look at how to put the Cycle2 plugin from M. Alsup to good use. Cycle2 provides some nice transition effects between slides and offers lots of configuration options. The Cycle2 plugin is flexible and can hold many types of content. It can even gracefully handle content of different sizes and/or different aspect ratios, which the two sliders we've built so far could not.

There are options to include controls for your site visitors to move forward and backward, to pause the slideshow when the mouse is hovered over it, and to add pagination to allow site visitors to move easily to a specific slide. Additionally, there are options to allow touch gestures, to animate different transition effects, to include pagination or thumbnail navigation, and more. Compared to the Basic Slider, Cycle2 has dozens of more options. Cycle2 even has its own plugins that we can add to get more functionality, making it super flexible and adaptable to many different situations. In fact, in the rest of this chapter, we'll look at building three very different types of sliders and slideshows, all with the Cycle2 plugin.

Unlike most other plugins, the Cycle2 plugin relies almost entirely on HTML markup. Apart from attaching Cycle2 and any of its plugins to your page, you often don't have to open a single JavaScript file or write a single line of JavaScript.

## Time for action – building a slideshow with Cycle2

Follow these steps to build your first Cycle2 slideshow:

**1.** We'll get started by creating a basic HTML document and associated files and folders just like we did in *Chapter 1, Designer, Meet jQuery*. In the body of the HTML document, we'll create a container `<div>` and then wrap the markup for each slide in a `<div>`:

```
<div class="cycle-slideshow">
  <div class="slide">
    <a href="http://en.wikipedia.org/wiki/Agua_Azul">
      <img src="images/AguaAzul.jpg">
    </a>
  </div>
  <div class="slide">
    <a href="http://en.wikipedia.org/wiki/Burney_Falls">
      <img src="images/BurneyFalls.jpg">
    </a>
  </div>
  . . .
</div>
```

Notice that we've used a class `cycle-slideshow` on the container `<div>` and then a class `slide` on the `<div>` elements that contain the markup for each of our individual slides. These are important for the Cycle2 plugin. Remember that this plugin requires us to write little or no JavaScript at all—instead, it relies on HTML markup, classes, and attributes so we have to be precise.

**2.** Now, we'll use the technique we've used before to make sure our slideshow content looks great even for our site visitors who have JavaScript disabled. First, add the `jsOff` class to the `<body>` tag:

```
<body class="jsOff">
```

Next, open up your `scripts.js` file and add the line of jQuery that will remove that class for our site visitors who actually do have JavaScript enabled:

```
$(document).ready(function(){
  $('body').removeClass('jsOff').addClass('jsOn');
});
```

In this case, the slideshow is simply visually highlighting content that's available elsewhere on the page and that the slideshow images won't actually provide a lot of value for site visitors with JavaScript disabled. We'll just hide the slideshow for those visitors. Add these styles in styles.css:

```
.jsOff .cycle-slideshow {
  display: none;
}
```

**3.** Now that we've taken care of site visitors without JavaScript, let's get the slideshow working for those who do have it. We need to download the Cycle2 plugin. We'll find that in the jQuery plugins repository at `http://plugins.jquery.com/cycle2/`. Click on the large orange **Download now** button. Save the file to your own `scripts` folder.

**4.** Now, we need to attach the script to our HTML page. At the bottom of the HTML file, after jQuery, add a `<script>` tag to include the Cycle2 plugin:

```
<script src="scripts/jquery.js"></script>
<script src="scripts/jquery.cycle2.min.js"></script>
<script src="scripts/scripts.js"></script>
</body>
</html>
```

**5.** Next, we need to let the Cycle2 plugin know which elements are wrapping our individual slides. By default, Cycle2 assumes that our slideshow is made up of just images, but we've wrapped each of our images in a link and in a `<div>` block with the class `slide`. To let Cycle2 know what our slide container is, we'll just add a data attribute named `data-cycle-slides` to the slideshow container. The value for that attribute is a jQuery selector. Find the `<div>` block with the `cycle-slideshow` class in your HTML file and add the appropriate data attribute:

```
<div class="cycle-slideshow" data-cycle-slides="> div.slide">
```

In this case, I'm using the direct descendent selector (`>`) to find all the `<div>` element with a class of `slide`.

If you refresh the page in the browser, you'll see that the slideshow now works. It's just that simple to get the Cycle2 plugin set up and working. We've created a simple image slideshow with a fading transition. That's perfectly acceptable, but Cycle2 gives us lots of additional options, so let's see how to add additional features and adjust the settings.

**6.** Since each of the slides links the site visitors to a page with more information, let's pause the slideshow when site visitors hover over the slideshow with their mouse. This will ensure that they always get sent to the page they intended. We just have to add another data attribute to the slideshow container. Since we'll be adding a few of these, let's start breaking them up for easy readability:

```
<div class="cycle-slideshow"
  data-cycle-slides="> div.slide"
  data-cycle-pause-on-hover="true"
</div>
```

In this case, we're adding a data attribute called `data-cycle-pause-on-hover`, and we're setting the value equal to `true`. Refresh the page in the browser and try to hover your mouse over the slideshow. You'll see that the slideshow pauses until you move your mouse elsewhere.

**7.** Next, let's add some next and previous controls so that our site visitors can move through the slideshow at their own pace. Inside the `<div>` element with the class `cycle-slideshow`, but before our first `<div>` with the class `slide`, we'll add two new `<div>` elements:

```
<div class="cycle-slideshow"
data-cycle-slides="> div.slide"
data-cycle-pause-on-hover="true">
```

```
<div class="cycle-prev"></div>
<div class="cycle-next"></div>
  <div class="slide">
  ...
```

The Cycle2 plugin will automatically look for `<div>` elements with the classes `cycle-next` and `cycle-prev` and enable those as controls for the slideshow. It's then up to us to style those with CSS to appear how and where we want them. You can also place content inside those `<div>` elements, irrespective of whether you'd like to type words or include images. We'll use CSS-generated content here.

We'll place the next and previous button on top of the slideshow on the left and right sides. Here's the CSS we'll use to accomplish that. First, we'll limit the width of the slideshow to the width of the largest item, which in this case is 800 pixels:

```
.cycle-slideshow {
  max-width: 800px;
}
```

Next, we'll style and position the controls:

```
.cycle-prev,
.cycle-next {
  cursor: pointer;
  font-size: 6em;
  margin-top: -0.6em;
  opacity: 0.4;
  position: absolute;
  text-shadow: 0 0 4px rgba(0,0,0,0.8);
  top: 50%;
  transition: opacity 0.3s;
  z-index: 102;
}

.cycle-prev:hover,
.cycle-next:hover {
  opacity: 0.9;
}

.cycle-prev {
  left: 0.1em;
}

.cycle-prev:before {
  content: '\276E';
}
```

```
.cycle-next {
  right: 0.1em;
}

.cycle-next:before {
  content: '\276F';
}
```

We're using the `:before` pseudoclass to add an angle bracket to the controls, so now the site visitors can use these to move forward or backward through the slideshow.

8. We've made it easy to move forward and backward through the slideshow for our site visitors on desktop devices, but what about those on touch-enabled devices? They don't get the benefit of pausing the slideshow on hover, so control over the slideshow is even more important for them. They can surely use those next and previous buttons just like everybody else, but we can also provide them with the ability to move through the slideshow by swiping across the screen. To enable the swiping motion for touch-enabled devices, we just have to add a `data-cycle-swipe` attribute and set it to `true`:

```
<div class="cycle-slideshow"
  data-cycle-slides="> div.slide"
  data-cycle-pause-on-hover="true"
  data-cycle-swipe="true">
```

**9.** Now, it would be nice to provide a bit more information about each of our slides. Let's include an overlay that contains a title and a line or two with description about each one. First, we'll add the data to each slide. We'll do this by adding the `data-cycle-title` and `data-cycle-desc` attributes to each of the slides:

```
<div class="slide" data-cycle-title="Agua Azul"
   data-cycle-desc="Tumbal&aacute;, Chiapas, Mexico">
   <a href="http://en.wikipedia.org/wiki/Agua_Azul">
     <img src="images/AguaAzul.jpg">
   </a>
</div>
```

It's important to add these two data attributes to the container of each slide rather than to an element inside the container. Go through each of the slides and add these two data attributes.

**10.** We've got the data, so now we just need a place to display it. Inside the `<div>` element with the class as `cycle-slideshow`, but before the first `<div>` element with the class `slide`, add a `<div>` element with class `cycle-overlay`, as shown in the following code:

```
<div class="cycle-slideshow"
   data-cycle-slides="> div.slide"
   data-cycle-pause-on-hover="true"
   data-cycle-swipe="true"   >
   <div class="cycle-prev"></div>
   <div class="cycle-next"></div>
   <div class="cycle-overlay"></div>
   <div class="slide" data-cycle-title="Agua Azul" data-cycle-
desc="Tumbal&aacute;, Chiapas, Mexico">
   ...
```

Refresh the page in the browser, and you'll see that the title and description that we added to each slide element now appears beneath the slideshow.

**11.** That's a good start, but let's style the overlay with a bit of CSS to display it on top of the slideshow:

```
.cycle-overlay {
   background: rgba(0,0,0,0.6);
   bottom: 0;
   left: 0;
   position: absolute;
   right: 0;
   z-index: 101;
}
```

**12.** Using Chrome's web tools, we can see the markup created by the Cycle2 plugin to display the title and description. Each line is simply wrapped in a `<div>` element without a `class` or an `id` value.

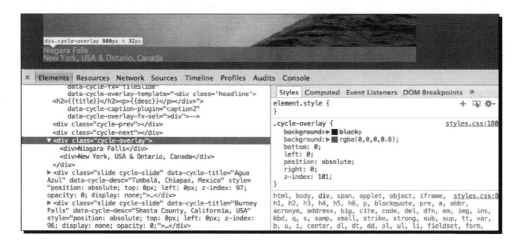

While we could technically use CSS pseudoclasses or advanced CSS selectors to select each of those `<div>` elements individually, it would make our CSS much easier to write if we had some control over that markup and could wrap the title in a heading tag and the description in a paragraph tag.

Good news! Cycle2 does give us a way to specify which HTML tags should be used to mark up the overlay content by passing an HTML template in a data attribute. We'll use the `data-cycle-overlay-template` attribute and we'll pass it the markup we'd like to use for our overlays:

```
<div class="cycle-slideshow"
  data-cycle-slides="> div.slide"
  data-cycle-pause-on-hover="true"
  data-cycle-swipe="true"
  data-cycle-overlay-template="<div class='headline'>
    <h2>{{title}}</h2><p>{{desc}}</p></div>">
```

You can see that we've used the `{{title}}` token to show Cycle2 where to display the bit of content we've designated as the title and then the `{{desc}}` token to tell Cycle2 where to display the bit of content that makes up the description for each slide. Now, we can jump back over to our `styles.css` file and write a bit of CSS to style this new markup:

```
.headline {
  color: white;
  padding: 1em;
}
```

```css
.headline h2 {
  color: white;
  font-size: 2em;
  line-height: 1.125;
}

.headline p {
  font-style: italic;
  line-height: 1.5;
}
```

This gives us a gorgeous-looking result that anyone would be proud of:

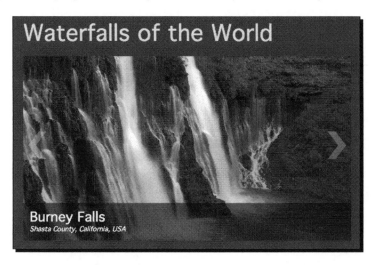

Our slideshow is looking pretty good, but we've got a few more tricks up our sleeves that we can use to make it even better:

13. While the fading transition animation is nice, let's use something a bit fancier. On the **Demos** page at `http://jquery.malsup.com/cycle2/demo/`, you can view the different transitions that are available for the Cycle2 plugin. Let's take a look at how to use and customize the tile transition.

First, we have to download the Tile Transition plugin and attach it to our page. The optional plugins for Cycle2 are not found in the jQuery plugins' repository like the core plugin—they need to be downloaded from the Cycle2 download page at `http://jquery.malsup.com/cycle2/download/`. Head over there and find the link for the **Production** version of the Tile Transition plugin in the table of transition plugins.

## Transition Plugins

| | | Production | Development | Demo Link |
|---|---|---|---|---|
| Carousel | A plugin for displaying slides in a carousel. A carousel slideshow differs from a normal slideshow in that it displays multiple images at a time while advancing them one-by-one. | Download (2kb) | Download (6kb) | Demo |
| Flip | A plugin for transitioning slides via CSS3 transformations. | Download (1kb) | Download (2kb) | Demo |
| IE-Fade | A fade/fadeout plugin for old versions of IE. This plugin corrects issues that arise when cleartype is used with opacity. | Download (1kb) | Download (1kb) | |
| ScrollVert | A vertical scroll plugin. Similar to the *scrollHorz* transition effect, but moves slides vertically. | Download (1kb) | Download (1kb) | Demo |
| Shuffle | A plugin which supports the classic Cycle Shuffle animation. The shuffle animation is somewhat like moving a card from the top of a deck of cards to the back of the deck, or vice versa. | Download (1kb) | Download (2kb) | Demo |
| Tile | A plugin for tile-based slide transitions. Tile animations break images into smaller sections and transition them out piece by piece. Interesting effects can be achieved by changing the direction, tile count, and speed of the transitions. | Download (1kb) | Download (4kb) | Demo |

Save the file to your own `scripts` folder. Then, open up your HTML file and attach the Tile Transition plugin at the bottom of the file, after the Cycle2 plugin, as shown in the following code:

```
<script src="scripts/jquery.js"></script>
<script src="scripts/jquery.cycle2.min.js"></script>
<script src="scripts/jquery.cycle2.tile.min.js"></script>
<script src="scripts/scripts.js"></script>
</body>
</html>
```

14. Next, we have to tell our slideshow to use the newly available tile transition. To do that, we'll add another data attribute to the parent container of our slideshow. In your HTML file, find the `<div>` element with `cycle-slideshow` as the class value, and add the `data-cycle-fx` attribute set to `tileSlide`:

```
<div class="cycle-slideshow"
  data-cycle-slides="> div.slide"
  data-cycle-pause-on-hover="true"
  data-cycle-swipe="true"
  data-cycle-overlay-template="<div class='headline'>
    <h2>{{title}}</h2><p>{{desc}}</p></div>"
  data-cycle-fx="tileSlide">
```

Refresh the page in the browser, and you'll see that the transition between slides now uses the sliding tile transition.

If you prefer, you could switch that to a blinds-style transition by specifying `tileBlind` as the value for the `data-cycle-fx` attribute:

```
<div class="cycle-slideshow"
  data-cycle-slides="> div.slide"
  data-cycle-pause-on-hover="true"
  data-cycle-swipe="true"
  data-cycle-overlay-template="<div class='headline'>
    <h2>{{title}}</h2><p>{{desc}}</p></div>"
  data-cycle-fx="tileBlind">
```

**15.** By default, the tile transition breaks each slide into seven vertical tiles. However, we have the option to change both the number of tiles and the orientation of the tiles by adding a few more data attributes to our slideshow. Here, we're using 13 horizontal tiles in a blinds animation:

```
<div class="cycle-slideshow"
  data-cycle-slides="> div.slide"
  data-cycle-pause-on-hover="true"
  data-cycle-swipe="true"
  data-cycle-overlay-template="<div class='headline'>
    <h2>{{title}}</h2><p>{{desc}}</p></div>"
  data-cycle-fx="tileBlind"
  data-cycle-tile-count="13"
  data-cycle-tile-vertical="false">
```

Experiment with the available options for the slideshow transition and find one you like best. Feel free to experiment with some of the other transition plugins as well.

**16.** Now that we have a fancy transition effect in place for the slides, notice the way the text in the overlay changes. It waits until the animated transition is complete, and then just snaps to the new value when the next slide is displayed. Let's animate that too.

Luckily, Cycle2 makes that easy to do too! There's another optional plugin for Cycle2 called Caption2 that allows us to control the transitions for the overlay. Head to the downloads page for Cycle2 (`http://jquery.malsup.com/cycle2/download/`) and click on the link to download the **Production** version of the Caption2 plugin. Save the file to your own `scripts` folder, then open your HTML file and attach the new plugin in the footer:

```
<script src="scripts/jquery.js"></script>
<script src="scripts/jquery.cycle2.min.js"></script>
<script src="scripts/jquery.cycle2.tile.min.js"></script>
<script src="scripts/jquery.cycle2.caption2.min.js"></script>
<script src="scripts/scripts.js"></script>
</body>
</html>
```

**17.** Next, we'll add some data attributes to our slideshow to control the transitions for the overlay. We have to tell our slideshow to use the Caption2 plugin, so we'll start by adding the `data-cycle-overlay-plugin` attribute equal to `caption2`:

```
<div class="cycle-slideshow"
  data-cycle-slides="> div.slide"
  data-cycle-pause-on-hover="true"
  data-cycle-swipe="true"
  data-cycle-overlay-template="<div class='headline'>
    <h2>{{title}}</h2><p>{{desc}}</p></div>"
  data-cycle-fx="tileSlide"
  data-cycle-tile-count="9"
  data-cycle-caption-plugin="caption2">
```

If you refresh the page in the browser, you'll see that the entire overlay now fades out as soon as the slide transition begins and then fades back in with the new value. Let's allow the translucent black background for the overlay to stay in place and for just the text itself to fade out and back in. To achieve this, we'll add another data attribute to the slideshow to specify which element in the overlay should be animated:

```
<div class="cycle-slideshow"
  data-cycle-slides="> div.slide"
  data-cycle-pause-on-hover="true"
  data-cycle-swipe="true"
```

```
      data-cycle-overlay-template="<div
class='headline'><h2>{{title}}</h2><p>{{desc}}</p></div>"
      data-cycle-fx="tileSlide"
      data-cycle-tile-count="9"
      data-cycle-caption-plugin="caption2"
      data-cycle-overlay-fx-sel=">div">
```

Now, if you refresh the page in the browser, you'll see that the overlay container stays visible, but just the text inside fades out and back in with each slide transition. This helps the slideshow feel more cohesive and makes it feel as if the overlay is a part of the slideshow.

We've already seen quite a lot of what the Cycle2 plugin can do, but we've barely scratched the surface! Let's next take a look at how we can create an image carousel with the Cycle2 plugin.

# The Cycle2 carousel

Cycle2 is flexible; you're not limited to simple slideshows. You can put Cycle2 to use to create a carousel that shows multiple images at one time. Let's take a look at how we might create a carousel of thumbnail images.

## Time for action – building a Cycle2 carousel

Follow these steps to create a carousel with the Cycle2 plugin.

1.  We'll get started, as we usually do, with using the HTML document and associated files and folders just like we did in *Chapter 1*, *Designer, Meet jQuery*. First up, we'll get the HTML markup for our carousel set up. Our HTML markup will be similar to the markup for the slideshow we set up in the previous example. We need a container `<div>` to hold the slideshow. Then, we also need individual `<div>` elements inside the external container for each individual slide or image that will appear in our slideshow:

```
<div class="cycle-slideshow">
  <div class="slide">
    <a href="http://en.wikipedia.org/wiki/Agua_Azul">
      <img src="images/AguaAzul.jpg">
    </a>
  </div>
  <div class="slide">
    <a href="http://en.wikipedia.org/wiki/Burney_Falls">
      <img src="images/BurneyFalls.jpg">
    </a>
  </div>
```

```
<div class="slide">
  <a href="http://en.wikipedia.org/wiki/Deer_Leap_Falls">
    <img src="images/Deer_Leap_Falls.jpg">
  </a>
</div>
  ...
</div>
```

Our markup here is similar to the previous example but a bit simpler. Since we're using thumbnail images, we aren't going to be using text overlays. So we can skip the extra data attributes for those.

2. Now, we'll take just a moment to consider those users who have JavaScript disabled. Our thumbnails are linking them off to more information about each of those slides, so let's show them these images as a grid. First, add the `jsOff` class to the `<body>` tag:

```
<body class="jsOff">
```

Next, let's pop into our `styles.css` file and write a bit of code that's going to display those thumbnails nicely for site visitors without JavaScript:

```
.jsOff .cycle-slideshow .slide {
  display: inline-block;
  padding: 0.5em;
}
```

The users with JavaScript disabled will see the page as shown in the following screenshot:

It's nothing extra fancy, but these visitors can still see the thumbnail images and can click on each one to see more information, so it fulfills our purpose. They'll never know what they're missing. Finally, we have to open our `scripts.js` file and add a bit of code to remove the `jsOff` class for site visitors who do have JavaScript enabled:

```
$(document).ready(function(){
  $('body').removeClass('jsOff').addClass('jsOn');
});
```

This isn't anything we haven't seen before. With the non-JavaScript case out of the way, let's take a look at creating and animating our carousel for everyone else.

**3.** First up, let's download and attach the Cycle2 plugin to our HTML page. This is available for download in the jQuery plugin repository or also from the download page of the Cycle2 documentation (`http://jquery.malsup.com/cycle2/download/`). Save the file to your `scripts.js` folder and then attach it in the footer of your HTML document after jQuery but before your `scripts.js` file:

```
<script src="scripts/jquery.js"></script>
<script src="scripts/jquery.cycle2.min.js"></script>
<script src="scripts/scripts.js"></script>
```

Now, you might expect to see a thumbnail-sized slideshow if you refresh the page in the browser at this point, but that's not the case. This is because Cycle2, by default, expects a collection of images inside the parent container, but we've wrapped each of our images in a link and a `<div>` element with the `slide` class. We just have to tell Cycle2 that we're using this alternate markup. In the HTML file, find the `<div>` element with the `cycle-slideshow` class and add the correct data attribute as shown in the following code:

```
<div class="cycle-slideshow"
  data-cycle-slides="> div.slide">
  <div class="slide">
  ...
```

Just like we did last time, we'll break the data attributes out onto individual lines to make them easier to read. Here, we've added the `data-cycle-slides` attribute and set the value equal to the selector for each of our individual slides. The thumbnail-sized slideshow will look like the one shown in the following screenshot:

Now, if you refresh the page in the browser, you'll see that you have a thumbnail-sized slideshow. Let's turn that into a carousel.

**4.** We need to add a Cycle2 plugin—the Carousel Transition plugin. Don't forget that while the Cycle2 plugin itself is available in the jQuery plugins' repository, the additional plugins that add the functionality are not. Additional Cycle2 plugins are only available from the Cycle2 downloads page at `http://jquery.malsup.com/cycle2/download/`. Head over there and find and download the **Production** version of the Carousel Transition plugin. Save it to your own `scripts` folder.

**5.** Next, open up `index.html` and attach the carousel plugin at the bottom of the file, after the Cycle2 plugin, but before your `scripts.js` file:

```
<script src="scripts/jquery.js"></script>
<script src="scripts/jquery.cycle2.min.js"></script>
<script src="scripts/jquery.cycle2.carousel.min.js"></script>
<script src="scripts/scripts.js"></script>
</body>
</html>
```

**6.** Now, we need to add a data attribute to our slideshow container, so Cycle2 knows we want to use a different transition effect. Find the `<div>` element with the `cycle-slideshow` class and add the `data-cycle-fx` attribute set to `carousel`:

```
<div class="cycle-slideshow"
  data-cycle-slides="> div.slide"
  data-cycle-fx="carousel">
```

Now, if you refresh the page in the browser, you'll see that you have a carousel, as shown in the following screenshot:

You'll see that the carousel automatically advances one image every second or so. That's nice, but it would be even nicer to put 100 percent of the control of the carousel in the hands of our site visitors.

7.  Let's disable the automatic animations. This way, site visitors won't be distracted by the images marching across their screen unexpectedly. To do this, we just have to add a data attribute. Find the `<div>` element with the class `cycle-slideshow` and add the `data-cycle-timeout` attribute in it. We can use this attribute on any Cycle2 slideshow to specify how long to wait between animations. In this case, we don't want any animations at all, so we'll set it equal to `0`:

```
<div class="cycle-slideshow"
  data-cycle-slides="> div.slide"
  data-cycle-fx="carousel"
  data-cycle-timeout="0">
```

8.  Now that we've removed the automatic animations, our site visitors have no way to access any of the slides that aren't visible on page load. Let's fix this by adding some previous and next buttons.

    By default, if we add the same code we added last time for the next and previous buttons, they'll both be shown under the carousel as they are in the demos on the Cycle2 documentation site:

That's okay, but we're designers! Let's place our buttons to the left and right of the slideshow. Also, let's use graphic images instead of text. Here's the look we're going for:

Can you push Cycle2 that far and customize it to such an extent? You bet you can! Let's see how to accomplish this.

**9.** First up, we have to add some space around the slideshow to make room for the buttons. We also need a way to position those buttons on either side of the slideshow. To accomplish this, we'll wrap a new `<div>` element around the entire slideshow:

```
<div class="slideshow-wrap">
  <div class="cycle-slideshow"
    data-cycle-slides="> div.slide"
    data-cycle-fx="carousel"
    data-cycle-timeout="0"
    >
    <div class="slide">
      <a href="http://en.wikipedia.org/wiki/Agua_Azul">
        <img src="images/AguaAzul.jpg">
      </a>
    </div>
    . . .
  </div>
</div>
```

Then, jump over to `styles.css` and style that new container:

```
.slideshow-wrap {
  position: relative;
}
```

That's all we need to set the `position` attribute to `relative` so that we can easily position items inside the container.

**10.** Next, we need to add some space on the left and right sides of the slideshow so we've got space to include the buttons. In the `styles.css` file, add a margin to the `div` element that contains the slideshow:

```
.cycle-slideshow {
  margin: 0 3.5em 0 3em;
}
```

Don't forget the users with JavaScript disabled. The margin won't be necessary for them, so let's remove that for the no-JavaScript case:

```
.jsOff .cycle-slideshow {
  margin: 0;
}
```

**11.** Now that we've made space for them, let's add our next and previous buttons. We don't want them to be inside the slideshow because we need more control. Instead, we'll place them after the slideshow, but inside that wrapper `<div>` element we added:

```
<div class="slideshow-wrap">
  <div class="cycle-slideshow"
    data-cycle-slides="> div.slide"
    data-cycle-fx="carousel"
    data-cycle-timeout="0"
    >
    <div class="slide">
      <a href="http://en.wikipedia.org/wiki/Agua_Azul">
        <img src="images/AguaAzul.jpg">
      </a>
    </div>
    ...
  </div>
  <div id="prev"><div class="button-wrap"></div></div>
  <div id="next"><div class="button-wrap"></div></div>
</div>
```

Notice that we're adding another `<div>` element inside those next and previous buttons. We'll use that to style the buttons just the way we'd like. Now, we've got our next and previous buttons, but because they're not inside the slideshow, Cycle2 doesn't even know about them yet. We just have to tell Cycle2 that we'd like to use those new `<div>` elements as the next and previous buttons. We'll do that by adding a couple of more data attributes to the `<div>` element with the class `cycle-slideshow`:

```
<div class="cycle-slideshow"
  data-cycle-slides="> div.slide"
  data-cycle-fx="carousel"
```

```
data-cycle-timeout="0"
data-cycle-next="#next"
data-cycle-prev="#prev">
```

We'll use the `data-cycle-next` and `data-cycle-prev` data attributes and set them to be equal to selectors for whatever elements we'd like to use as the next and previous buttons.

**12.** Now, our next and previous buttons work to control the slideshow in theory, but as we haven't styled them with CSS yet, we can't actually see them to click and try them out.

Before we get started with styling those buttons, let's remember our visitors without JavaScript again. Those buttons won't be of any help to them, so let's tuck them out of view:

```css
.jsOff #next,
.jsOff #prev {
  display: none;
}
```

Now, we can get to work on styling our previous and next buttons for everyone else. First, set the size and position of each of the buttons:

```css
#next,
#prev {
  bottom: 0;
  cursor: pointer;
  overflow: hidden;
  position: absolute;
  top: 0;
  width: 3em;
}

#next {
  right: 0;
}

#prev {
  left: 0;
}
```

This bit of code absolutely positions the buttons to either the left or the right of the slideshow, in the space we created for them when we added a margin to the slideshow container. It also sets the width of the buttons to 3 em and makes them equal in height to the height of the slideshow.

**13.** Now, remember that extra button-wrap container we placed inside each of our buttons? We're going to use that to create the half-circle buttons. Here are the styles to apply:

```css
.button-wrap {
  background: #4fc1e9;
  border-radius: 50%;
  bottom: 0;
  position: absolute;
  top: 0;
  width: 6em;
}

#next .button-wrap {
  right: 0;
}

#prev .button-wrap {
  left: 0;
}
```

Let's take a look at this to be sure you understand what's going on. First up, we're setting the background color as bright blue. By setting the `border-radius` value to `50%`, we're creating a circle shape. Next, we absolutely position the blue circle and set its width to twice the width of the parent container. Essentially, we're creating a complete circle but only showing half of the circle. The circle, along with its attributes, is diagrammatically shown as follows:

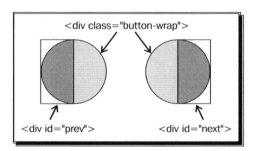

**14.** Now, let's add a hover style and make the blue part a slightly darker shade when the buttons are hovered over:

```css
#next .button-wrap:hover,
#prev .button-wrap:hover {
  background: #38afda;
}
```

That's simple enough—it's just a simple background color change. But what if we wanted a quick animation from color to color? All we have to do is go back to the CSS element where we originally defined the background color and add a CSS transition property:

```
.button-wrap {
  background: #4fc1e9;
  border-radius: 50%;
  bottom: 0;
  position: absolute;
  top: 0;
  transition: background-color 0.3s;
  width: 6em;
}
```

Now, if you hover over the buttons, you'll see an animation that takes 0.3 seconds to change from the default background color to the hover background color.

**15.** Our carousel is looking pretty good so far, but we do need to add some arrows to those buttons to make their functionality clearer. Remember that clever technique for creating triangles with CSS? We'll put that to use here again. Let's define a slightly transparent white triangle for each button:

```
#next .button-wrap:before,
#prev .button-wrap:before {
  border-style: solid;
  content: '';
  margin-top: -0.866em;
  position: absolute;
  top: 50%;
}

#next .button-wrap:before {
  border-width: 0.866em 0 0.866em 1em;
  border-color: transparent transparent transparent
rgba(255,255,255,0.5);
  right: 1em;
}

#prev .button-wrap:before {
  border-width: 0.866em 1em 0.866em 0;
  border-color: transparent rgba(255,255,255,0.5) transparent
transparent;
  left: 1em;
}
```

We're absolutely positioning the arrow to appear in the middle of our half-circle button, and then adjusting the border widths and colors to produce the triangle.

**16.** The only thing left to do is to add a hover effect to the triangles. Since the button color is changing, we can emphasize that difference by also changing the triangles to be less transparent when hovered over:

```
#next .button-wrap:hover:before {
  border-left-color: rgba(255,255,255,0.8);
}

#prev .button-wrap:hover:before {
  border-right-color: rgba(255,255,255,0.8);
}
```

Again, if we wanted to animate that color change, we can use the CSS transition property. But since we now have two things changing, we could actually just make a simple change to the transition line we wrote earlier to animate both the button background color and the triangle color:

```
.button-wrap {
  background: #4fc1e9;
  border-radius: 50%;
  bottom: 0;
  position: absolute;
  top: 0;
  transition: all 0.3s;
  width: 6em;
}
```

Rather than animating only the background color, we've animated anything that might change—this will cover the background animation for the button itself as well as the arrow color. If we changed other properties when hovered over, those would be animated as well.

We've created a very nice carousel, but we could definitely improve upon it. What if our carousel were just a tool to navigate a set of full-size images? Let's take a look at how we can combine a carousel and a slideshow.

# Combining a carousel with a slideshow

Not only can you include more than one Cycle2 slideshow on a single page, you can also set up those slideshows to "talk" to one another. Let's take a look at how we can set up a carousel to act as a controller for a slideshow. Here's an example of what we'll be building:

Clicking on one of the thumbnails in the carousel will load the full-size version of that image in the slideshow section.

## Setting up the carousel

To make this a little bit easier to digest, we're going to break the process of creating the carousel/slideshow combo into three pieces. In this first piece, we'll get the carousel set up and working and look at the special considerations we have to make to ensure that it will work flawlessly with our slideshow component.

## Time for action – creating the carousel controller

Follow these steps to create a Cycle2 carousel that can act as a controller for a slideshow:

1.  First, we'll create the carousel. Once we have that on the page and it's functioning, we'll add the slideshow and then connect them together.

    Here's the HTML markup we'll use for the slideshow:

    ```
    <div id="carousel">
      <div class="cycle-slideshow">
    ```

```
        <div>
          <a href="images/AguaAzul.jpg">
            <img src="images/AguaAzul-thumb.jpg" width="140"
height="100">
          </a>
        </div>
        <div>
          <a href="images/BurneyFalls.jpg">
            <img src="images/BurneyFalls-thumb.jpg" width="140"
height="100">
          </a>
        </div>
        <div>
          <a href="images/Deer_Leap_Falls.jpg">
            <img src="images/Deer_Leap_Falls-thumb.jpg" width="140"
height="100">
          </a>
        </div>
        </div>
</div>
```

We'll wrap the entire slideshow in a `<div>` element with the ID of `carousel`. We'll use this `<div>` element for styling purposes and also in our JavaScript to allow us to select items in the carousel or the slideshow without having to select both.

This markup is a bit different than the markup we used for our last carousel. Rather than linking to a page with more information about each image, we're going to link the thumbnail-size of the image to the full-size image.

2. Now, let's take a minute to consider how our page will work for site visitors who don't have JavaScript enabled. The basic functionality we're looking for is to view the full size of each image when we click on the thumbnail. That's easy enough to handle, and the HTML markup we've set up for the carousel will already handle that.

Add the `jsOff` class to your `<body>` tag. Then, open up the `styles.css` file and style the carousel thumbs:

```css
.jsOff .cycle-slideshow div {
  display: inline-block;
  padding: 0.5em;
}
```

Now, if you refresh the page in the browser, you'll see that you have a grid of thumbnails, as shown in the following screenshot:

Visitors without JavaScript will see a grid of thumbnails. When they click on a thumbnail, they'll see the full-size version of that image. They can then use the back button on the browser to return to this page and view the next thumbnail.

3. Now that we have those site visitors taken care of, let's dive into the interactive version for the site visitors that do have JavaScript. Open the `scripts.js` file and add a bit of code that we've seen several times now to remove the `jsOff` class and replace it with a `jsOn` class:

```
$(document).ready(function(){
  $('body').removeClass('jsOff').addClass('jsOn');
});
```

4. Next, we'll attach the JavaScript files that we'll need in order to get the carousel working. Just as with the previous carousel, we'll need the Cycle2 plugin itself and the Carousel Transition plugin. Place both of those files into your `scripts` folder. Then, head down to the bottom of the HTML file and attach those scripts after jQuery but before your `scripts.js` file:

```
<script src="scripts/jquery.js"></script>
<script src="scripts/jquery.cycle2.min.js"></script>
<script src="scripts/jquery.cycle2.carousel.min.js"></script>
<script src="scripts/scripts.js"></script>
</body>
</html>
```

**5.** Now, let's add the data attributes to the `<div>` element that contains our carousel to get it working just the way we need. We'll need the `data-cycle-slides` attribute so that Cycle2 knows what markup we're using for our individual slides, and we'll need to specify that we want to use the carousel transition effect with the `data-cycle-fx` attribute:

```
<div class="cycle-slideshow"
  data-cycle-slides="> div"
  data-cycle-fx="carousel">
```

If you refresh the page in the browser, you'll see that we're on our way—we now have a functioning carousel:

Now, let's modify the carousal to suit our needs. For that, perform the following steps:

**6.** First, we don't want the carousel to advance automatically, so add the `data-cycle-timeout` attribute and set this to `0`:

```
<div class="cycle-slideshow"
  data-cycle-slides="> div"
  data-cycle-fx="carousel"
  data-cycle-timeout="0">
```

This will prevent the default automatic advance through the slides.

**7.** Now that we've taken the default animation away, we need to provide a way for our site visitors to get to all the slides in the carousel. We'll add a previous button and a next button. First, add the HTML markup for the buttons. These should be inserted after the closure of the `<div>` element with the class `cycle-slideshow` but before the closure of the `<div>` element with the ID `carousel`:

```
<div id="carousel">
  <div class="cycle-slideshow"
    data-cycle-slides="> div"
    data-cycle-fx="carousel"
    data-cycle-timeout="0">
    <div>
      <a href="images/AguaAzul.jpg">
```

```
      <img src="images/AguaAzul-thumb.jpg"
        width="140" height="100">
    </a>
  </div>
  ...
</div>
<div class="cycle-prev cycle-button">
  <div class="button-wrap"></div>
</div>
<div class="cycle-next cycle-button">
  <div class="button-wrap"></div>
</div>
</div>
```

**8.** Next, we have to tell Cycle2 which elements on our page will be acting as our next and previous buttons. We can do that by adding two additional data attributes to our carousel:

```
<div class="cycle-slideshow"
  data-cycle-slides="> div"
  data-cycle-fx="carousel"
  data-cycle-timeout="0"
  data-cycle-prev="#carousel .cycle-prev"
  data-cycle-next="#carousel .cycle-next">
```

The value of these data attributes is the jQuery (or CSS) selector for the elements. Now, these two new HTML elements are activated as next and previous buttons, but we can't see them on our HTML page yet since we haven't applied any CSS styles.

**9.** We'll apply similar styles as we did in the last carousel example. In `styles.css`, let's add a margin to the carousel to make room for the next and previous buttons on either side:

```
#carousel .cycle-slideshow {
  margin: 0 3.5em;
}
```

Now that we've got space for them, we can position our next and previous buttons on either side of the carousel:

```
#carousel {
  margin: 1em 0;
  position: relative;
}

.cycle-button {
  bottom: 0;
```

```
  cursor: pointer;
  overflow: hidden;
  position: absolute;
  top: 0;
  width: 3em;
}

.cycle-next {
  right: 0;
}

.cycle-prev {
  left: 0;
}
```

**10.** Now, we can style the `<div>` element with the `button-wrap` class that's inside each of our button containers:

```
.button-wrap {
  background: #4fc1e9;
  border-radius: 50%;
  bottom: 0;
  position: absolute;
  top: 0;
  transition: all 0.3s;
  width: 6em;
}

.cycle-next .button-wrap {
  right: 0;
}

.cycle-prev .button-wrap {
  left: 0;
}
```

Just like we did last time, we're using the technique of creating a circle with CSS and then only showing 50 percent of the circle to create a half-circle-shaped button. Next, we'll change the background color of those buttons when our site visitor hovers over them:

```
.cycle-button .button-wrap:hover {
  background: #38afda;
}
```

**11.** We'll use the same CSS technique we used last time to add triangles to these buttons:

```css
.cycle-button .button-wrap:before {
  border-style: solid;
  content: '';
  margin-top: -0.866em;
  position: absolute;
  top: 50%;
}

.cycle-next .button-wrap:before {
  border-width: 0.866em 0 0.866em 1em;
  border-color: transparent transparent transparent
rgba(255,255,255,0.5);
  right: 1em;
}

.cycle-prev .button-wrap:before {
  border-width: 0.866em 1em 0.866em 0;
  border-color: transparent rgba(255,255,255,0.5) transparent
transparent;
  left: 1em;
}
```

Also, just like last time, we'll add a hover style to these new triangles as well:

```css
.cycle-next .button-wrap:hover:before {
  border-left-color: rgba(255,255,255,0.8);
}

.cycle-prev .button-wrap:hover:before {
  border-right-color: rgba(255,255,255,0.8);
}
```

If you refresh the page in the browser, you'll see that we now have a working carousel that looks pretty similar to the carousel we built the first time.

We do need to make a few changes to our carousel now to get it ready for acting as the controller for the slideshow. It's just a few more data attributes that we need to add to the slideshow.

**12.** However, let's take a minute to think about our users without JavaScript. They won't get any use from the next and previous buttons, and it's probably best to just hide those from them:

```
.jsOff .cycle-button {
  display: none;
}
```

When we're connecting a carousel with a slideshow, we have a few things to consider that we wouldn't have to think about if we were only building a carousel. The first problem we have to solve is what we'll call the indexing problem. Let me explain what that problem is, and then explain how we can solve it.

The carousel and slideshow we're working within the code examples for this book each contain eight different slides. If we create a carousel with thumbnails and then a slideshow with full-size images and put those images in exactly the same order, then we can use a simple index association to match the thumbnails with the full-size images. In other words, we know that if the site visitor clicks on the first thumbnail in the carousel, we should show them the first image in the slideshow. When they click on the third thumbnail in the carousel, we should show them the third image in the slideshow, and so on. So what's the problem?

If you click on the next button on this carousel repeatedly, you'll see that the set of slides inside it loops—you can repeatedly click on the next button until you return to the first slide.

We didn't have to do any extra work to make that happen—this is a feature that the developer of the Cycle2 plugin thought out and made happen for us. However, this feature works by creating some extra copies of the slides inside the carousel and then using jQuery to cleverly move them around as needed so that it appears that the carousel just moves infinitely. However, Cycle2 slideshows only show one slide at a time, so there's no need to add extra copies of the individual slides to make them work. The fact that the carousel has extra slides while the slideshow does not can make things difficult when we want to build a combo.

The eight slides we're placing into the carousel become 41 slides when Cycle2 finishes making all of its magic happen on the page. If the site visitor clicks on the fifteenth image in the carousel, we don't have a fifteenth image in the slideshow to send them off to, and our carousel/slideshow combo breaks.

**13.** Luckily, we can solve this problem really easily by telling our carousel not to loop infinitely, by adding a data attribute called `data-allow-wrap`:

```
<div class="cycle-slideshow"
  data-cycle-slides="> div"
  data-cycle-fx="carousel"
  data-cycle-timeout="0"
  data-cycle-prev="#carousel .cycle-prev"
  data-cycle-next="#carousel .cycle-next"
  data-allow-wrap="false">
```

Now, because our carousel isn't wrapping infinitely, there's no need for Cycle2 to create extra copies of our slides, and we can easily associate thumbnails in the carousel with images in the slideshow.

**14.** However, if you click the next button on the carousel repeatedly, you'll see that the thumbnails keep moving over, until there's just one image left, as shown in the following screenshot:

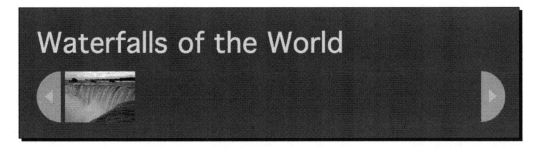

This feels really awkward, so let's force the carousel to always show us five slides. We can do that with another data attribute:

```
<div class="cycle-slideshow"
  data-cycle-slides="> div"
  data-cycle-fx="carousel"
  data-cycle-timeout="0"
  data-cycle-prev="#carousel .cycle-prev"
  data-cycle-next="#carousel .cycle-next"
  data-allow-wrap="false"
  data-cycle-carousel-visible="5">
```

Now, once our final thumbnail is visible, the carousel stops advancing forward. Nice, except that the thumbnails are all bunched up, as shown in the following screenshot:

Luckily, that's an easy fix for this too. If we just add the `data-cycle-carousel-fluid` data attribute and set it to `true`, Cycle2 will take care of spacing out our five thumbnails to fill the space nicely:

```
<div class="cycle-slideshow"
  data-cycle-slides="> div"
  data-cycle-fx="carousel"
  data-cycle-timeout="0"
  data-cycle-prev="#carousel .cycle-prev"
  data-cycle-next="#carousel .cycle-next"
  data-allow-wrap="false"
  data-cycle-carousel-visible="5"
  data-cycle-carousel-fluid="true">
```

This gives us a nice result, as shown in the following screenshot, and it's responsive too!

Now that we've got our carousel set up and working, let's layer in the slideshow component.

## Adding the slideshow

Congratulations to us! We've got a gorgeous-looking carousel set up and working, and we've already solved some of the problems we might encounter when connecting our carousel and our slideshow together.

With the carousel out of the way, let's dive into adding the slideshow component. After this, we'll connect them so they work together.

## Time for action – adding the slideshow

Follow these steps to set up the slideshow component of our carousel/slideshow combo:

1. As usual, we'll get started with the HTML markup for our slideshow. Since we want the slideshow to be visible above the carousel, we'll place the slideshow into the code before the carousel code. Everything will work just fine if you choose to do things the other way around. Here's the HTML structure for the slideshow:

```
<div id="slideshow">
  <div class="cycle-slideshow">
    <div data-cycle-title="Agua Azul"
      data-cycle-desc="Tumbal&aacute;, Chiapas, Mexico">
      <img src="images/AguaAzul.jpg"></div>
    <div data-cycle-title="Burney Falls"
      data-cycle-desc="Shasta County, California, USA">
      <img src="images/BurneyFalls.jpg"></div>
    <div data-cycle-title="Deer Leap Falls"
      data-cycle-desc="Dingmans Ferry, Pennsylvania, USA">
      <img src="images/Deer_Leap_Falls.jpg"></div>
    ...
  </div>
</div>
```

We're including the `data-cycle-title` and `data-cycle-desc` attributes in the container for each of the slides because we want to use those later on to show an overlay just like we did when we built our previous slideshow.

We've also wrapped the entire slideshow in a `<div>` element with the ID of `slideshow` to make it easy to select elements inside the slideshow for either CSS or JavaScript purposes.

2. We don't want the slideshow and the carousel to butt up against one another, so we'll go into `styles.css` and add a bit of space around both the components:

```
#carousel,
#slideshow {
  margin: 1em 0;
  position: relative;
}
```

Also, we've added a margin on the left and right sides of the carousel to make room for the next and previous buttons. To keep things nicely aligned, we should add this same margin around the slideshow portion. Find the line in `styles.css` where you added the left and right margin around the carousel and apply the same style to the slideshow:

```
#carousel .cycle-slideshow,
#slideshow .cycle-slideshow {
  margin: 0 3.5em;
}
```

3.  Now, just like we always do, we'll take a moment now to think about how this slideshow should look and behave for site visitors without JavaScript. For the visitors who do have JavaScript, we're loading up the full-size version of the image in the slideshow when they click on the thumbnail. A similar behavior that we can accomplish for visitors without JavaScript would be what we already built in the carousel section—we'll show them a grid of images that link to the full-size version of the images. For this, it would make sense to just hide the slideshow portion of our combo altogether for users without JavaScript. Add this to `styles.css`:

```
.jsOff #slideshow {
  display: none;
}
```

4.  Our slideshow won't work until we tell Cycle2 the markup for our slides. Just like we've done before, we'll add the `data-cycle-slides` attribute:

```
<div class="cycle-slideshow"
  data-cycle-slides="> div">
```

Now, if you refresh the page in the browser, you'll see that we have a working slideshow.

**5.** Just like with the carousel, we don't want automatic animation to happen since we want our site visitors to have complete control over the slideshow. We'll use the `data-cycle-timeout` data attribute to turn that off:

```
<div class="cycle-slideshow"
  data-cycle-slides="> div"
  data-cycle-timeout="0">
```

**6.** Next, let's get the overlay with the title and description working for our slideshow. We'll add a `<div>` element to contain our overlay at the bottom of our slideshow after the closure of the `<div>` element with the class `cycle-slideshow`, but before the closure of `<div>` element with the ID `slideshow`:

```
<div id="slideshow">
  <div class="cycle-slideshow"
    data-cycle-slides="> div"
    data-cycle-timeout="0">
    <div data-cycle-title="Agua Azul"
      data-cycle-desc="Tumbal&aacute;, Chiapas, Mexico">
      <img src="images/AguaAzul.jpg"></div>
    <div data-cycle-title="Burney Falls"
      data-cycle-desc="Shasta County, California, USA">
      <img src="images/BurneyFalls.jpg"></div>
    ...
  <div id="overlay" class="cycle-overlay"></div>
</div>
```

Now, we just have to tell Cycle2 that this is the container we'd like to use for the overlay. We'll do that with a data attribute:

```
<div class="cycle-slideshow"
  data-cycle-slides="> div"
  data-cycle-timeout="0"
  data-cycle-overlay="#overlay">
```

If you refresh the page in the browser now, you'll see that the text we specified as the `data-cycle-title` and `data-cycle-desc` attributes on each slide are now displayed below the slideshow, as shown in the following screenshot:

7. Next, we need to style that text. Just like last time, we want to specify a different bit of HTML to be used to mark up that text because the default markup is a bit challenging to style with CSS. We'll pass the `data-cycle-overlay-template` attribute with the HTML we want to use:

```
<div class="cycle-slideshow"
  data-cycle-slides="> div"
  data-cycle-timeout="0"
  data-cycle-overlay="#overlay"
  data-cycle-overlay-template="<div class='headline'>
    <h2>{{title}}</h2><p>{{desc}}</p></div>">
```

Then, we'll jump back over to `styles.css` and add some CSS to style that overlay:

```
.cycle-overlay {
  bottom: 0;
  left: 0;
  position: absolute;
  right: 0;
  z-index: 101;
}
```

```
.headline {
  background: rgba(0,0,0,0.6);
  color: white;
  margin: 0 4em;
  padding: 1em;
}

.headline h2 {
  color: white;
  font-size: 2em;
  line-height: 1.125;
}

.headline p {
  font-style: italic;
  line-height: 1.5;
}
```

Now, if you refresh the page in the browser, you can see that the overlay is close to the final position we want, but it seems just a bit off:

This is happening because our image isn't centered inside the stage area of the slideshow. Let's take a look at how we can fix that.

8. Cycle2 has a Center plugin that will allow us to center content vertically, horizontally, or both inside the slideshow area. This can be one method of nicely handling slides that are of different sizes or aspect ratios. In this case, we want to bump the images of the slideshow over so that they're centered. Head to the Cycle2 downloads page (http://jquery.malsup.com/cycle2/download/) and download the **Production** version of the Center plugin and save it to your scripts folder. Then, attach it at the bottom of index.html:

```
<script src="scripts/jquery.js"></script>
<script src="scripts/jquery.cycle2.min.js"></script>
<script src="scripts/jquery.cycle2.carousel.min.js"></script>
<script src="scripts/jquery.cycle2.center.min.js"></script>
<script src="scripts/scripts.js"></script>
</body>
</html>
```

Now, we just have to add a data attribute to the slideshow to tell Cycle2 that we want to horizontally center the slides:

```
<div class="cycle-slideshow"
  data-cycle-slides="> div"
  data-cycle-timeout="0"
  data-cycle-overlay="#overlay"
  data-cycle-overlay-template="<div
class='headline'><h2>{{title}}</h2><p>{{desc}}</p></div>"
  data-cycle-center-horz="true">
```

If you refresh the page in the browser, you'll see that the overlay now matches up with our slides because our slides are properly centered in the stage area.

Now, our slideshow and our carousel look good; the only thing left to do is get them talking to each other.

# Connecting the carousel and the slider

In this final section, we'll take a look at how to connect the carousel with the slider so that clicking on a thumbnail in the carousel loads up the full-size version of the image in the slideshow. Once that's finished, we'll make some final adjustments that will add some nice touches.

## Time for action – connecting the carousel and the slider

Follow these steps to connect the carousel and the slider:

1. We've done a lot so far with Cycle2 without writing much jQuery to make it all happen. We've finally found something we want to do with Cycle2 that will require us to write a few lines of jQuery. We want to load the full-size image in the slideshow when our site visitor clicks on the thumbnail in the carousel. So we'll get started with `scripts.js` by selecting all the slides in the carousel. Add the code to select those inside the document ready method, after the bit of code that we're using to change the `<body>` class:

```
$(document).ready(function(){
  $('body').removeClass('jsOff').addClass('jsOn');

  $('#carousel .cycle-slide');
});
```

This little bit of code won't change anything on our page, but now we've got all the thumbnails in the carousel and we can work with them. The `cycle-slide` class is added to each individual slide in a slideshow by the Cycle2 plugin.

2. We want the slides in the slideshow to change when the site visitor clicks on those thumbnails in the carousel, so we need to add a `click` event to those thumbnails:

```
$(document).ready(function(){
  $('body').removeClass('jsOff').addClass('jsOn');

  $('#carousel .cycle-slide').on('click', function(){
    // here's what happens when we click on a thumbnail
  });
});
```

Now, we're all set to take some action when our site visitor clicks on a thumbnail, so let's think about what we need to do.

**3.** Each of our thumbnails is wrapped in a link to the full-size image, but we don't want to send people off to that link if they have JavaScript enabled. The first thing we'll do is cancel this default action:

```
$('#carousel .cycle-slide').on('click', function(e){
  e.preventDefault();
});
```

Notice that we made a change at the end of the first line. We added an e argument inside the parentheses after my function. Recall that this is the event that we're working with.

Then, inside the function, we can call a method of that event to change what happens. We're calling a method called preventDefault() that cancels the default action. In this case, it will prevent the opening of the full-size image in the browser window. We want to write our own action that will happen when a site visitor clicks, so we don't want that default action to happen.

If you refresh the page in the browser now and click on one of the thumbnails in the carousel, you'll see that nothing happens. Let's write a new action.

**4.** When a site visitor clicks on one of the carousel thumbnails, the first thing we need to do is figure out the index of the thumbnail. Remember earlier we talked about how there are eight slides in the carousel and eight slides in the slideshow? When we click on the third thumbnail, we want to show the third image in the slideshow. In order to be able to that, we need to know what is the number of the thumbnail the site visitor clicked. This number is called the index.

So, the next step of our action is figuring out the index of the thumbnail that the site visitor clicked. We'll set up a variable for that and call it index:

```
$('#carousel .cycle-slide').on('click', function(e){
  e.preventDefault();
  var index;
});
```

Remember, a variable is just an empty container. We've created an empty container named index. Now, let's figure out how to put the index of the thumbnail into that container.

**5.** The Cycle2 plugin actually gives us a pretty nice way to figure out which thumbnail was clicked. The thumbnail gets stored as data attached to the carousel container. So, the first thing we'll do is select the carousel container:

```
$('#carousel .cycle-slide').on('click', function(e){
  e.preventDefault();
  var index = $('#carousel .cycle-slideshow');
});
```

**6.** Now that we've got that container, we just need to access the data that's attached to it. To do that, we'll use jQuery's `data()` method, and we'll use `cycle.API` that the Cycle2 plugin has provided us:

```
$('#carousel .cycle-slide').on('click', function(e){
  e.preventDefault();
  var index = $('#carousel .cycle-slideshow').
    data('cycle.API');
});
```

The `cycle.API` is just a programmer-speak for some handy bits of information that the Cycle2 plugin makes available to us. This is also the information that Cycle2 and the Cycle2 plugins themselves use to make the magic happen. You can take a look at the assorted information available to us by looking at the Cycle2 API documentation page at `http://jquery.malsup.com/cycle2/api/advanced.php`

Now, chances are that there's going to be a lot of information there that you don't understand—that's okay. We'll just need to understand some of it to get the functionality we want.

**7.** In this case, the bit of information we'd like to get from Cycle2 is the index of the thumbnail that was clicked. We'll ask for that with the `getSlideIndex()` method:

```
$('#carousel .cycle-slide').on('click', function(e){
  e.preventDefault();
  var index = $('#carousel .cycle-slideshow').
    data('cycle.API').getSlideIndex(this);
});
```

It's not terribly important to understand exactly how this works. Just know that when a thumbnail in the carousel is clicked, we now know exactly which slide it was.

**8.** Now that we've got the index of the clicked thumbnail, we have to figure out how to tell the slideshow to show that slide. We also have to tell the carousel that we want that thumbnail to be moved to the prime position. That is refreshingly easy. We'll get started by selecting the slideshows:

```
$('#carousel .cycle-slide').on('click', function(e){
  e.preventDefault();
  var index = $('#carousel .cycle-slideshow').data('cycle.API').
getSlideIndex(this);
  $('.cycle-slideshow');
});
```

**9.** Now, we can call the `cycle()` method and tell it what we'd like to do. In this case, we want to tell the slideshow to go to the slide that matches the index:

```
$('#carousel .cycle-slide').on('click', function(e){
  e.preventDefault();
  var index = $('#carousel .cycle-slideshow').data('cycle.API').
getSlideIndex(this);
    $('.cycle-slideshow').cycle('goto', index);
});
```

That's it, just a couple of lines of code. If you refresh the page in the browser, you'll see that when you click on one of the thumbnails, it loads up the full-size version of that image in the slideshow and also moves that thumbnail to the first position as long as we're not too close to the end.

Now, let's take a look at a few things we can do to make the experience of using our slideshow/carousel combo even better.

**10.** It's not terribly clear which thumbnail in the carousel represents the currently selected thumbnail. We can fix that with a bit of CSS. Open `styles.css` and add a few lines to style the thumbnails:

```
#carousel .cycle-slide img {
  border: 2px solid transparent;
  display: block;
  opacity: 0.7;
}

#carousel .cycle-slide-active img {
  border-color: #38AFDA;
  opacity: 1;
}
```

In this case, we are fading out the thumbnails that aren't selected and then showing the selected thumbnail at full opacity and with a blue border. By assigning a 2px transparent border to the unselected thumbnails, we assure that there won't be any awkward 2px jumping when the border is applied. Rather than adding and removing the border, we're just changing the color of the border.

And where does that `cycle-slide-active` class come from? It's added for us by the Cycle2 plugin. Refresh the page, and your slideshow should look like the following screenshot:

Now, it's easy to identify at a glance which thumbnail is selected.

11. Remember how we removed the infinite looping of the carousel? We had to do that in order to make the carousel work as a controller for the slideshow, but we're not doing a very good job of communicating to our site visitor that they've reached the end of the carousel and further clicking isn't going to advance them any further.

    We can fix that by adding some CSS styles for disabled carousel buttons. In `styles.css`, add an alternate style for the buttons if they're disabled:

```
.cycle-button.disabled {
  opacity: 0.5;
}
```

In this case, we'll to fade those out to communicate that they're no longer active. The `disabled` class is added to those buttons for us by the Cycle2 plugin.

***12.*** Finally, our slideshow/carousel combo doesn't currently behave very nicely when we have a narrower window, like our site visitors might have on a tablet or a mobile phone. Let's shrink the images nicely to fit in the space available:

In `styles.css`, **add this bit of code:**

```
.cycle-slideshow img {
  height: auto;
  max-width: 100%;
}
```

Refresh the page in the browser and make the window narrower. You'll see that our slideshow now behaves pretty nicely and fits inside the screen.

Phew! That was quite a lot of work and it was pretty involved! But you made it through. Thanks for sticking with me.

# Summary

In this chapter, we took a look at five different ways in which we can deal with slideshows and sliders on websites. We started off by building a simple crossfading slideshow from scratch without using a plugin. Next, we took a look at implementing the Basic Slider, which while being basic, has enough options and the ability to change its appearance via CSS, making it a great fit for many different types of projects.

For those projects that require fancy transition effects and even more options, we worked through three different types of sliders that we can build with the Cycle2 plugin. This flexible and extensible plugin will come in handy for many different types of slideshows on many different projects.

Next, we'll take a look at some techniques to use when working with responsive designs.

# 7

# Working with Responsive Designs

*The last couple of years have seen a rise in the popularity of an approach to designing websites called **responsive design**. Coined by Ethan Marcotte, the term refers to websites that respond to the viewport size of your website visitor. You can learn more about responsive design in Marcotte's article at* `http://alistapart.com/article/responsive-web-design`*. Whether site visitors are viewing your website on a mobile device, a tablet, a netbook, or a huge desktop screen, the website detects the viewport size and responds by adjusting layouts, font sizes, image sizes, and more to optimize the website for that particular viewport size.*

*While most of the magic of responsive design happens with media queries and other CSS, JavaScript can help to enhance the experience even further for our website visitors. Some elements and layouts aren't easily adapted to the viewport size with just CSS. JavaScript can fill in and help us take our responsive designs to the next level.*

In this chapter, we'll cover the following topics:

- ◆ Using the FitVids plugin to fit video players to the viewport
- ◆ Turning a drop-down menu into a responsive menu
- ◆ Building a tiled layout to display image galleries in responsive designs

# Using FitVids for responsive videos

Video players are one of the handful of elements on a website that don't readily respond to being resized easily with just CSS. However, video players are so popular that we need a way to fit those into our responsive designs.

jQuery and the FitVids plugin come to the rescue. This simple little script automatically sizes your videos to fit inside any container, whether that's a page or a column on your site.

## Time for action – resizing videos

Perform the following steps to make your videos respond to the viewport size:

**1.** We'll get started as we usually do by creating a basic HTML document and the associated files and folders just like we did in *Chapter 1, Designer, Meet jQuery*. In the body of the HTML document, we'll create a few sections. In each section, we'll include a place to put a video, a title, and a short description, as shown in the following code:

```
<div class="content">
  <h1>Favorite Videos</h1>
  <section>
    <div class="video">
    </div>
    <div class="description">
      <h1>Maru Being Maru</h1>
      <p>A video of Maru, the cutest cat in Japan,
        playing with a box.</p>
    </div>
  </section>
  <section>
    <div class="video">
    </div>
    <div class="description">
      <h1>Candy apple shaped soft candy</h1>
      <p>RRCherryPie demonstrates how to use a candy kit to
        make adorable candy that looks like miniature candy
        apples.</p>
    </div>
  </section>
</div>
```

2.  Next, we want to add our videos. I'm going to choose one video from Vimeo and one video from YouTube. Feel free to select your favorite videos to use for this example. Each video service offers a way to embed videos by copying and pasting a short bit of code. Just copy the following code to embed your selected video into the `<div>` element with `class` of `video`:

```
<div class="video">
  <iframe src="//player.vimeo.com/video/5056857" width="500"
    height="333" frameborder="0" webkitallowfullscreen
    mozallowfullscreen allowfullscreen></iframe>
</div>
<div class="description">
  <h1>Maru Being Maru</h1>
  <p>A video of Maru, the cutest cat in Japan,
    playing with a box.</p>
</div>
```

If you want to view your videos while working on files on your own computer, you'll have to make a small adjustment to the provided embed code for both Vimeo and YouTube. Both services remove the `http:` protocol from the beginning of the `src` attribute to ensure that their videos can be embedded without any issues on both secure (`https`) and unsecure (`http`) websites. To view your videos on local files, you just have to restore `http:` as follows:

```
<iframe src="http://player.vimeo.com/
video/5056857"
    width="500" height="333" frameborder="0"
    webkitallowfullscreen mozallowfullscreen
    allowfullscreen></iframe>
```

This will enable you to view the videos while looking at your local files.

3.  Next, let's add some styles to nicely display our videos and descriptions. As we'll be making our videos responsive, let's go ahead and style the layout to be responsive, starting with the mobile layout first. At narrow screen widths, we'll want the description to be displayed below the video. Open your `styles.css` file and add the few lines shown in the following code snippet to style your section elements:

```
.content section {
  margin: 1em 0;
}

.content section h1 {
```

```
    font-size: 1.5em;
    margin: 0 0 0.5em 0;
}

section .video {
    box-sizing: border-box;
}

section .description {
    box-sizing: border-box;
    padding: 0.5em 0 0 0;
}
```

We're going to add just a bit of space around each section by adding a top and bottom margin. Then, we'll include some simple styles for the video title and description. Now, view the page in the browser and make the browser window narrow to test your layout. You should see something like the following screenshot:

Our text is doing just what we wanted and is wrapping to fit within the browser window. The videos aren't resizing correctly though. That's okay—we'll take care of those later after we've set up our responsive layout in CSS only.

**4.** Next, we'll add some media queries to the CSS files so that when the screen gets wider, the text will appear next to the videos rather than underneath them. In your `styles.css` file, add the following styles:

```
@media (min-width: 24em) {
  section .video {
    float: left;
    width: 50%;
  }
  section .description {
    float: right;
    padding: 0 0 0 1em;
    width: 50%;
  }
}

@media (min-width: 36em) {
  section .video {
    width: 75%;
  }
  section .description {
    width: 25%;
  }
}
```

When the screen is at least 24 em wide, we'll divide the screen in two equal-width (50%) columns—one column will hold our video and another column will hold the title and description for the video. We're working with ems rather than pixels because we need a flexible unit when working with responsive designs. Ems or rems are better suited to responsive designs than pixel measurements.

When the screen is even wider, at least 36 em wide, we'll let the video take up 75 percent of the width and leave 25 percent for the title and description.

The only thing we need to do to our CSS code now is to make sure that we're containing the floats inside each section. That's easy enough to do—just add the following code snippet to your `styles.css` file:

```
.content section:after {
  clear: both;
  content: '';
  display: table;
}
```

Now if you open the page in a browser and adjust the width from narrow to wide, you'll see the layout adjusted as shown in the following screenshot:

However, our videos aren't adjusting correctly, which is frustrating. In fact, the videos are often covering up the text because they're too wide for the layout.

5. We'll use the FitVids jQuery plugin to resize the videos so that they fit correctly inside our responsive layout. First of all, we need to download the plugin. You won't find FitVids inside the jQuery plugin repository, but it is hosted on GitHub. There's a brief page with some demos at `http://fitvidsjs.com`; scroll down the page to find the link to download the plugin from GitHub. Follow that link, then click on the **Download Zip** button.

**6.** Unzip the folder and take a look at the files inside. The following screenshot shows the contents of the folder:

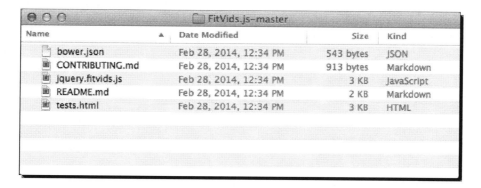

This is a pretty simple plugin, so there's not a whole lot here. We've already seen the bower.js file in other plugins and know that we can safely ignore that. There's a README file with some information about the plugin. The CONTRIBUTING file has some information for developers who might want to contribute towards making the plugin better. That leaves us with the tests.html file and jquery.fitvids.js. The HTML file, as you can probably guess, is just a file with several different videos embedded from different video services to show them working inside a responsive design. The JavaScript file is our plugin. Copy jquery.fitvids.js to your own scripts folder.

**7.** Next, we'll attach the plugin to our HTML page. At the bottom of the file, add a `<script>` tag to include the plugin after jQuery, but before your own scripts.js file:

```
<script src="scripts/jquery.js"></script>
<script src="scripts/jquery.fitvids.js"></script>
<script src="scripts/scripts.js"></script>
</body>
</html>
```

**8.** Finally, we have to write a bit of JavaScript to tell FitVids to resize our videos correctly. Open your scripts.js file and add the document ready statement:

```
$(document).ready(function(){
  // Our code will go here
});
```

**9.** A quick look at the documentation for the video shows us that we need to select whatever HTML element it is that contains our video or videos and then call the `fitVids()` method. We've wrapped each of our videos in a `div` element with `class` of `video`, so this is what we'll select. Use the following code to select the correct element and call the `fitVids()` method:

```
$(document).ready(function(){
  $('.video').fitVids();
});
```

Now, if you refresh the page in the browser and try resizing the window to different widths, you'll see that the videos resize correctly to fit within the responsive layout that we've created, as shown in the following screenshot:

## What just happened?

We used the FitVids jQuery plugin to resize videos embedded from Vimeo and YouTube to fit within a responsive layout. Now, no matter what width our screen is, the videos display at the perfect size, and the plugin is both small and easy to use. After setting up a responsive layout, include the plugin file, select the HTML element that contains your videos, and then call the `fitVids()` method. The plugin takes care of everything else to make the videos resize fluidly to fit within a responsive layout.

## Pop quiz – choosing breakpoints for responsive design

Q1. Which of the following is the best approach to choosing breakpoints for a responsive design?

1. Set breakpoints to the pixel widths of the most popular devices.
2. Always use the same three breakpoints for consistency across websites.
3. Set breakpoints where your content starts to look and feel awkward.
4. Choose breakpoints at random.

# Responsive menus

In *Chapter 4, Building an Interactive Navigation Menu*, we made great use of the Superfish plugin to create animated drop-down and fly-out menus. The gorgeous menus we can create with Superfish are nice, but they're not going to work very nicely for us if we're making a responsive design. On wider screen sizes, the menus will work great, but as we start to use smaller screens like those found on mobile devices, we'll lose all the benefits of the Superfish plugin.

A convention is quickly being established for responsive menus: on screen sizes too small to display a full menu bar, the menu is collapsed to a single three-line character (☰), sometimes accompanied by the word **Menu**. This character is most often referred to as a **hamburger**, but might also be called a **same-o** or **navigation drawer**. When the hamburger is clicked, the menu opens and is available for exploration to our site visitor.

We'll take a look at how we can combine the MeanMenu jQuery plugin with Superfish to create a menu that works well, no matter what screen size our site visitors are using.

## Time for action – making our menu responsive

We'll get started with the custom-designed menu we created in the section *The hoverIntent plugin* of *Chapter 4, Building an Interactive Navigation Menu*. Then, we'll perform the following steps to make that menu work for responsive designs:

***1.*** We're going to use the MeanMenu plugin from MeanThemes to make our menu responsive. The MeanMenu plugin is available from GitHub at `https://github.com/weare2ndfloor/meanMenu`. Head over there and find the **Download Zip** button in the right-hand side column to download a ZIP file of all the files we'll need to get the MeanMenu working.

***2.*** Now that we've downloaded that ZIP file, let's open it up and take a look at what's inside:

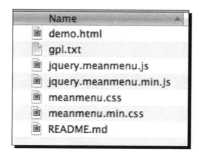

This is pretty straightforward. We have a demo HTML file to show us the MeanMenu plugin in action. There's a copy of the GPL license. There are the JavaScript and CSS files for the menu, along with a minified copy of each. And finally, there's a README file with some documentation.

3. First of all, we'll get the JavaScript we need copied to our own project and attached to our HTML file. Copy `jquery.meanmenu.min.js` to your own `scripts` folder, then attach it at the bottom of your HTML file before your own `scripts.js` file, as follows:

```
<script src="scripts/jquery.js"></script>
<script src="scripts/hoverIntent.js"></script>
<script src="scripts/superfish.js"></script>
<script src="scripts/jquery.meanmenu.min.js"></script>
<script src="scripts/scripts.js"></script>
</body>
</html>
```

4. Next, we need some CSS code to style the menu. We're going to end up with three different types of CSS code:

- The first one is CSS that applies to our menu items at all times. These items are things such as `font-family`, `background-color`, `color`, and so on. Our menu is going to have the `.sf-menu` class at all times, so we can use that to prepend our selectors for CSS that should always apply.

- Then, we have CSS that only applies to our menu on smaller screens where the menu is collapsed to a hamburger. The MeanMenu plugin adds a class of `mean-container` to the `<body>` tag when the MeanMenu is displayed. We can use that class to prepend our selectors for CSS that should only apply to the collapsed menu.

- And lastly, we have CSS that only applies to our menu on larger screens where the full menu bar is visible. We can add a CSS class of `super-nav` to the `<nav>` tag that wraps our menu. Then we can use this class to prepend our CSS selectors for the full menu to be sure they only apply when the full menu is visible. This is achieved as follows:

```
<nav class="super-nav">
  <ul id="sfNav" class="sf-menu">
    <li><a href="#">Papilionidae</a>
    ...
    </li>
  </ul>
</nav>
```

**5.** Let's get started by taking the styles we've already written for our menu and dividing them up into universal navigation styles and styles used only for wider screens where the full menu is visible. These styles will replace the styles we've already written in our CSS file to style our menu. The following styles are the universal styles for the menu:

```css
.sf-menu {
  background: white;
}

.sf-menu:after {
  clear: both;
  content: '';
  display: table;
}
```

Next, we have some universal styles for the first level of the menu:

```css
.sf-menu li {
  position: relative;
}

.sf-menu li:hover {
  background: #a0d468;
}

.sf-menu a {
  color: #444;
  display: block;
  padding: 1.5em 1em;
  position: relative;
  text-decoration: none;
}

.sf-menu a:hover {
  background: #a0d468;
  color: white;
}
```

The following are some universal styles for the second level of the menu:

```css
.sf-menu ul {
  background: #a0d468;
  z-index: 99;
}
```

```
.sf-menu ul li:hover {
  background: #8cc152;
}


.sf-menu ul a:hover {
  background: #8cc152;
}


.sf-menu li:hover > ul {
  display: block;
}
```

Finally, we have some universal styles for the third level of the menu:

```
.sf-menu ul ul {
  background: #8cc152;
}


.sf-menu ul ul li:hover {
  background: #7bb140;
}


.sf-menu ul ul a:hover {
  background: #7bb140;
}
```

6.  Next up, we'll get those styles that apply just to the large-screen version of our menu. We'll start off with general menu styles, as follows:

```
nav.super-nav {
  margin: 2em 1em;
}


.super-nav .sf-menu {
  border-radius: 7px;
}
```

Then, we'll write some styles for the first level of the navigation. Notice how each selector includes the .super-nav class at the beginning to make sure these styles only apply when the full menu is visible:

```
.super-nav .sf-menu li {
  white-space: nowrap;
}
```

```
.super-nav .sf-menu > li:first-child,
.super-nav .sf-menu > li:first-child a {
  border-top-left-radius: 7px;
}


.super-nav .sf-menu > li {
  float: left;
}
```

Next up, we have some styles for the second level of the navigation:

```
.super-nav .sf-menu ul {
  border-bottom-right-radius: 7px;
  border-bottom-left-radius: 7px;
  display: none;
  left: 0;
  min-width: 12em;
  position: absolute;
  top: 100%;
}


.super-nav .sf-menu ul > li:last-child,
.super-nav .sf-menu ul > li:last-child a {
  border-bottom-left-radius: 7px;
  border-bottom-right-radius: 7px;
}
```

Then, we have some styles for the third level:

```
.super-nav .sf-menu ul ul {
  border-top-right-radius: 7px;
  top: 0;
  left: 100%;
}


.super-nav .sf-menu ul ul > li:first-child,
.super-nav .sf-menu ul ul > li:first-child a {
  border-top-right-radius: 7px;
}


.super-nav .sf-menu ul ul > li:last-child,
.super-nav .sf-menu ul ul > li:last-child a {
  border-bottom-right-radius: 7px;
}
```

Finally, we have some styles for the extras—mainly the arrows that show whether a menu item is hiding a submenu:

```css
.super-nav .sf-arrows .sf-with-ul {
  padding-right: 2.5em;
}

.super-nav .sf-arrows .sf-with-ul:after {
  border: 5px solid transparent;
  border-top-color: #444;
  content: '';
  height: 0;
  margin-top: -3px;
  position: absolute;
  right: 1em;
  top: 50%;
  width: 0;
}

.super-nav .sf-arrows > li > .sf-with-ul:focus:after,
.super-nav .sf-arrows > li:hover > .sf-with-ul:after {
  border-top-color: white;
}

.super-nav .sf-arrows ul .sf-with-ul:after {
  margin-top: -5px;
  margin-right: -3px;
  border-color: transparent;
  border-left-color: #e7f2dc;
}

.super-nav .sf-arrows ul li > .sf-with-ul:focus:after,
.super-nav .sf-arrows ul li:hover > .sf-with-ul:after {
  border-left-color: white;
}
```

7. Now, the only thing left to style is the collapsed menu that will be visible only on narrower screens. For that, we can use the CSS code that was supplied with the MeanMenu plugin as a template and just customize it to suit our needs.

As we're going to change the styles quite a lot to fit our design, we'll copy the MeanMenu CSS code to our own `styles.css` file, and then modify it to suit our needs. Starting from the CSS code provided with a jQuery plugin is a great way to customize the appearance without having to do all the legwork of figuring out what styles are needed on your own. We'll start by writing some general styles for the MeanMenu container, as follows:

```css
a.meanmenu-reveal {
  display: none;
}

.mean-container .mean-bar {
  background: white;
  padding: 0.222em 0;
  min-height: 2.531em;
  position: relative;
  width: 100%;
  z-index: 999999;
}
```

We'll hide the button to reveal the menu and then use JavaScript later to only show it when we need it.

**8.** Now we'll style the reveal button to look just the way we'd like:

```css
.mean-container a.meanmenu-reveal {
  color: #444;
  cursor: pointer;
  display: block;
  font-size: 18px;
  height: 1.5em;
  line-height: 1.5;
  padding: 13px 13px 11px 13px;
  position: absolute;
  right: 0;
  text-decoration: none;
  text-indent: -9999em;
  top: 0;
  width: 1.5em;
}

.mean-container a.meanmenu-reveal span {
  background: #444;
  display: block;
  height: 0.198em;
  margin-top: 0.198em;
  width: 100%;
}
```

**9.** Next, we'll write some styles for the different levels of the menu, when the mobile version is visible:

```css
.mean-container .mean-nav {
  background: white;
  margin-top: 2.25em;
  width: 100%;
}

.mean-container .mean-nav ul {
  width: 100%;
}

.mean-container .mean-nav ul li {
  position: relative;
  width: 100%;
}

.mean-container .mean-nav ul li:after {
  clear: both;
  content: '';
  display: table;
}

.mean-container .mean-nav ul li a {
  border-bottom: 1px solid rgba(160, 212, 104, 0.3);
  color: #444;
  display: block;
  padding: 1em 5%;
  text-align: left;
  text-decoration: none;
  width: 90%;
}

.mean-container .mean-nav ul li:hover a,
.mean-container .mean-nav ul li a:hover {
  color: white;
}

.mean-container .mean-nav ul li li a {
  border-bottom: 1px solid rgba(255,255,255,0.5);
  padding: 1em 10%;
  width: 80%;
}
```

```
.mean-container .mean-nav ul li.mean-last a {
  border-bottom: none;
  margin-bottom: 0;
}


.mean-container .mean-nav ul li li li a {
  width: 70%;
  padding: 1em 15%;
}


.mean-container .mean-nav ul li li li li a {
  width: 60%;
  padding: 1em 20%;
}


.mean-container .mean-nav ul li li li li li a {
  width: 50%;
  padding: 1em 25%;
}
```

**10.** Now, we can write some styles for the reveal and hide buttons for the menu:

```
.mean-container .mean-nav ul li a.mean-expand {
  border: none;
  height: 1.688em;
  padding: 0.75em;
  position: absolute;
  right: 0;
  text-align: center;
  top: 0;
  width: 1.688em;
  z-index: 2;
}


.mean-container .mean-nav ul li a.mean-expand:hover {
  background: none;
}


.mean-container .mean-push {
  clear: both;
  float: left;
  width: 100%;
}
```

**11.** Finally, we'll finish up with some general styles for the mobile menu:

```
.mean-nav .wrapper {
  width: 100%;
}


.mean-container .mean-bar,  .mean-container .mean-bar * {
  box-sizing: content-box;
}
```

**12.** Phew! That was a lot of CSS, but really these plugins do their job so well, most of the work in getting these menus to work is getting all the CSS code properly sorted out. Now that we've got that out of the way, let's open up our `scripts.js` file and add a line to call the `meanmenu()` method for our menu, as follows:

```
$(document).ready(function(){
  $('#sfNav').superfish({
    animation: {
      height: 'show'
    }
  });

  $('nav').meanmenu();
});
```

Now, if you refresh the page in the browser and make the window narrow, you'll see that the Superfish navigation bar disappears and is replaced by a hamburger menu, as shown in the following screenshot:

Clicking on the hamburger opens up the menu for further exploration, as follows:

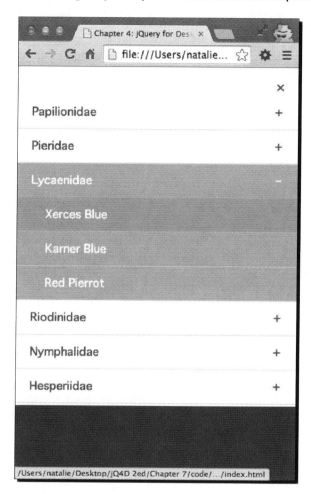

13. Now, let's take a look at how we can use some of the options supplied with the MeanMenu plugin to adjust our menu to work just the way we'd like.

First of all, let's figure out how narrow the screen will look when the MeanMenu plugin kicks in. By default, MeanMenu will replace the full navigation when the screen is 480 pixels wide or less. However, our menu is pretty wide and starts to wrap to a new line way before that. Testing out the menu by adjusting the browser width, we can see that we'll need MeanMenu to replace the full navigation bar for screens that are about 880 pixels or narrower.

Each navigation bar is unique, so it's important to test your navigation bar, and in fact, all of your content, to see at which screen widths it starts to look or feel awkward. Rather than setting breakpoints at the widths of specific devices that happen to be popular right now, use your design and content to determine where the breakpoints should be placed. This way, your design will remain fresh, relevant, and usable no matter which devices and screen sizes are popular in the following year or in the next five years.

To adjust the width for MeanMenu, we'll use the `meanScreenWidth` option, as follows:

```
$('nav').meanmenu({
  meanScreenWidth: '880'
});
```

**14.** Next up, the MeanMenu plugin uses a hamburger as the symbol that will open the menu, and then a letter X as the character that will close the menu. The multiplication symbol (×) is more aesthetically pleasing, so let's switch the close symbol. We can use the `meanMenuClose` option to set the close symbol to whatever character we'd like, as shown in the following code:

```
$('nav').meanmenu({
  meanScreenWidth: '880',
  meanMenuClose: '\xD7'
});
```

Wait, `\xd7`? What is that? It's a peculiar JavaScript way of writing special characters such as the multiplication sign. How are you supposed to know what that special code is? Head on over to `http://www.charbase.com/` and do a quick search for the character you're looking for. A search for `multiplication` easily turns up our multiplication sign and you can see that a **JavaScript Escape** value is listed. You just have to copy and paste it into your JavaScript to produce the special character.

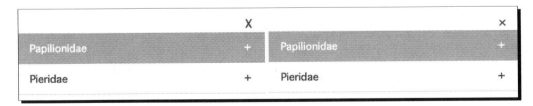

On the left, you can see the menu with the letter X as the close symbol, and on the right with the multiplication sign. The difference is subtle, but the multiplication symbol feels more like a close button.

**15.** Finally, as the hyphen (-) character used to collapse submenu items is a bit too small, let's replace it with an em dash to make it a larger and more noticeable target. We can use the `meanContract` option to set this:

```
$('nav').meanmenu({
  meanScreenWidth: '880',
  meanMenuClose: '\xD7',
  meanContract: '\u2014'
});
```

Again, we're using the special **JavaScript Escape** for that character. The following screenshot shows the difference between using a hyphen (-) and an em dash (—):

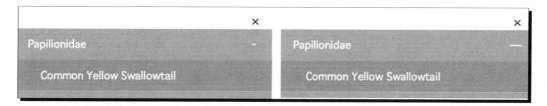

You can see that the em dash is significantly larger than the hyphen, and makes it easier to tap or click on the character to collapse the submenus again. Now the menus work well for all site visitors, no matter what screen size they happen to be using.

## What just happened?

We took our custom, animated drop-down menu that we created in *Chapter 4, Building an Interactive Navigation Menu*, and updated it to make it ideal for use in responsive designs. We used the MeanMenu plugin to help us handle the transition between the full menu and the responsive menu. The responsive menu is replaced with a hamburger icon, which when clicked or tapped opens the full menu.

## Have a go hero – create a custom menu

Now that you've seen how to work with MeanMenu and Superfish, design and build your own custom menu. Customize the appearance, the animations, the size at which it collapses to the mobile menu, and so on.

# Creating a tiled layout

In a tiled layout, or a masonry layout, HTML elements are fit together like bricks in a wall rather than the strict grid layouts we can create with just CSS. With CSS, we're limited to layouts as shown in the following figure:

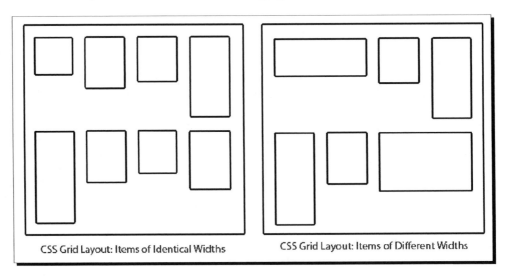

CSS Grid Layout: Items of Identical Widths          CSS Grid Layout: Items of Different Widths

This is a perfectly acceptable way to lay out our content; our site visitors can view all of the content without a problem. However, if we add JavaScript to the mix, we can improve those layouts a bit by making them fit together as shown in the following figure:

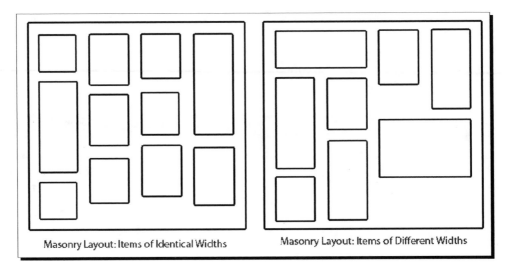

Masonry Layout: Items of Identical Widths          Masonry Layout: Items of Different Widths

Tiled layouts or masonry layouts can help to close up gaps left by items of different heights. Tiled layouts are great for situations where our site visitors are browsing through lots of graphical content—such as a photo gallery. They're less ideal for situations where site visitors might be looking for something specific or where the content is less graphical—such as a list of search results.

To accomplish our tiled layout, we'll be using the excellent Masonry library by David DeSandro.

## Time for action – creating a masonry layout

Perform the following steps to create a tiled layout:

1. We'll get started by creating a basic HTML document and the associated files and folders just like we did in *Chapter 1, Designer, Meet jQuery*. In the body of the HTML document, we'll set up a container with a series of repeating elements inside. We'll use a list (`<ul>`) as the container and individual list items (`<li>`) inside for the repeating elements. Inside each list item, we'll place an image and some text that describes that image, as follows:

```
<div class="content">
  <h1>Cats of the World</h1>
</div>

<ul class="container">

  <li class="cat">
    <figure>
      <img src="images/siamese.jpg">
      <figcaption>
        <h2>Siamese</h2>
      </figcaption>
    </figure>
    <div class="info">
      <div class="traits">
        <dl>
          <dt>Country</dt>
          <dd>Thailand</dd>
        </dl>
        <dl>
          <dt>Coat</dt>
          <dd>Short</dd>
        </dl>
        <dl>
```

```
            <dt>Pattern</dt>
            <dd>Colorpoint</dd>
         </dl>
      </div>
    </div>
  </li>
  ...
</ul>
```

We're using an HTML5 `<figure>` element to hold the image itself and a caption for the image inside a `<figcaption>` element. Next, we created an area where we can share some more details about the image.

Create at least a dozen similar list items inside the container so that you'll be able to see the difference made once we apply the Masonry script.

2.  Next, we'll style our list items. Open up your `styles.css` file and add the following lines:

```css
.cat {
  background: white;
  border-radius: 5px;
  color: #434a54;
  margin: 5% 0;
  vertical-align: top;
  width: 100%;
}
```

We're going to style our layout responsively, starting with mobile layout first. At small screen sizes, we want each list item to fill the width of the screen.

3.  Next, we'll add a media query to display the items in two columns for slightly wider screens. Add the following code snippet to your `styles.css` file:

```css
@media (min-width:30em) {
  .container {
    font-size: 0.75em;
  }
  .cat {
    display: inline-block;
    margin: 3% 1%;
    width: 44%;
  }
}
```

First, we'll make the font size a bit smaller to make sure that our text fits into the narrow columns. Next, we set our individual items to `display: inline-block`, which lines them up, add a bit of a margin, and set a width.

**4.** Next, let's create a three-column layout for wider screens. Add the following code snippet to your `styles.css` file:

```
@media (min-width:45em) {
  .cat {
    margin: 2% 1%;
    width: 30%;
  }
}
```

Since the `display: inline-block` declaration will still apply at this width, all we have to do is adjust the width and margins of our individual items.

**5.** Finally, if the screen is wide enough, we can set the font size back to full size. Add the following code snippet to your `styles.css` file:

```
@media (min-width:60em) {
  .container {
    font-size: 1em;
  }
}
```

Now, if you view your page in the browser and change the width of the window, you'll see the layout changes from one column, at narrow widths, to two columns, as the window gets wider, to three columns, as it gets even wider. Have a look at the following screenshot:

However, our images are overflowing their containers and the text isn't very readable. Let's style those items next.

**6.** We're going to position the image caption over the image and ensure that the images don't overflow their containers. Add the following code snippet to your `styles.css` file:

```css
.cat img {
  border-radius: 5px 5px 0 0;
  height: auto;
  width: 100%;
}

.cat figure {
  position: relative;
}

.cat figcaption {
  background: linear-gradient(to bottom,
    rgba(0,0,0,0.65) 0%,rgba(0,0,0,0) 100%);
  border-radius: 5px 5px 0 0;
  position: absolute;
  top: 0;
  width: 100%;
}

.cat figcaption h2 {
  color: white;
  font-size: 2.25em;
  margin: 0;
  padding: 0.25em;
}
```

As we can't be sure that all the images will be dark enough at the top for a white headline to be visible, we'll add a dark gradient as a background on the `<figcaption>` element to make sure the text is visible. Then, we'll position the caption at the top of each image. If you refresh the page in a browser now, the layout is easier to see:

**7.** Next up, let's style the text underneath each image. To make sure it's flexible, we'll use a table-like layout. Add the following code snippet to your `styles.css` file:

```css
.cat .info {
  display: table;
  width: 100%;
}

.cat .traits {
  display: table-row;
}

.cat .traits dl {
  display: table-cell;
  line-height: 1.125;
  padding: 1em 0.5em;
  text-align: center;
  vertical-align: top;
  width: 33%;
}

.cat .traits dt {
  color: #aab2bd;
  font-size: 0.75em;
},

.cat .traits dd {
  font-size: 1.125em;
}
```

This lines up our three bits of information about each image in a neat row under the image, as shown in the following screenshot:

Because we've set the widths in percentages, this row of text will flex with our layout and always fit nicely into three columns beneath the image.

At this point, we have a responsive grid layout that's perfectly acceptable for our site visitors who may not have JavaScript enabled. Next, let's take a look at using JavaScript to switch this to a tiled layout for those site visitors who do have JavaScript enabled.

8. We're going to use the Masonry library. Masonry is not a jQuery plugin—it will work with or without jQuery. In our case, we're going to use jQuery because it makes it just a bit easier to work with. First of all, head over to `http://masonry.desandro.com/` to get the documentation and download for Masonry. To download the file we need, click on the **Download masonry.pkgd.min.js** button.

   This opens the JavaScript file right in your browser window. You can right-click on it and then click on **Save As** or from the **File** menu, click on **Save** to save the file to your own `scripts` folder.

9. Next, we need to attach the Masonry file to our HTML file. At the bottom of the document, add the file between jQuery and your own `scripts.js` file, using the following highlighted line of code:

```
<script src="scripts/jquery.js"></script>
<script src="scripts/masonry.pkgd.min.js"></script>
<script src="scripts/scripts.js"></script>
```

10. Now open your `scripts.js` file and add the document ready statement, as follows:

```
$(document).ready(function(){
    // Our code will go here
});
```

11. When we use Masonry with jQuery, it can work just like a jQuery plugin—we can select an element, then call the `masonry()` method on that element. The element we select is the container of all of our items. In our case, it's the `<ul>` element with a `class` selector of container. Select that element and call the `masonry()` method, as follows:

```
$(document).ready(function(){
    $('.container').masonry();
});
```

**12.** While that's technically all we need to get a tiled layout to work, David DeSandro, Masonry's author, recommends that we always set two options that will help Masonry perform better. These two options are `columnWidth` and `itemSelector`. The `columnWidth` option sets a width for the columns in the layout and `itemSelector` helps Masonry identify which items we want to tile in our layout. The `itemSelector` option is easy enough—we want to use the list items inside our container, to which we've assigned a `class` selector of `cat`. Add this option to your `scripts.js` file, as follows:

```
$(document).ready(function(){
  $('.container').masonry({
    itemSelector: '.cat'
  });
});
```

**13.** However, this `columnWidth` option is a little more problematic as we're using a responsive layout—we don't want to set a fixed width for our items. Luckily, Masonry makes this easy too. We can use an item inside our list to set the `columnWidth` option—Masonry will then calculate the width of all items based on whatever width our selected item is. Go back to your list of items in the HTML file and select a list item—the first item is as good as any; as in this case, all of our items are of the same width. Now, add a `class` of `gridsize` to that item, as follows:

```
<ul class="container">

  <li class="cat gridsize">
      . . .
  </li>
</ul>
```

**14.** Now, we can tell Masonry to use the width of that item to calculate our `columnWidth` option:

```
$(document).ready(function(){
  $('.container').masonry({
    columnWidth: '.gridsize',
    itemSelector: '.cat'
  });
});
```

Now if you refresh the page in the browser, you'll see that the grid layout has been transformed into a responsive tiled layout:

What's more, Masonry has a lovely transition animation that floats the items to their new positions after we resize the browser window.

## What just happened?

We took an ordinary CSS grid layout and transformed it into a tiled layout with the help of the Masonry JavaScript library. Items now move upward to fill in vertical gaps, which helps to make a grid of items of different heights appear more pleasing to the eye. The Masonry library makes creating these layouts super-simple, especially when we pair it with the jQuery library. For site visitors without JavaScript enabled, the items will appear in a usable CSS grid layout.

## Creating a tiled layout with items of different widths

The tiled layout we created works well as long as all of our items have the same width, but what if our elements have different widths? Let's take a look at how we'd go about setting up such a layout.

We're going to keep working with the tiled layout example we set up in the section *Time for action – creating a masonry layout*.

# Time for action – creating a tiled layout with different width items

Perform the following steps to take the tiled layout we've already created and to make it work for items with different widths:

1. First, we need to create items of different widths. A few of the items in the layout have images that are landscape rather than portrait orientation, which means those items appear particularly small in the layout. Let's make those the width of two columns so they stand out more. Go back to the HTML file for the list of items and add a class of w2 to each item that will now be two columns wide:

```html
<li class="cat w2">
  <figure>
    <img src="images/himalayan.jpg">
    <figcaption>
      <h2>Himalayan</h2>
    </figcaption>
  </figure>
  <div class="info">
    ...
  </div>
</li>
```

2. Next, open your styles.css file and style these items with a wider width. As all items are of full width at narrow screen sizes, we only have to add the new width for wider screens inside our media queries as follows:

```css
@media (min-width:30em) {
  .container {
    font-size: 0.75em;
  }
  .cat {
    display: inline-block;
    margin: 3% 1%;
    width: 44%;
  }
  .cat.w2 {
    width: 89%;
  }
}
```

Where did we get that value of 89%? We want our block to be as wide as two columns. Each of our columns is 44 percent wide, so two of them would be 88 percent wide. However, there is also a 1 percent margin between the single width images, so *44 percent + 1 percent + 44 percent = 89 percent.* For the widest screens, have a look at the following code:

```
@media (min-width:45em) {
  .cat {
    margin: 2% 1%;
    width: 30%;
  }
  .cat.w2 {
    width: 61%;
  }
}
```

Again, we're making the width double and accounting for the 1 percent margin, so *30 percent + 1 percent + 30 percent = 61 percent.*

3. Finally, we just have to make sure that the item we're using to define the `columnWidth` option is a single-column item rather than one of the new two-column wide items. Make sure that you've selected an item that doesn't have the `w2` class to have the `gridsize` class, as follows:

```
<li class="cat gridsize">
  ...
<li>
<li class="cat w2">
  ...
</li>
```

Now, if you refresh the page in the browser, you'll see that a handful items are two columns wide rather than one at wider screen sizes:

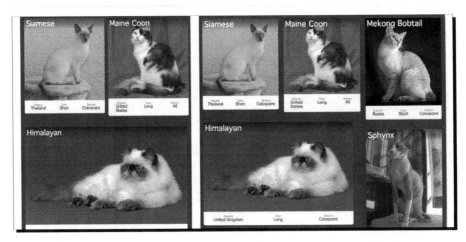

## *What just happened?*

We took the tiled layout that we already created and modified it so that not all of our items share the same width. Now we can see how Masonry fills in gaps and creates a pleasing layout even if our items share different widths as well as different heights. All we needed to do was select a handful of our items and modify their width in the CSS code—Masonry takes care of the rest.

# Summary

In this chapter, we took a look at some jQuery plugins and one JavaScript library that can make it just a little bit better to work with responsive designs. First, we took a look at how we can use the FitVids jQuery plugin to make the videos resize correctly inside responsive designs. Then we took our animated drop-down menu originally created in *Chapter 4*, *Building an Interactive Navigation Menu*, and made it work inside responsive designs with the help of the MeanMenu plugin. Finally, we took at look at how to build responsive tiled layouts with the help of the Masonry JavaScript library.

Next up, we'll look at some different ways that jQuery can help us work with images in a better way, including images inside responsive layouts.

# 8
# Getting the Most from Images

*Working with images in a responsive design world has presented a whole new set of challenges and opportunities. We need to balance optimizing performance along with taking advantage of new capabilities and gorgeous image display on retina screens with minimizing bandwidth for those on slower connections. It's a great idea to have several tools in your toolbox that will help you work with images in a robust and flexible way. We'll be looking at a few tools to deal with images.*

In this chapter, we'll cover the following topics:

- ◆ Using lazy loading of images so that images are only downloaded if they're scrolled into view
- ◆ Using image zoom to allow site visitors to enlarge the part of an image they're most interested in
- ◆ Using fullscreen background images and slideshows

## Lazy loading images

Imagine you want to build a responsive page with many big, gorgeous images. What are the things you need to consider to be sure that the page is as flexible and optimized as possible? First, it would be nice if we only loaded the images when needed; if a page has twenty large images but a site visitor never scrolls down the page to see more than the first two or three of them, why load all twenty? Second, it would be great if we could load high-resolution images for those who use retina displays to ensure that the images look as clear and crisp as possible.

There are a few proposals in the works within the upcoming HTML5 specification that will build some of this functionality into HTML. At the time of writing this book, nothing has been decided for sure, though many different solutions have been proposed. In the meantime, we can build websites that address these issues with jQuery, using the Unveil plugin from Luís Almeida.

It's important that this is one case where we cannot use progressive enhancement. If we create a page with several image tags, we can't prevent those images from loading with jQuery—all the images will load no matter what. So for this example, we're going to use the principle of graceful degradation. The page will still work for users with JavaScript disabled— when they view the page, we'll load the regular resolution of each image.

## Time for action – lazy loading images

Perform the following steps to create a page of images that load the correct resolution only when needed:

1. We'll get started by creating a basic HTML document and associated files and folders just like we did in *Chapter 1*, *Designer, Meet jQuery*. Inside the body of the HTML document, we'll add a series of images using the new HTML5 `figure` and `figcaption` elements, as shown in the following code:

```
<figure>
  <img src="images/loading.gif" />
  <figcaption>
    <a href="http://www.public-domain-image.com/
      wallpapers-public-domain-images-pictures/
      a-bench-for-resting.jpg.html" title
      ="A bench for resting">A bench for resting</a>
      by Steve Hillebrand, U.S. Fish and Wildlife Service
  </figcaption>
</figure>
```

Note that we've used a small, animated `.gif` image as a placeholder rather than the image we actually want to display. We'll be replacing this later with the actual image. You'll want to add at least four or five images to the page to appreciate the effect that Unveil makes possible.

2. Next, we need to add some information about the paths to the regular resolution and high-resolution images. We'll use the new HTML5 `data` attributes to add this data to our placeholder image, as follows:

```
<figure>
  <img src="images/loading.gif" data-src="images/
    bench.jpg" data-src-retina="images/bench-2x.jpg" />
  . . .
</figure>
```

   Add a `data-src` attribute that contains the path to the regular resolution image. If you also have a high-resolution image suitable for retina displays, you can add the path to this image inside a `data-src-retina` attribute. Note that the high-resolution image is optional—Unveil will work just fine if you exclude high-resolution images.

3. Now, we can add a bit of CSS to style our images. Open up your `styles.css` file and add the following styles:

```
figure {
  margin: 2.531em auto;
  max-width: 800px;
  text-align: center;
}

figcaption {
  line-height: 1.125;
  padding: 0.75em 0 1.5em 0;
}

figure img {
  border-radius: 5px;
  display: inline-block;
  height: auto;
  max-width: 100%;
}
```

This bit of code just centers the list of images on the page and adds some spacing between each image and caption pair. If you look at the page in a browser at this point, you'll just see the loading image repeated down the page, each with a caption beneath, as shown in the following screenshot:

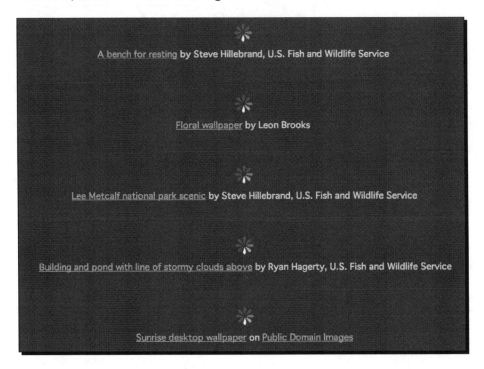

A bench for resting by Steve Hillebrand, U.S. Fish and Wildlife Service

Floral wallpaper by Leon Brooks

Lee Metcalf national park scenic by Steve Hillebrand, U.S. Fish and Wildlife Service

Building and pond with line of stormy clouds above by Ryan Hagerty, U.S. Fish and Wildlife Service

Sunrise desktop wallpaper on Public Domain Images

4. Now, we need to add the jQuery plugin and the code that will replace these `.gif` images with the actual images. The Unveil plugin is hosted on GitHub at `https://github.com/luis-almeida/unveil`—just as we've done before with plugins hosted on GitHub, click on the **Download ZIP** button in the right-hand side column.

Unzip the folder and take a look inside it. You should recognize what's inside by now—`bower.json` for those using Bower, an `img` directory and `index.html` file to demo the plugin at work, a jQuery file, a `README.md` file with information about the plugin, and then the development and production versions of the Unveil plugin , as shown in the following screenshot:

| Name | ▲ | Date Modified | Size | Kind |
|---|---|---|---|---|
| bower.json | | Sep 22, 2013, 12:20 PM | 84 bytes | JSON |
| ▶ img | | Sep 22, 2013, 12:20 PM | -- | Folder |
| index.html | | Sep 22, 2013, 12:20 PM | 10 KB | HTML |
| jquery-1.9.1.min.js | | Sep 22, 2013, 12:20 PM | 93 KB | JavaScript |
| jquery.unveil.js | | Sep 22, 2013, 12:20 PM | 1 KB | JavaScript |
| jquery.unveil.min.js | | Sep 22, 2013, 12:20 PM | 945 bytes | JavaScript |
| README.md | | Sep 22, 2013, 12:20 PM | 3 KB | Markdown |

jQuery and jQuery plugins are being updated all the time. As new browsers are released with new support and capabilities, and as JavaScript, HTML, and CSS are further developed, new versions of jQuery and plugins are released to keep pace with the change. On one hand, this is a great news—jQuery and accompanying plugins get faster and more powerful all the time. On the other hand, it can be tough to keep up with all the changes. All versions of the plugins referenced were current at the time of writing the book, but you might find some differences when you work through the exercises. Plugin developers are usually very good at documenting the changes and updates, so don't be afraid to read through the documentation so you can understand what's changed and what adjustments you might need to make.

5. Copy `jquery.unveil.js` to your own `scripts` folder. Then, attach it in your HTML file at the bottom, between jQuery and your own `scripts.js` file, as follows:

```
<script src="scripts/jquery.js"></script>
<script src="scripts/jquery.unveil.js"></script>
<script src="scripts/scripts.js"></script>
```

6. Now, we're ready to put the script into action. Open your `scripts.js` file and add the document ready statement:

```
$(document).ready(function(){
  // Our code will go here
});
```

7. Inside the document ready statement, add the following line of code to select the images and call the `unveil()` method:

```
$(document).ready(function(){
  $('img').unveil();
});
```

In this case, our page is very simple and we want to select all the images on the page. You might find yourself in situations where you want to select just the images inside a certain container, or images with a certain class assigned to them. Just adjust your selector accordingly.

If you refresh the page at this point, you'll see that the loading animations are replaced with either the regular or high-resolution images, depending on whether you're currently using a retina display, as shown in the following screenshot:

A bench for resting by Steve Hillebrand, U.S. Fish and Wildlife Service

8. So far, our page appears to be working pretty well, but there are a few things we can do to make it even better. First, what about the users who have JavaScript disabled? The way the page is set up now, they'll only see the loading animations. Let's get that fixed so that it gracefully degrades.

After each image, add a `<noscript>` element. Inside the tags, we'll add a regular old HTML image tag, as follows:

```
<figure>
  <img src="images/loading.gif" data-src
    ="images/bench.jpg" data-src-retina
    ="images/bench-2x.jpg" />
  <noscript><img src="images/bench.jpg"></noscript>

  . . .
</figure>
```

Now, visitors who have JavaScript disabled can see our images, but they'll also see the loading `.gif` image above each one. Let's hide these images for them.

**9.** Inside the HTML document, add a `class` selector of `jsOff` to the `body` tag, using the following line of code:

```
<body class="jsOff">
```

Then, in the `styles.css` file, add a bit of CSS to hide those loading `.gif` images if the body has the `jsOff` class, as shown in the following code:

```
.jsOff figure > img {
  display: none;
}
```

Finally, inside the `scripts.js` file, add a bit of code to remove this class from the body—the code in the class will only run if JavaScript is enabled:

```
$(document).ready(function(){
  $('body').removeClass('jsOff');
  $('img').unveil();
});
```

Now, our page degrades gracefully for those site visitors who don't have JavaScript enabled—they'll see the list of images just fine. The majority of users will benefit from having the correct resolution of image loaded and improved performance from the images only loaded when and as needed, but those without JavaScript will never know what they're missing. For them, the experience will seem complete.

**10.** We can also take the effect one step further for those site visitors who have JavaScript enabled. We can fade in the image rather than just popping them onto the page. The `unveil()` method will let us set some options.

First, we can set a threshold option—how far from appearing on the screen should an image be before we start the process of downloading and displaying it? Let's set a threshold of 200 pixels—when an image is 200 pixels from appearing on the screen, we'll start loading it:

```
$('img').unveil(200);
```

Next, we can write a function to be called when it's time to unveil or load an image. The following code shows what we'll do to fade an image in:

```
$('img').unveil(200, function(){
  $(this).hide().fadeIn();
});
```

This bit of code will select the image tag and hide it, then fade in the real image as soon as it's loaded. If you refresh the page in the browser now, you'll see the images fade on to the page rather than just appear.

## What just happened?

We set up a page with many large images so that it only loaded the images when needed, thereby helping to improve performance and reduce the load on our server. We are also loading a high-resolution version of our image for those site visitors who might be using a retina display capable of displaying our images at a higher resolution. We used the Unveil plugin by Luís Almeida to accomplish all of that in just a few lines of code. Note that the images load very quickly, even if they're large, when you're viewing a page on your own computer. To get a real feel for the difference this plugin makes, you might want to try uploading your page to a server and accessing it via the Web.

## Pop quiz – building accessible pages

Q1. We've learned about both progressive enhancement and graceful degradation. Why are these principles important when working with JavaScript?

1.  They allow site visitors with disabilities to access and use the pages we build.

2.  They allow search engines to correctly index the pages we build.

3.  They allow site visitors on less-capable devices to use the pages we build.

4.  They allow site visitors with JavaScript disabled to access and use the pages we build.

5.  All of the above.

# Creating zoomable images

Sometimes, we include a small image to maintain a nice layout and fit more content on the screen, but our site visitors might want to see a larger image to see more details. One way of handling this is showing the full-size image in a lightbox, like we did in *Chapter 5, Showing Content in Lightboxes*. However, another option we have is to zoom in on the image right where it is. Our site visitor can move their mouse to move around the image to see the details. On touch screens, they can use their finger to drag over the image and zoom in.

To accomplish this, we'll use the jQuery Zoom plugin by Jack Moore. You might recognize Jack Moore's name; he is also the author of the Colorbox plugin we used in *Chapter 5, Showing Content in Lightboxes*.

# Time for action – creating zoomable images

Perform the following steps to create zoomable images on your HTML pages:

**1.** We'll get started by creating a basic HTML document and the associated files and folders just like we did in *Chapter 1, Designer, Meet jQuery*. You'll need two sizes of the same image—I've found that if the smaller image is approximately one-third the size of the larger image, the zoom functionality works very well. Inside the body of the HTML document, we'll add an image and some information about the image, as follows:

```html
<article>
  <figure>
    <img src="images/aster.jpg" height="1004" width
      ="1024" alt="Aster">
  </figure>
  <div class="flower-info">
    <h2>Aster</h2>
    <p>Aster is a genus of flowering plants in the family
      Asteraceae. Its circumscription has been narrowed,
      and it now encompasses around 180 species, all but
      one of which are restricted to Eurasia; many species
      formerly in Aster are now in other genera of the tribe
      Astereae.</p>
  </div>
</article>
```

**2.** Next, we'll style this HTML document. For small screens, we'll show the image with the information underneath. For wide screens, we'll show the image on the left-hand side and the text on the right-hand side of the screen. Open your `styles.css` file and add the following styles:

```css
article {
  margin: 2.25em 0;
}

article:after {
  clear: both;
  content: '';
  display: table;
}

figure {
  margin: 0 0 1em 0;
  max-width: 100%;
}
```

```
figure img {
  height: auto;
  max-width: 100%;
}

@media (min-width:36rem) {
  figure {
    float: left;
    margin: 0 2.25em 0 0;
    max-width: 50%;
  }
}

.flower-info {
  overflow: hidden;
}

article h2 {
  font-size: 2.25em;
  line-height: 1.125;
  margin: 0 0 0.75em 0;
}

article p {
  line-height: 1.5;
  margin: 0 0 1.5em 0;
}
```

Now, if you view the page in the browser, you'll see the images and accompanying text are nicely styled and the layout adjusts nicely to the width of the screen, as shown in the following screenshot:

**3.** Next, we need to get the Zoom plugin. Head over to `http://www.jacklmoore.com/zoom/` where you'll find the download as well as the documentation for the plugin. Click on the **Download** link under the two sample zoomable images to download the ZIP file.

**4.** Unzip the file. Inside it, you'll find all the usual files—a `README.md` file, some samples, and so on. Look for `jquery.zoom.min.js` and copy it to your own `scripts` folder.

**5.** Now, we need to attach the Zoom plugin file to our HTML file. At the bottom of the file, between jQuery and your own `scripts.js` file, add the plugin file as follows:

```
<script src="scripts/jquery.js"></script>
<script src="scripts/jquery.zoom.min.js"></script>
<script src="scripts/scripts.js"></script>
```

**6.** Next, we'll jump into our `scripts.js` file and add a bit of code to get the zoom working for the image. Get started by adding the document ready statement:

```
$(document).ready(function(){
    // Our code will go here
});
```

**7.** To get the zoom working, we need to select the element that actually wraps our image, rather than the image itself. In our case, we've wrapped our image in a `<figure>` element, so this is what we'll select. Then, we'll call the `zoom()` method, as follows:

```
$(document).ready(function(){
    $('figure').zoom();
});
```

**8.** Now, there's just one thing that the Zoom plugin needs to know from us in order to work—we have to tell Zoom the path to the larger version of our image. We can do that by passing in a `url` option as follows:

```
$(document).ready(function(){
    $('figure').zoom({
        url: 'images/lg-aster.jpg'
    });
});
```

If you refresh the page in the browser now and move your mouse over the image, you'll see the zoom in effect. As you move your mouse over the image, the zoom effect moves over different areas of the image, allowing you to see the details in all parts of the image.

**9.** It feels a bit strange that as we move the mouse cursor over the image, we're just seeing the default cursor. A few browsers have started supporting some new cursors, including the `zoom-in` cursor. Let's add a few lines of CSS to show this cursor instead of the default for the browsers that have this capability. Inside your `styles.css` file, add the following styles for the `img` element:

```
figure img {
  cursor: -webkit-zoom-in;
  cursor: -moz-zoom-in;
  cursor: zoom-in;
  height: auto;
  max-width: 100%;
}
```

Now, if you're using a browser with support for this new cursor, when you move your mouse over the image, you'll see a magnifying glass icon instead of the default cursor:

## What just happened?

We created a zoomable image using the Zoom plugin by Jack Moore. We created a page with a smaller version of the image along with some text that describes the image. Then, we added the plugin and a few lines of code. Now, when we move our mouse over the image, you'll see the larger version of the image appear.

# Zooming in on multiple images

While the Zoom plugin was simple and easy to use, the plugin will only work as long as we have just one image that's zoomable. If we want to have multiple images on a single page, then we have to make some modifications.

Remember when we passed the `url` option to the `zoom()` method? We added a `url` option that points to the larger version of the image—this image name is now hardcoded in our JavaScript. If you add a second image to the page, you'll find that when you try to zoom in on it, you'll see the first image rather than the second.

Let's take a look at how we can address this issue and also make our JavaScript more portable and flexible.

## Time for action – creating multiple zoomable images

We'll keep working with the files we created in the example to create zoomable images—with just a few modifications; we'll be able to place as many zoomable images on the page as we like. Perform the following steps to create multiple zoomable images:

1.  Inside the HTML file, add a few more images and accompanying text. The CSS code we wrote earlier is flexible enough to handle multiple blocks of code. We're going to make just one small change to the HTML file. In the `<img>` element, we'll add an HTML5 `data` attribute that contains the path to the larger version of the image, as shown in the following code:

    ```
    <article>
      <figure>
        <img src="images/chamomile.jpg" height="879"
          width="1024" alt="Chamomile" data-lgsrc
          ="images/lg-chamomile.jpg">
      </figure>
      <div class="flower-info">
        <h2>Chamomile</h2>
        <p>...</p>
      </div>
    </article>
    ```

2.  Next, we need to modify the JavaScript that we wrote earlier so that it's a bit more flexible. Inside the document ready statement, remove the code we wrote earlier so that your `scripts.js` file looks like the following code snippet:

    ```
    $(document).ready(function(){

    });
    ```

3. Each individual image has its own accompanying larger image that should be shown when we zoom in. We'll need to step through each image, one at a time, and collect the appropriate image path. To do this, we'll use the jQuery's `each()` method. This gets started as follows:

```
$(document).ready(function(){
    $('figure').each();
});
```

4. Inside the `each()` method, we'll run a function that will find the unique file path and then assign it inside the `zoom()` method. This just means that we're going to go through each image on the page and tell the Zoom plugin which big image to show when we zoom in. Add a function inside `each()`, as follows:

```
$(document).ready(function(){
    $('figure').each(function(){
    });
});
```

5. The first thing we'll do inside the function is get the path to the larger image. We'll create a variable to hold the path. Remember that a variable is just an empty container. We're creating a convenient place to store the file path, as follows:

```
$(document).ready(function(){
    $('figure').each(function(){
        var filePath;
    });
});
```

6. Now, we need to get the file path to the larger image and store it in the variable. Recall that we added a `data` attribute to the `<img>` element. As we're working with the `<figure>` element that wraps the `<img>` element, we'll have to find the image. This is achieved by adding a line of code as follows:

```
$(document).ready(function(){
    $('figure').each(function(){
        var filePath = $(this).find('img');
    });
});
```

7. Now that we have the image, we can use the handy `jQuery data()` method to get the value of that `data` attribute we added to our HTML file:

```
$(document).ready(function(){
    $('figure').each(function(){
        var filePath = $(this).find('img').data('lgsrc');
    });
});
```

**8.** Now that we've got the path to the large file, we can call the `zoom()` method for each image and use our `filePath` variable for the path to the large image, as shown in the following code:

```
$(document).ready(function(){
  $('figure').each(function(){
    var filePath = $(this).find('img').data('lgsrc');
    $(this).zoom({
      url: filePath
    });
  });
});
```

This is the same function we wrote earlier in the example with just one image. The only difference is that we're using this variable to pass in the correct large image for each image on the page. If you refresh the page now, you'll see that multiple images each zoom into the correct larger image when you move your mouse over.

## What just happened?

We made some modifications to our earlier code so that we can create multiple zoomable images on each page. First, we added the path to the larger image as a `data` attribute in the HTML. Then, we modified our JavaScript to loop through each image individually and assign the correct larger image to be used for the zooming effect. Now, our page can work with one image or with a dozen images or even with 100 images. We've structured our JavaScript in a flexible way that's not dependent on the number of images we have on the page. This gives us the ability to edit the HTML file to add or remove images without having to rewrite the JavaScript.

# Using fullscreen backgrounds

For websites where we're emphasizing imagery, using a single image as a fullscreen background image is a great way to create a visual punch. However, there are a few challenges we have to overcome, which are as follows:

- We need to fill the entire background of the page, no matter what screen size or device our site visitor uses, without gaps or repetition
- We need to minimize the file size of the images to increase speed and performance
- We need to maintain the proportions of the image without distorting it, while still scaling it to best fit the current window size
- We need the image to appear at an acceptable quality level, without visible degradation

CSS3 has introduced the `background-size` property, which we can use to proportionally scale an image to the window size. This works pretty well in the browsers that have support for this new property (check `http://caniuse.com/#search=background-size` for the latest information on support) but even in browsers with support, we'll see a JPG background image load progressively. Let's take a look at how we can use jQuery to support more browsers, scale the images perfectly, and also include a lovely fade-in effect for the image once it's completely loaded.

We'll be using Jay Salvat's Vegas Background plugin, which has a variety of features that make it flexible and easy to work with.

**Reducing image file sizes**

When using large, fullscreen images, there are a couple of nifty techniques you can use to get the smallest file size possible. First, in your image editing program, increase the size of the images to at least twice their normal size (some developers use three or four times their normal size), then save for Web as a JPG file with zero percent image quality. This produces a very large, low-quality image that will be scaled down for nearly all browsers and will appear crisp, clean, and indistinguishable from a high-quality image for most of your site visitors. Best of all, the file size will be very small.

Also, before using your images on the Web, use an image compression tool such as ImageOptim (`http://imageoptim.com/`), JPEGmini (`http://www.jpegmini.com/`), or RIOT (`http://luci.criosweb.ro/riot/`) to compress them as much as possible without affecting the quality.

# Time for action – creating a fullscreen background image

Perform the following steps to create a page with a fullscreen background image:

**1.** We'll get started by creating a basic HTML document and the associated files and folders just like we created in *Chapter 1, Designer, Meet jQuery*. Inside the HTML document, we'll add just a few lines of text, as shown in the following code:

```
<div class="content">
  <h1>Seychelles</h1>
  <p>Seychelles, officially the Republic of Seychelles,
    is a 155-island country (as per the Constitution)
    spanning an archipelago in the Indian Ocean,
    whose capital, Victoria, lies some 1,500 kilometres
    (932 mi) east of mainland Southeast Africa,
    northeast of the island of Madagascar.</p>
</div>
```

2. Next, we'll add a few styles for this text. To make sure it's readable over the photo background, let's add a transparent black background to the `div` element with a `class` selector of `content`, as shown in the following code:

```
.content {
  background: black;
  background: rgba(0,0,0,0.5);
  margin-top: 4em;
  padding: 2em;
}
```

3. As our page is so simple, it's already time to start working with our JavaScript. Head over to `http://vegas.jaysalvat.com/` where you can find the download and documentation for the Vegas plugin. To download it, click on the **DOWNLOAD VEGAS** link near the bottom-right corner of the screen. Unzip the folder and take a look inside the folder; you will see the contents as shown in the following screenshot:

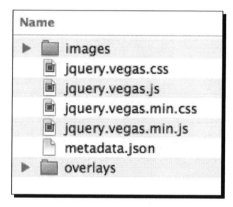

Note that this plugin doesn't contain a sample HTML file like most of the plugins we've worked with so far—just the files we'll need to get the plugin working. Inside the `images` folder, you'll find a `loading.gif` file. Copy this file to your own `images` folder. Copy the entire `overlays` folder to your own project directory. Then, copy `jquery.vegas.min.css` to your own `styles` folder and copy `jquery.vegas.min.js` to your own `scripts` folder.

When you're finished, your own project directory should look like the following screenshot:

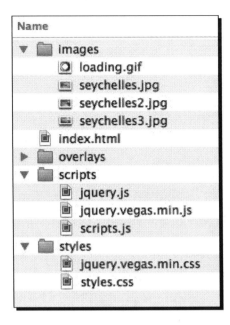

The `images` folder contains both the `loading.gif` file copied from the Vegas download folder, along with any images that you'll be working with to create fullscreen backgrounds.

4. Next, attach the Vegas style sheet at the top of the HTML file, after your own style sheet, as shown in the following code:

```html
<head>
  <title>Chapter 8: Fullscreen Background</title>
  <link rel="stylesheet" href="styles/styles.css">
  <link rel="stylesheet" href="styles/jquery.vegas.min.css">
</head>
```

5. Attach the Vegas plugin file at the bottom of the HTML file, after jQuery but before your own `scripts.js` file:

```html
<script src="scripts/jquery.js"></script>
<script src="scripts/jquery.vegas.min.js"></script>
<script src="scripts/scripts.js"></script>
</body>
</html>
```

6. Now, it's time to open up the `scripts.js` file to write some JavaScript. Get started with the document ready statement, as follows:

```
$(document).ready(function(){
  // Our code will go here
});
```

7. Next, we'll call the Vegas plugin. Vegas works just a bit differently from many of the other plugins we've seen so far. We don't have to select an element in our document that we want to work with. The following code shows how to call the `vegas()` method:

```
$(document).ready(function(){
  $.vegas();
});
```

8. Then, we just have to pass in some options. First, we'll use the `src` option to tell Vegas which image to use as the background:

```
$(document).ready(function(){
  $.vegas({
    src: 'images/seychelles.jpg'
  });
});
```

Note that the path to the image is relative to the HTML file, not to the `scripts.js` file where we're writing this code.

9. We want the image to fade on to the page rather than progressively downloading as the JPG files usually do, so we'll pass another option, `fade`:

```
$(document).ready(function(){
  $.vegas({
    src: 'images/seychelles.jpg',
    fade: 2000
  });
});
```

The number we pass to the `fade` option should be the number of milliseconds the fading action will take—2000 milliseconds is 2 seconds. If you refresh the page in the browser, you'll see a solid background color until the image fades in for 2 seconds. If you try resizing the browser window, you'll see that the image responds just as we'd like; it scales to best fit the window without distorting and stays centered.

**10.** The Vegas plugin has an additional handy option available that is tremendously helpful when we're using images as fullscreen backgrounds—overlays. Inside the `overlays` folder, you'll find 15 different PNG files—each one creates a different pattern when used to fill an area—dots, stripes, checks, grids, and so on. By laying one of these patterns over our background images, we can help disguise or hide any image degradation that might be visible when our images are stretched to fill larger screens. These overlay patterns also help darken our background images, to make the text content on top just a bit easier to read. To add an overlay to our background image, we'll just chain the overlay options, as follows:

```
$(document).ready(function(){
  $.vegas({
    src: 'images/seychelles.jpg',
    fade: 2000
  })('overlay', {
    src: 'overlays/03.png'
  });
});
```

Just like the background image itself, we have an `src` option for the overlay. Again, the path to the overlay is relative to the HTML document, not the JavaScript document where you're writing this code. I've selected `03.png` as my overlay of choice, but feel free to experiment with all the 15 options provided with the plugin or to create one of your own.

Now, if you refresh the page in the browser, you'll see the subtle overlay pattern on the image.

## What just happened?

We used the Vegas plugin to create a flexible, scalable fullscreen background image for our HTML page. We added options for the image to fade in for 2 seconds and also added an overlay to the image that helps to darken it just a bit and also to hide any image degradation that might happen, particularly on large screens. When we resize the window, the image resizes while remaining centered and doesn't distort.

## Creating a fullscreen slideshow

In addition to creating perfectly responsive fullscreen background images, the Vegas plugin will also allow us to create fullscreen background slideshows. Let's take a look at how we can take this same HTML file and create a fullscreen slideshow behind the text rather than just a single fullscreen image.

# Time for action – creating a fullscreen slideshow

We'll keep working with the files that we created in the *Time for action – creating a fullscreen background image* section. The only change we'll need to make to create a slideshow rather than a single fullscreen background image is to our `scripts.js` file. To do so, perform the following steps:

**1.** Open `scripts.js` and remove the `src` and `fade` options from the `vegas()` method, as shown in the following code:

```
$(document).ready(function(){
  $.vegas({

  })('overlay', {
    src: 'overlays/03.png'
  });
});
```

**2.** Next, we need to tell Vegas that we want to use a slideshow. Before we pass in the options object, tell Vegas to use a slideshow, as shown in the code:

```
$(document).ready(function(){
  $.vegas('slideshow', {

  })('overlay', {
    src: 'overlays/03.png'
  });
});
```

Note that this slideshow option is outside the curly braces.

**3.** We'll pass in the slideshow options we want to use, inside the curly braces. First, let's add `delay`. This tells Vegas how long to display each image in the slideshow. As the slideshow takes up the entire screen, it works best if the slideshow is slow. We'll let each image be displayed for 5 seconds or 5000 milliseconds, as shown in the code:

```
$(document).ready(function(){
  $.vegas('slideshow', {
    delay: 5000
  })('overlay', {
    src: 'overlays/03.png'
  });
});
```

**4.** We'll tell Vegas which images we want to use in our slideshow. We'll do that with the `backgrounds` option, as shown in the following code:

```
$(document).ready(function(){
  $.vegas('slideshow', {
    delay: 5000,
    backgrounds: []
  })('overlay', {
    src: 'overlays/03.png'
  });
});
```

Don't forget to add a comma after the delay option to separate it from the `backgrounds` option. We've added a pair of square brackets as the value for the `backgrounds` option. Square brackets denote an array—an **array** is just a collection of values instead of a single value. As our slideshow is going to contain multiple background images, we'll use an array to make sure Vegas knows about each one.

**5.** Inside the array, we'll pass some information about each of our images inside curly braces. We need the path to each image, along with how long the animation for each image will be:

```
$(document).ready(function(){
  $.vegas('slideshow', {
    delay: 5000,
    backgrounds: [
      { src: 'images/seychelles.jpg', fade: 2000 },
      { src: 'images/seychelles2.jpg', fade: 2000 },
      { src: 'images/seychelles3.jpg', fade: 2000 }
    ]
  })('overlay', {
    src: 'overlays/03.png'
  });
});
```

Again, because the slideshow is occupying the entire page, it's best if the transition between the images is slow—here, we allow 2 full seconds for the image to change.

Now if you refresh the page in the browser, you'll see that our single fullscreen background image has been replaced by a fullscreen slideshow. Experiment with the `delay`, `fade`, and `overlay` options to find the combination that works best for the images that you're using.

## *What just happened?*

We modified the settings of the Vegas plugin to create a fullscreen slideshow on our page's background rather than just a single fullscreen background image. Just like the single background image, the slideshow is responsive and resizes flawlessly as we resize our browser window. We were able to set the amount of time each image in the slideshow should be visible for, and we were also able to pass in an array of images to use in the slideshow along with the duration of the transition animation for each one.

# Summary

In this chapter, we took a look at few techniques for working with images in responsive designs. First, we set up lazy loading so that images will only be loaded if and when they are required. Then, we took a look at adding the ability to zoom in images to get more detail. Finally, we looked at how to create both fullscreen background images and fullscreen background slideshows. Armed with this knowledge, we can create even more flexible and more full-featured responsive pages. Next, we'll take a look at ways to make our typography just as flexible and responsive.

# 9
# Improving Typography

*A lot of the responsive design tutorials that you'll find on the Web tend to be very focused around images, videos, and column layouts. But the backbone of most websites is the text content—this is where having some knowledge and skills around typography and making typography more responsive is especially useful. If you can make the content on a website a visual delight and a pleasure to read, you're more likely to draw in regular readers than if your text content is poorly set and difficult to read.*

In this chapter, you'll learn:

- How to use the FitText plugin to size headlines responsively according to the width of the browser window
- How to use the SlabText plugin to create perfectly-sized multiline blocks of text
- How to use the Lettering.js plugin to fine-tune kerning and apply special text effects
- How to use the ArcText plugin to set text on a curve

## Sizing headlines perfectly

With the recent rise in the popularity of responsive design, some designers have pointed out that the Web is responsive by default—we've made the Web unresponsive by setting fixed widths in layouts. That's partially true. Text on the Web will automatically flow to best fit its container, but that can sometimes lead to awkward line breaks and line lengths (or measures) that make reading difficult.

While we can use CSS and media queries to fix some of these issues, adding a little bit of JavaScript magic into the mix can allow us to accomplish things that we wouldn't be able to accomplish with CSS alone. Let's take a look at resizing headlines to accommodate the width of the screen. This can be really helpful to prevent awkward line breaks in headings.

**Modular scale**

To create visual harmony and text that's set with precision, give the modular scale a try. A modular scale is a mathematical scale of numbers that share the same relation to one another. When you choose numbers from the scale to set your font sizes, line heights, column widths, margins, and padding, you'll create typography that's more professional and aesthetically pleasing. Tim Brown, the type manager at TypeKit, has produced `http://modularscale.com`—a tool that enables anyone to calculate a scale and produce gorgeous typography. Links to several articles on `http://modularscale.com` will help you understand and use a modular scale more effectively for setting your typography.

## Time for action – sizing headlines to the screen width

Perform the following steps to create headlines that resize according to the width of the browser window:

1. We'll get started by creating a basic HTML document and associated files and folders just like we did in *Chapter 1, Designer, Meet jQuery*. Inside the HTML document, we're going to create a bit of text with a headline, as follows:

```
<div class="content">
  <h1>What is Typography?</h1>
  <p>Typography is the art ...</p>
</div>
```

2. Inside `styles.css`, some basic CSS that is applied helps to set the size of the heading, the paragraph, and padding and margin around both elements. If you take a look at the sample code included with the book, you'll see the following bit of CSS that styles basic text elements:

```
.content p {
  line-height: 1.5;
  margin: 1.125em 0;
}

.content h1 {
  font-size: 3.375em;
  line-height: 1.125;
  margin: 1.125em 0 0.5em 0;
}
```

For our site visitors without JavaScript, this bit of text is perfectly acceptable, no matter what their screen width happens to be. The text of both the paragraph and the headline simply reflows as the browser window resizes, as shown in the following screenshot:

However, by using in the FitText plugin, we gain a little more control over the headline, and we can resize it fluidly so that it will fill the width of the screen.

3. You'll find documentation and download links for FitText at http://fittextjs. com/. Just click on the **Download on GitHub** link to be redirected to GitHub. Once you're on GitHub, just click on the **Download ZIP** button as we've done with other plugins that we've downloaded from GitHub.

4. Unzip and open the ZIP file. Look for jquery.fittext.js and copy it to your own scripts folder. Then, in the HTML file, add the FitText file at the bottom, after jQuery but before your own scripts.js, as follows:

```
<script src="scripts/jquery.js"></script>
<script src="scripts/jquery.fittext.js"></script>
<script src="scripts/scripts.js"></script>
</body>
</html>
```

5. Open your scripts.js file and get started by adding the document ready statement, as follows:

```
$(document).ready(function(){
  // Our code will go here
});
```

6. Next, we'll select the element we'd like to resize and then call the fitText() method. Make sure you pay careful attention to the letter T in the middle of the method name—it won't work if you forget that:

```
$(document).ready(function(){
  $('h1').fitText();
});
```

7. Now, if you refresh the page in the browser, you'll see that the headline resizes according to the browser window's width, but it's not working exactly the way we want, as shown in the following screenshot:

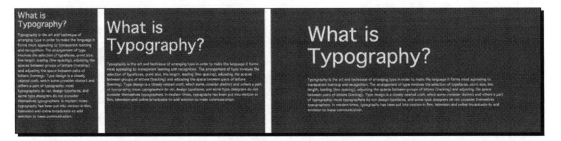

While the text is resizing with the browser window, it's a little too big and is spread over two lines. Let's take a look at how we can fine-tune FitText and gain a bit more control over the resizing of text.

8. FitText includes what the developers of the plugin call "the compressor." It's basically the ability to control how aggressive FitText is about resizing the text. The default value is 1, but we can pass a new value to the fitText() method. Often, it's a matter of trying out a few different values to find the one that works best for your particular situation:

```
$(document).ready(function(){
    $('h1').fitText(1.1);
});
```

9. In addition to the control we gain from passing values for the compressor, we can also set minimum and maximum font sizes for the text. In this example, our body text is set to the browser's default font size, and we'd like our heading to always be just a tad larger than the body text so that we don't end up with a headline that's actually smaller than the body text. After the compressor, we can pass the fitText() method a settings object to set the minimum font size to 1.2em:

```
$(document).ready(function(){
    $('h1').fitText(1.1, {minFontSize: '1.2em'});
});
```

Now, even if our screen were to get very narrow, the heading's font size would always be 20 percent larger than that of the body text, even if it means that the text will wrap onto a second (or even third) line. FitText also includes a maxFontSize setting, but we won't need to use it in this example.

If you refresh the page in the browser, you'll see that the headline now appears on a single line and the font resizes to best fit the current width of the browser window, while never going below 1.2 em:

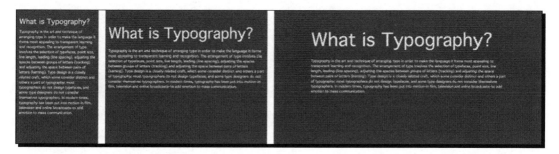

## *What just happened?*

We used the FitText plugin to resize our headline so that it always fits neatly on one single line. We learned how to adjust the Compressor for more control over the resizing and also learned how to set minimum and maximum font sizes for the headline to make sure that it stays within the boundaries that we set. In this example, we set a minimum font size of On one line please to ensure that the headline is always larger than the body text. FitText is only intended to be used for headlines—it will significantly impact the performance of your website if you attempt to use it for your body text or for all the text on the page. Stick to using FitText to create impactful, bold headlines.

## Creating bold text blocks

FitText is ideal for situations where we want to resize a headline to best fit the screen size, but what if want to take this a step further and create blocks of perfectly-sized text, as shown in the following screenshot:

We could wrap bits of our headline in some `<span>` tags and then set individual font sizes for each one, but handling the rewrapping of the text at different font sizes would be difficult, if not impossible. That's where the fabulous SlabText plugin comes in. SlabText will automatically calculate the best places to insert line breaks and then resize the text to perfectly fill each line. Let's take a look at how it works.

## Time for action – creating a bold text block with SlabText

Perform the following steps to break a headline into multiple lines, all resized to fit the width perfectly:

1. We'll get started by creating a basic HTML document and associated files and folders just like we did in *Chapter 1, Designer, Meet jQuery*. Inside the HTML document, we're going to place a headline as follows:

```
<header>
  <h1>Pride &amp; Prejudice</h1>
</header>
```

2. Next, we'll add some styles to style our headline the way we'd like. Open your `styles.css` file and add the following lines:

```
header {
  margin: 5.063em 0;
}


header h1 {
  line-height: 1.125;
  margin: 0;
  padding: 0;
  text-transform: uppercase;
}

h1 {
  font-size: 3.375em;
}
```

We've removed any default margins or padding from the `<h1>` element. We'll use the `<header>` element to add white space around our headline instead. Also, note that we used a unitless number for our line-height value. Unitless line heights allow these values to cascade down the DOM in a more elegant and useful manner.

We've set `text-transform` to `uppercase` since the SlabText effect is more visually impactful if we're using uppercase letters.

**3.** Next, we need to download the SlabText plugin and get it attached to our HTML page. You'll find the SlabText plugin in the jQuery plugins repository at `http://plugins.jquery.com/slabtext/`. Just click on the big orange **Download now** button to download the ZIP file. Unzip it, locate the `jquery.slabtext.min.js` file inside the `js` folder, and copy it to your own `scripts` folder.

Now, at the bottom of your HTML file, add the `<script>` tag to include the file after jQuery, but before your own `scripts.js` file, as shown in the code:

```
<script src="scripts/jquery.js"></script>
<script src="scripts/jquery.slabtext.min.js"></script>
<script src="scripts/scripts.js"></script>
```

**4.** The SlabText plugin also includes some CSS that we'll need for the plugin to work as expected. You'll find a `slabtext.css` file inside the `css` folder. We could copy this file to our own project and attach the file to our HTML page, but it's only a few lines. We'll get better performance on our pages if we reduce the number of external files we include, so instead, let's open up that CSS file, copy the code that's there, and add it to our own `styles.css` file as shown in the code:

```css
.slabtexted .slabtext {
  display: -moz-inline-box;
  display: inline-block;
  white-space: nowrap
}

.slabtextinactive .slabtext {
  display: inline;
  font-size: 1em !important;
  letter-spacing: inherit !important;
  *letter-spacing: 0 !important;
  white-space: normal;
  word-spacing: inherit !important;
  *word-spacing:0 !important;
}

.slabtextdone .slabtext {
  display: block;
  line-height: 0.9;
}
```

**5.** Now, open your `scripts.js` file and add the document ready statement as follows:

```
$(document).ready(function(){
  // Our code will go here
});
```

**6.** SlabText works like most other jQuery plugins; we select an element and then call the `slabText()` method. In this case, we want to work with the `<h1>` element:

```
$(document).ready(function(){
  $('h1').slabText();
});
```

If you refresh the page in the browser, you'll see that the text now expands to fill the horizontal space. If you resize the browser window, you'll see that the text size is recalculated and at narrower widths, even broken into two lines, each of equal length, as shown in the following screenshot:

**7.** Many typography experts recommend using the best ampersand (**&**) you possibly can—and the ampersand that's included with the font we're using here (Geneva) is a bit flat and boring. The SlabText plugin automatically wraps ampersands in a `<span>` element with an `amp` class. We can use this class to style the ampersand in a nicer style. In your `styles.css` file, add the following lines of code:

```
.amp {
  font-family: Baskerville, 'Goudy Old Style', Palatino,
    'Book Antiqua', serif;
  font-size: 1.125em;
  font-style: italic;
  font-weight: normal;
}
```

This is the font style that is recommended by Dan Cederholm to style ampersands on the Web. If you refresh the page in the browser now, you'll see our ampersand replaced by a much nicer and more visually interesting ampersand, as shown in the following screenshot:

**8.** We've created a nice text effect, but this bit of text is rather short. Let's take a look at how this effect might work with a longer bit of text. Open your `index.html` file and add another headline:

```
<header>
    <h1>The Importance of Being Earnest: A Trivial Comedy for
    Serious People by Oscar Wilde</h1>
</header>
```

If you refresh the page in the browser now, you'll see that this headline breaks into multiple lines, all of which fill the width of the page. However, the line breaks are a bit awkward, and the resizing of text feels random and strange, as shown in the following screenshot:

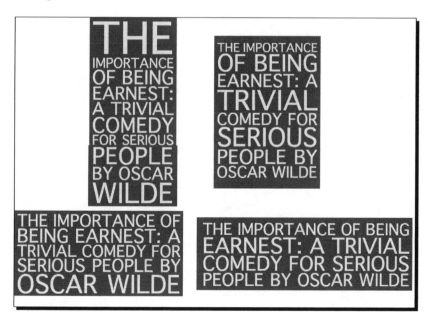

9. Luckily, the SlabText plugin provides a way for us to have control over where the text is broken into lines. We can do that by just wrapping each line in a `<span>` element with the `class` selector of `slabtext`. Inside `index.html`, add some `<span>` tags around the text as follows:

```
<header>
  <h1>
    <span class="slabtext">The Importance of Being</span>
    <span class="slabtext">Earnest:</span>
    <span class="slabtext">A Trivial Comedy for Serious People</span>
    <span class="slabtext">by Oscar Wilde</span>
  </h1>
</header>
```

Now, if you refresh the page in the browser, you can see that our line breaks make more visual sense, as shown in the following screenshot:

The line breaks are the same, no matter how wide or narrow the browser window is.

10. Wrapping each line in its own `<span>` tag also gives us the opportunity to style each line a bit differently. Inside the `index.html` file, add classes for the line numbers to each `<span>` element:

```
<header>
  <h1>
    <span class="slabtext line1">The Importance of Being</span>
    <span class="slabtext line2">Earnest:</span>
    <span class="slabtext line3">A Trivial Comedy
      for Serious People</span>
    <span class="slabtext line4">by Oscar Wilde</span>
  </h1>
</header>
```

**11.** We can use these new classes to add some additional styles to the lines of text. For example, let's take the first and third lines and make them green and set them in the same `font-family` style that we used for the ampersand earlier. In the `styles.css` file, add the following styles:

```css
.line1, .line3 {
  color: #a1d36e;
  font-family: Baskerville, "Times, Times New Roman", serif;
}
```

Refresh the page in the browser, and you'll see that the first and third lines of text are green and are in a serif typeface:

All lines of text still resize correctly to fill the width of the screen.

**12.** So far, we've tried a few different techniques. What if we have a case where we want to control just one line break in the text and allow the others to happen naturally? If we add the author to our first example headline, our code will look as follows:

```html
<header>
  <h1>Pride &amp; Prejudice by Jane Austen</h1>
</header>
```

We'd always want to have a line break between the title and the author, but within the title and within the author, we'd want the line breaks to happen naturally.

If we wrap the title and the author each in a `<span>` element, like we did in the previous example, each of those lines will resize to always fill the screen width. **Pride & Prejudice** won't wrap to two lines at narrow screen widths.

The solution is to wrap each bit of text in its own tag and then call the `slabText()` method on both elements. Change the HTML markup as follows:

```html
<header>
  <h1>Pride &amp; Prejudice</h1>
  <h2>by Jane Austen</h2>
</header>
```

**13.** Next, we need to add a few new styles to `styles.css` to account for the `<h2>` element:

```
header h1, header h2 {
  line-height: 1.125;
  margin: 0;
  padding: 0;
  text-transform: uppercase;
}

h2 {
  font-size: 2.25em;
}
```

**14.** The last thing to do is to modify the `scripts.js` file to call `slabText()` on both levels of heading:

```
$(document).ready(function(){
  $('h1, h2').slabText();
});
```

Refresh the page in the browser and try changing the window width. You'll see that both the title and the author name resize themselves to fit the width, and each of them wraps to a new line when it seems best to do so.

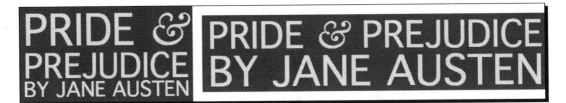

## What just happened?

We took a look at using the SlabText plugin to create large blocky headlines. We saw how to control the line breaks in the headline by using `<span>` tags inserted in the headline or by using multiple HTML elements. SlabText takes care of recalculating the correct font size for each line of the headline so that it fills the width of the container. We use the SlabText plugin by selecting the elements we want to work with and calling the `slabText()` method.

Q1. When we're using plugins such as FitText and SlabText to resize text, it's best to use this functionality on which types of text?

1. The entire text on the page—everything should be sized together for consistency.

2. Just the text in the main content area.

3. Headlines and other short, important bits of text such as pull quotes.

4. Just the text in the footer.

# Styling individual letters

Next, we'll take a look at the Lettering.js plugin, which gives us fine-tuned control over individual characters. Just like the FitText and SlabText plugins, we'll reserve the power of Lettering.js for headlines. Our webpage would suffer some pretty serious performance issues if we tried to use it for all the text on the page. Stick to applying these text effects to text that deserves extra attention—items such as headlines and pull quotes.

## Time for action – using Lettering.js to style letters

Perform the following steps to use the Lettering.js plugin:

*1.* We'll get started by creating a basic HTML document and associated files and folders, just like we did in *Chapter 1, Designer, Meet jQuery*. Inside the HTML document, we need a headline to work with. It's nice to also have at least a bit of text on the page as well in order to really understand how our headline will look with other text on the page:

```
<div class="content">
  <h1>Alice&#8217;s Adventures in Wonderland</h1>

  <section>
    <h2>CHAPTER I. Down the Rabbit-Hole</h2>
    <p>Alice was beginning to get very tired of sitting by her
      sister on the bank, and of having nothing to do:
      once or twice she had peeped into the book her sister
      was reading, but it had no pictures or conversations in it,
      &lsquo;and what is the use of a book,&rsquo; thought Alice
      &lsquo;without pictures or conversations?&rsquo;</p>
  </section>
</div>
```

Note that we've used a typographically correct apostrophe in the headline. As we're paying close attention to typography in this chapter, we'll try to use all the correct characters instead of the shortcuts that so often get used on the Web.

2.  We've already got default styles set for content in our default style sheet, so we don't have to write any special styles just yet. We can head over to `http://letteringjs.com/` to get the download file and documentation for the Lettering.js plugin. Follow the **DOWNLOAD ON GITHUB** link and then click on **Download ZIP** to get the files you'll need.

3.  Unzip the file, find `jquery.lettering.js` inside, and copy it to your own `scripts` folder. Then, at the bottom of the HTML file, attach the Lettering.js plugin after jQuery, but before your own `scripts.js` file, as follows:

    ```
    <script src="scripts/jquery.js"></script>
    <script src="scripts/jquery.lettering.js"></script>
    <script src="scripts/scripts.js"></script>
    ```

4.  Open `scripts.js` and add the document ready statement, as follows:

    ```
    $(document).ready(function(){
      // Our code will go here
    });
    ```

5.  Next, we need to call the `lettering()` method. We want to add the capabilities of Lettering.js to our header, so we'll select the `<h1>` element:

    ```
    $(document).ready(function(){
      $('h1').lettering();
    });
    ```

6.  If you refresh the page in the browser, you'll see that it appears as though nothing has changed on the page. However, if you open the Inspector tools in Safari or Chrome, or Firebug in Firefox, you'll see that each individual character in the heading is now wrapped in a `<span>` tag with a numbered class, as shown in the following screenshot:

```
▼ <div class="content">
  ▼ <h1>
      <span class="char1">A</span>
      <span class="char2">l</span>
      <span class="char3">i</span>
      <span class="char4">c</span>
      <span class="char5">e</span>
      <span class="char6">'</span>
      <span class="char7">s</span>
      <span class="char8"> </span>
      <span class="char9">A</span>
      <span class="char10">d</span>
      <span class="char11">v</span>
      <span class="char12">e</span>
      <span class="char13">n</span>
      <span class="char14">t</span>
      <span class="char15">u</span>
      <span class="char16">r</span>
      <span class="char17">e</span>
      <span class="char18">s</span>
      <span class="char19"> </span>
      <span class="char20">i</span>
      <span class="char21">n</span>
      <span class="char22"> </span>
      <span class="char23">W</span>
      <span class="char24">o</span>
      <span class="char25">n</span>
      <span class="char26">d</span>
      <span class="char27">e</span>
      <span class="char28">r</span>
      <span class="char29">l</span>
      <span class="char30">a</span>
      <span class="char31">n</span>
      <span class="char32">d</span>
    </h1>
  ▶ <section>…</section>
  </div>
```

This is all that the Lettering.js plugin does. By wrapping each character in a span and giving each a unique class, it enables us to write CSS to style each character individually. But how can that be useful?

7. First up, it allows us to fine-tune kerning. For example, the gap between the letter **W** and the letter **o** in **Wonderland** is too large in many typefaces. We can close that up by selecting **o** (`char24`) and applying a negative left margin. In your `styles.css` file, add the following lines of code:

```
.char24 {
  margin-left: -0.05em;
}
```

Have a look at the following screenshot and find the difference in the words:

You can see in the bottom **Wonderland** text that the gap between **W** and **o** is smaller and the spacing between **W** and **o** feels consistent with the spacing between the remaining letters.

8. Another possibility is to add individual styles to each letter. We can add individual colors, background colors, background images, padding, margins, and so on. We can also use the new CSS3 capabilities to add box shadows, text shadows, transforms, transitions, gradients, and so on. Let's take a look at adding a bit of whimsy to the first word (**ALICE'S**) in our title. We'll get started by adding some styles that will apply to all the letters in that word in the `styles.css` file, as shown in the following code:

```
.char1, .char2, .char3, .char4, .char5, .char6, .char7 {
  border-radius: 50%;
  cursor: pointer;
  display: inline-block;
  margin: 0 0.125em;
  padding: 0.125em 0.25em;
  text-align: center;
  text-transform: uppercase;
  transition: all 300ms;
  width: 1em;
}
```

**9.** Next, we'll add some individual styles for each of those letters, as follows:

```
.char1 {
background: #fa6f57;
-webkit-transform: rotate(7deg);
}
.char2 {
background: #42b0d8;
-webkit-transform: rotate(-5deg);
}
.char3 {
background: #a1d36e;
-webkit-transform: rotate(12deg);
}
.char4 {
background: #967dd9;
-webkit-transform: rotate(-10deg);
}
.char5 {
background: #e75845;
-webkit-transform: rotate(-5deg);
}
.char6 {
background: #55c1e7;
-webkit-transform: rotate(4deg);
}
.char7 {
background: #ac94e9;
-webkit-transform: rotate(13deg);
}
```

We'll also style the :hover pseudoclass for each letter to add a bit of interactivity. When our site visitor moves their mouse over the letters, they'll see a subtle animation:

```
.char1:hover {
background: #a1d36e;
-webkit-transform: rotate(-8deg);
}
.char2:hover {
background: #967dd9;
-webkit-transform: rotate(10deg);
}
.char3:hover {
background: #e75845;
-webkit-transform: rotate(-3deg);
```

```
}
.char4:hover {
background: #55c1e7;
-webkit-transform: rotate(5deg);
}
.char5:hover {
background: #ac94e9;
-webkit-transform: rotate(10deg);
Improving Typography
}
.char6:hover {
background: #fa6f57;
-webkit-transform: rotate(-9deg);
}
.char7:hover {
background: #42b0d8;
-webkit-transform: rotate(-2deg);
}
```

Refresh the page in the browser and you'll see that the letters are encapsulated in differently colored circles and tilted in different directions:

When you move your mouse over each letter, they rotate and change background colors. Feel free to add your own styles and colors to each letter—the only limit to what you can accomplish is your own imagination.

## What just happened?

We applied the Lettering.js plugin to our headline. While the jQuery plugin itself doesn't actually make any changes to the appearance of the page, it does make it possible for us to style each individual letter with CSS. This allows us to fine-tune kerning and apply creative styles. Take a look through the gallery on `http://letteringjs.com/` to get a feel for what's possible. The plugin itself is very simple to use—just one line of JavaScript gets you up and running. After that, the remainder of the work is CSS.

## Have a go hero – creating fancy effects with Lettering.js

Take a look through the gallery for Lettering.js (`http://letteringjs.com`) and see whether you can recreate the effect of your choosing, or design your own special lettering effect and put the Lettering.js plugin to work to create your design. Use gradients, transforms, 3D transforms, box shadows, text shadows, border radii, or CSS animations to create your custom appearance.

# Setting text on a curve

Using CSS3 transforms, it would technically be possible to set text on a curve using the Lettering.js plugin. It would, however, require us to do quite a lot of calculations to get the letters arranged just so.

Thankfully, Pedro Botelho, author of the ArcText plugin, has figured out a way to let JavaScript do all the math for us. He started from the Lettering.js plugin, but then added the ability to set text perfectly to a curve of your choosing. The result is the ArcText plugin, which allows us to set any text on a curve of any radius.

## Time for action – setting text on a curve with the ArcText plugin

Perform the following steps to set text on a curve:

*1.* We'll get started by creating a basic HTML document and associated files and folders, just like we did in *Chapter 1, Designer, Meet jQuery*. Inside the HTML document, we'll add a heading, as follows:

```
<div class="content">
  <header id="ex1">
    <h1>A Tale of Two Cities</h1>
  </header>
</div>
```

*2.* Next, we'll download the ArcText plugin. The plugin is available through a tutorial on the Codrops blog by Tympanus. Head over to `http://tympanus.net/codrops/2012/01/24/arctext-js-curving-text-with-css3-and-jquery/` and click on the **DOWNLOAD SOURCE** button to get the ZIP file.

Unzip the file. Inside the `js` folder, you'll find the `jquery.arctext.js` file—copy this file to your own `scripts` folder.

**3.** At the bottom of the HTML file, attach the ArcText plugin, after jQuery but before your own `scripts.js` file, as follows:

```
<script src="scripts/jquery.js"></script>
<script src="scripts/jquery.arctext.js"></script>
<script src="scripts/scripts.js"></script>
</body>
</html>
```

**4.** Open the `scripts.js` file and add the document ready statement, as follows:

```
$(document).ready(function(){
   // Our code will go here
});
```

**5.** Next, we'll need to call the `arctext()` method. Select the headline and call the `arctext()` method, as follows:

```
$(document).ready(function(){
   $('h1').arctext();
});
```

Refresh the page in the browser and you'll see that the headline is now curved.

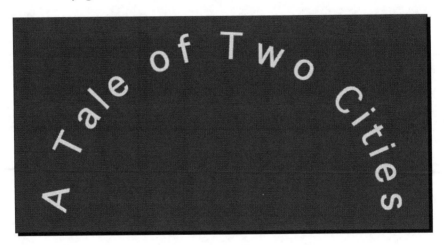

**6.** The curve we get by default might not be exactly what we wanted, so let's take a look at the options we have in the ArcText plugin. First, we have control over the `radius` document ready of the circle used to set the text. Let's try setting that to `500`, as shown in the following code:

```
$('h1').arctext({
   radius: 500
});
```

The following screenshot shows the change in the arc:

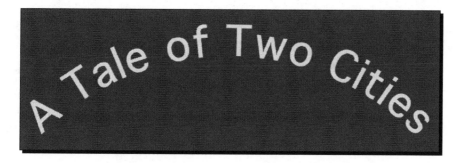

This gives us a much more gentle arc and is generally more readable. Feel free to experiment with different values to get the effect you'd like.

7. Next, we can control the direction of the arc. By default, the text arcs up, but we can also make it arc down. We use the `dir` option—if set to `1`, the curve bends upwards, and if set to `-1`, the curve bends downwards:

```
$('h1').arctext({
   radius: 500,
   dir: -1
});
```

Don't forget to include a comma between different options but no comma after the last option. The following screenshot shows the change in the arc:

8. By default, ArcText will rotate our letters to the curve. But we can turn that off if we wish to with the `rotate` option. If we set it to `false`, as follows, each letter remains vertical:

```
$('h1').arctext({
   radius: 500,
   rotate: false
});
```

The following screenshot shows the change in the letters on setting the rotation of letters to `false`:

9. The final option we have is one you're already familiar with. ArcText will optionally resize the arced text to best fit the width of its container. To use this option, just set `fitText` to `true`, as follows:

```
$('h1').arctext({
    radius: 500,
    fitText: true
});
```

Now, as you resize the browser window, the text will automatically resize to best fit into the available space.

Note that as the text gets larger, the arc's radius increases.

10. The arced headline looks just fine, but if we try to add other text to the page, we'll find that it overlaps with the arced text, as shown in the following screenshot:

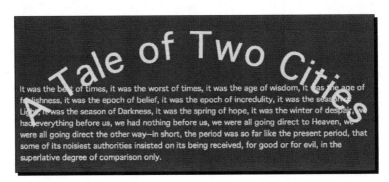

It's simple enough to correct this issue by adding a margin to the headline that contains the arced text. Inside `styles.css`, add the following style:

```
.content h1 {
  margin-bottom: 3em;
  text-align: center;
}
```

Now, if you refresh the page in the browser, you'll see that the body text added after the headline no longer overlaps, as shown in the following screenshot:

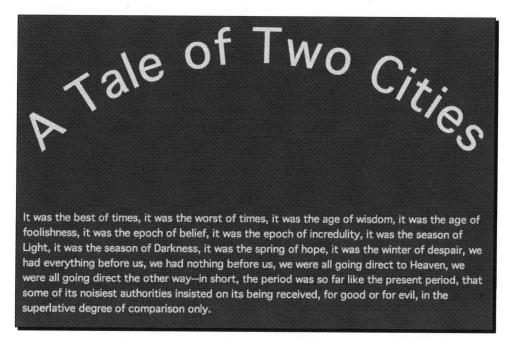

You can experiment with the margin value to find the value that best works for your text. Note that if you are using the `fitText` option, you'll want to set the margin in ems so that it will adjust in proportion to the font size at different screen widths.

## What just happened?

We used the ArcText plugin to set our text on a curve. The ArcText plugin automatically calculates the rotation and position of each letter in the headline for us to set it on a perfect arc. The options that are included allow us to control the direction of the arc and the radius of the arc, whether or not the letters are rotated, and whether or not the arced text is resized to best fit the screen. We gave all of these options a try. We also saw how we can adjust the margin of the arced text to avoid any subsequent text from overlapping.

# Summary

In this chapter, we took at look at several options we have to work with text inside responsive designs. We saw how we can make headlines resize automatically to fill the available space using the FitText plugin. We learned how to use the SlabText plugin to create blocky chunks of text. We tried using the Lettering.js plugin to fine-tune kerning and apply styles to individual letters. Finally, we learned how to set text on an arc using the ArcText plugin. Next, we'll explore some ways to present data beautifully in our designs with interactive data grids, graphs, and charts.

# 10
# Displaying Data Beautifully

*While you might not consider displaying data to be all that exciting, it is often crucial to present large amounts of data to site visitors in a way that makes it easy for them to understand, explore, and interact with in new ways. Finding new and better ways to display data helps to communicate complex principles effectively. Allowing site visitors to interact with data enables them to make their own discoveries. As we are presented with more and more data everyday, the field of data visualization grows. Let's take a look at some simple things we can do when working with large amounts of data to make it easier for our site visitors to consume and understand.*

In this chapter, we'll learn:

◆ How to turn an ordinary table into an interactive data grid using the DataTables jQuery plugin by Allan Jardine

◆ How to customize the appearance and behavior of the data grid using the jQuery UI ThemeRoller plugin

◆ How to use the jQuery Visualize plugin to use tables of data to create charts and graphs

# A basic data grid

We'll get started by using the DataTables plugin to create a basic data grid, keeping the default settings and the styles provided with the data grid. Data grids are most helpful when we have large amounts of data to present, and the site visitors might want to filter and sort the data in different ways to find the information they are looking for. Think, for example, of a list of flights; one site visitor might be interested in sorting the flights by the departure time to find the earliest possible departure, while another site visitor might want to sort the flights by duration of the flight to find the shortest possible flight. Presenting the data in an interactive data grid allows each site visitor to quickly and easily find just the information they're looking for in a sea of information. For site visitors with JavaScript disabled, they'll simply see a large table of data and will never know that they're missing out on the interactive features. All of the information will still be available to them.

## Time for action – creating a basic data grid

Let's take a look at how to turn a basic HTML table into an interactive data grid, as follows:

1. We'll get started as usual with our basic HTML file and associated files and folders, just like we did in *Chapter 1, Designer, Meet jQuery*. We'll fill the `<body>` element of our HTML document with the HTML markup for a large table of data. The DataTables plugin requires us to be careful and correct with our table markup, otherwise the DataTables features may not work as expected. We'll need to ensure that we use a `<thead>` element for the table's header, and a `<tbody>` element for the table's body. A `<tfoot>` element for the table's footer is optional. The following code is an abbreviated sample of the HTML markup for a table of the all-time best-selling books:

```
<table id="book-grid">
  <thead>
    <tr>
      <th>Title</th>
      <th>Author(s)</th>
      <th>Original Language</th>
      <th>First Published</th>
      <th>Approximate Sales</th>
    </tr>
  </thead>
  <tbody>
```

```
    <tr>
      <td>A Tale of Two Cities</td>
      <td>Charles Dickens</td>
      <td>English</td>
      <td>1859</td>
      <td>200 million</td>
    </tr>
    <tr>
      <td>The Lord of the Rings</td>
      <td>J. R. R. Tolkien</td>
      <td>English</td>
      <td>1955</td>
      <td>150 million</td>
    </tr>
    ...
  </tbody>
</table>
```

In the sample code for the book, you'll find that the table contains a total of 127 books, each marked up just as these are. Note that we've added an `id` value (`book-grid`) to the table element, we have used the `<th>` elements for the heading of each column, and we've enclosed these elements in a `<thead>` element. We've also used a `<tbody>` element to wrap all the rows in the table's body.

2.  Next, we'll download the DataTables plugin. Head over to `http://datatables.net`, where you'll find the plugin's downloads, documentation, and examples. Click on the **Download** link in the menu to go to the download page. Then, click on the **Download DataTables** button to download a ZIP file.

3.  Unzip the file and take a look inside the folder. There's a folder of `examples` with several different examples of the DataTables plugin in action. There's folder that provides extra functionality for advanced data tables—we won't be using any of those here. There's a `media` folder that contains `images`, `css`, and `js` resources. Next, a `Readme.md` file contains information on the plugin's creator, information for where to find the documentation, and so on. Finally, you'll find the license for the plugin and a few other files we've seen before and can safely ignore for now.

4.  We're going to be setting up a basic example, so we'll just need a couple of things for our own project. First, copy the contents of the `images` folder from the downloaded folder to your own `images` folder. Open the `css` folder and copy `jquery.dataTables.min.css` to your own `styles` folder. Finally, in the `js` folder, find the minified version of the plugin, `jquery.dataTables.min.js`, and copy it to your own `scripts` folder.

5.  Next, we'll get all the necessary files attached to our HTML page that contains our table. In the `<head>` section of the document, attach the CSS file before your own `styles.css` file, as follows:

```
<link rel="stylesheet" href="styles/jquery.dataTables.min.css"/>
<link rel="stylesheet" href="styles/styles.css"/>
```

6.  Inside `styles.css`, we have to add just one style for our table to make sure it fills the available width, and to adjust the text color for the table contents. The style is as shown in the following code:

```
table {
    color: #333;
    width: 100%;
}
```

7.  Next, at the bottom of the HTML document, attach the DataTables plugin in between the jQuery file and your own `scripts.js` file, as shown in the following code:

```
<script src="scripts/jquery.js"></script>
<script src="scripts/jquery.dataTables.min.js"></script>
<script src="scripts/scripts.js"></script>
</body>
</html>
```

8.  Next, open your `scripts.js` file, and inside a document ready statement, select the table and call the `dataTable()` method, as follows:

```
$(document).ready(function(){
    $('#book-grid').dataTable();
});
```

Now, if you refresh the page in the browser, you'll see that your table has been transformed into a data grid. You can select the number of items to view at one time, type into the search box to find specific table entries, and use the pagination controls at the bottom-right corner of the table to page through the data table's rows.

| | | | | |
|---|---|---|---|---|
| 紅樓夢/红楼梦 (Dream of the Red Chamber) | Cao Xueqin | Chinese | 1754 | 100 million |
| 狼图腾 (Wolf Totem) | Jiang Rong | Chinese | 2004 | 20 million |
| 中国社会主义经济问题研究 (Problems in China's Socialist Economy) | Xue Muqiao | Chinese | 1979 | 10 million |
| 于丹《论语》心得 (Confucius from the Heart) | Yu Dan | Chinese | 2006 | 10 million |
| Osudy dobrého vojáka Švejka za světové války (The Good Soldier Švejk) | Jaroslav Hašek | Czech | 1923 | 20 million |

## What just happened?

We set up a basic HTML table and turned it into an interactive data grid by attaching a CSS file and the DataTables plugin. We selected the table and called the `dataTable()` method to activate the DataTables plugin.

That was pretty easy, wasn't it? Of course, chances are that this lavender design doesn't fit the design of your site, so let's take a look at how we can customize the appearance of the data table.

# A customized data grid

The DataTables plugin is the first plugin we've used that has support for the jQuery UI ThemeRoller plugin. jQuery UI is a collection of widgets and interactions that make building complex applications easier and faster. Learning jQuery UI itself is beyond the scope of this book, but we'll take a look at how to use the jQuery UI ThemeRoller to create a custom theme for our data table. This same theme would apply to any jQuery UI widgets used on our page, as well as any jQuery plugins being used that include support for the jQuery UI ThemeRoller.

# Time for action – customizing the data grid

We'll pick up right from where we left off with our data table. If you'd like to save your basic data grid example, just save a copy of the files we created. Then, perform the following steps to customize the appearance of your data grid:

***1.*** Head over to `http://jqueryui.com/themeroller` where we'll take a look at the ThemeRoller plugin. Take a look at the following screenshot to see the page. In the left-hand side column, you'll find the controls for selecting a predefined theme or creating a custom theme, and the right-hand side wide column contains samples of several different types of widgets.

2. Click on the **Gallery** tab in the left-hand side column, and you'll see that you have dozens of choices of prebuilt ThemeRoller themes to choose from. As you click on different samples, you'll see the sample widgets in the right-hand side column update to reflect that style. I usually like to get started by selecting a prebuilt theme that's reasonably close to the color scheme or appearance that I want, and then I flip to the **Roll Your Own** tab to tweak it to suit my needs. For this example, I'm going to start with the **Cupertino** style.

After flipping to the **Roll Your Own** tab, you'll see that there are settings for fonts, colors, corners, headers, and so on. Make the adjustments you'd like in order to get the theme to look just the way you'd like. Feel free to play and experiment. If you go too far and get to something you don't like, it's easy to flip back to the **Gallery** tab and select the prebuilt theme again, stripped of any of your customizations, and then start again.

 Any of your customizations will be lost if you reselect a prebuilt theme. Once you get something you like, be sure to move on to step 3 to save it.

3. Once you've got your theme set up just the way you'd like, click on the **Download theme** button.

You'll find yourself on the **Download Builder** page, which might seem a little confusing. See, jQuery UI is so large and has so many different features to offer that the developers realize that forcing everyone to download the entire thing would be overkill. If you only wanted to use one widget, there'd be no need to download all the other widgets and effects. This page lets you pick and choose different components of jQuery UI so that you don't have to download more than you need.

In the **Version** section, go ahead and leave the version set to the default. Since we're just getting a theme, we'll just use the latest stable version.

Uncheck the **Toggle All** checkbox in the **Components** section. We won't need to download any of these components because we just want a theme.

Then, we'll leave the **Theme** settings at the bottom of the page at their defaults and click on the **Download** button to download a ZIP file.

4.  Unzip the file and take a look inside. You'll see that even though we got the simplest download we could, we still have quite a few files shown in the following screenshot:

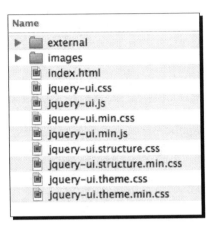

We've got an `external` folder that contains the jQuery library, an `images` folder that contains the images we'll need, and then several `.js` and `.css` files.

The only items we need are the `images` folder and the CSS for the theme you selected, which is contained in a file named `jquery-ui.theme.min.css`. Copy the CSS file to your `styles` folder and copy the `images` folder to your own `styles` folder. This is important—please be sure to nest the jQuery UI `images` folder inside your own `styles` folder.

5.  Next, we'll attach our theme's CSS file to our HTML file. Inside the `<head>` section, attach your theme's CSS file before the `jquery.dataTables.min.css` file we attached in the example of basic data grid, as follows:

```
<link rel="stylesheet" href="styles/
  jquery.dataTables_themeroller.css">
<link rel="stylesheet" href="styles/jquery.dataTables.min.css">
```

6.  Now, unfortunately, our theme's CSS file doesn't quite have all the styles we'll need for a nicely-styled data grid. After all, the jQuery UI developers have no way of knowing all the different types of widgets and plugins people will want to use, so there's no possible way they could cover every single case. Luckily, the DataTables plugin author, Allan Jardine, has already done some nice work for us in this area and has provided a CSS file with the styles we'll need to get our themed data grid to look its best.

You can read up on styling the DataTables plugin in the documentation that Allan Jardine has made available at `http://datatables.net/styling/`.

Back inside the DataTables plugin files, look inside the `css` folder that is inside the `media` folder to find the `jquery.dataTables_themeroller.css` file. Copy it to your own `styles` folder and update your `<link>` tag to link to point to this new CSS file instead of `jquery.dataTables.min.css`, as follows:

```
<link rel="stylesheet" href="styles/jquery-ui.theme.min.css">
<link rel="stylesheet" href="styles/jquery.dataTables_themeroller.css">
```

7.  Now, we just have to make a small update to our JavaScript code. We have to tell the `dataTable()` method that we want to use jQuery UI. Head back into your `scripts.js` file and we'll add a pair of curly brackets and pass a key/value pair to enable jQuery UI styling for our data table, as follows:

```
$(document).ready(function(){
  $('#book-grid').dataTable({
    'jQueryUI': true
  });
});
```

If you refresh the page in the browser now, you'll see that the data grid is now using a style that's consistent with the widgets we saw on the jQuery UI ThemeRoller page. Take a look at the following screenshot:

| Show 10 ⇕ entries | | | | Search: |
|---|---|---|---|---|
| Title ▴ | Author(s) ⇕ | Original Language ⇕ | First Published ⇕ | Approximate Sales ⇕ |
| A Brief History of Time | Stephen Hawking | English | 1988 | 10 million |
| A Message to Garcia | Elbert Hubbard | English | 1899 | 40 million |
| A Tale of Two Cities | Charles Dickens | English | 1859 | 200 million |
| A Wrinkle in Time | Madeleine L'Engle | English | 1962 | 10 million |
| And Then There Were None | Agatha Christie | English | 1939 | 100 million |
| Angels & Demons | Dan Brown | English | 2000 | 39 million |
| Anne of Green Gables | Lucy Maud Montgomery | English | 1908 | 50 million |
| Black Beauty: His Grooms and Companions: The autobiography of a horse | Anna Sewell | English | 1877 | 50 million |
| Catch-22 | Joseph Heller | English | 1961 | 10 million |
| Charlie and the Chocolate Factory | Roald Dahl | English | 1964 | 13 million |
| Showing 1 to 10 of 127 entries | | Previous 1 2 3 4 5 ... 13 Next | | |

**8.** Let's make some adjustments to Open `styles.css` and add some styles to add zebra-striping to the table as follows:

```
tr.odd td {
  background-color: #f5fbf0;
}

tr.even td {
  background-color: white;
}
```

I'm going with a pale green for odd rows and white for even rows to match the customized Cupertino style I selected earlier. Feel free to choose colors that match your own chosen theme.

**9.** Next, we'll change the color scheme for the currently sorted row. Add a style for this to `styles.css`. I'm going to change mine to a medium green, as follows:

```
tr.odd td.sorting_1 {
  background-color: #d4ebbc;
}
```

**10.** Finally, we can add the CSS code for the sorted even row in `styles.css`. I'm going to change this to a light green, as follows:

```
tr.even td.sorting_1 {
  background-color: #e5f3d6;
}
```

You can select your own colors that coordinate with your own chosen theme.

Now, if you refresh the page in the browser, you'll see that the zebra-striping pattern of the table fits with our ThemeRoller theme, as shown in the following screenshot:

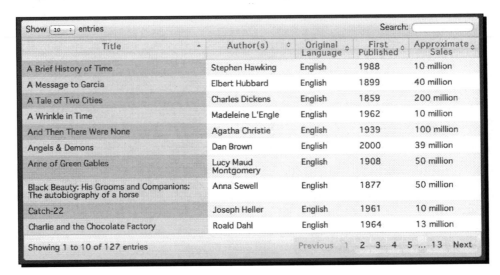

**11.** Our table could use a bit of help style-wise, so let's add a few more of our own custom styles to `styles.css` to get things to look a bit nicer, as shown in the following code:

```
th {
  cursor: pointer;
  vertical-align: middle;
}

th, td {
  padding: 0.5em;
}

td {
  border-bottom: 1px solid #c3e3a2;
}
```

These styles help to add a bit of space inside the table cells, a subtle border between rows, and help to fix the alignment of the table headers. The result is a much more readable table. Have a look at the following screenshot:

| Title ↕ | Author(s) ↕ | Original Language ↕ | First Published ↕ | Approximate Sales ↕ |
|---|---|---|---|---|
| A Brief History of Time | Stephen Hawking | English | 1988 | 10 million |
| A Message to Garcia | Elbert Hubbard | English | 1899 | 40 million |
| A Tale of Two Cities | Charles Dickens | English | 1859 | 200 million |
| A Wrinkle in Time | Madeleine L'Engle | English | 1962 | 10 million |
| And Then There Were None | Agatha Christie | English | 1939 | 100 million |
| Angels & Demons | Dan Brown | English | 2000 | 39 million |
| Anne of Green Gables | Lucy Maud Montgomery | English | 1908 | 50 million |
| Black Beauty: His Grooms and Companions: The autobiography of a horse | Anna Sewell | English | 1877 | 50 million |
| Catch-22 | Joseph Heller | English | 1961 | 10 million |
| Charlie and the Chocolate Factory | Roald Dahl | English | 1964 | 13 million |

Show [10 ▾] entries     Search: [　　　　　]

Showing 1 to 10 of 127 entries     Previous 1 2 3 4 5 ... 13 Next

**12.** We might decide that for this particular data table, the search function doesn't make sense. The DataTables plugin offers a way for us to disable individual features. To disable the search box filtering, we'll pass another key/value pair, as follows:

```
$(document).ready(function(){
  $('#book-grid').dataTable({
    'jQueryUI': true,
    'searching': false
  });
});
```

Refresh the page in the browser and you'll see that the search box has disappeared, as shown in the following screenshot:

| Show 10 entries | | | | | |
| --- | --- | --- | --- | --- | --- |
| Title | | Author(s) | Original Language | First Published | Approximate Sales |
| A Brief History of Time | | Stephen Hawking | English | 1988 | 10 million |

**13.** You've probably noticed that by default, DataTables is sorting our table by the first column in the ascending order, from A to Z. This might be fine in some cases, but in this case, since we're listing the all-time bestselling books, we probably want to sort the table to show the books with the highest sales first. We'll pass in a new key/value pair to specify which column should be used for the default sort and which direction the sort should go, as follows:

```
$(document).ready(function(){
  $('#book-grid').dataTable({
    'jQueryUI': true,
    'searching': false,
    'order': [[4, 'desc']]
  });
});
```

The key we're using is called `order`, and the value is the column number and sort direction inside two sets of square brackets. Don't forget that JavaScript starts counting at zero, not one. So the fifth column in our table is actually column 4. Then, we want the highest number at the top, so we pass `desc` for the descending order.

Refresh the page in the browser and you'll see that the books are now in order from the highest sales to lowest sales. Also, note that this default sort order doesn't affect your site visitor's ability to sort the table by any of the other columns in any order they'd like. The site visitor can still interact with your table. We're just redefining the default view in a way that makes the most sense for the data we're presenting.

## What just happened?

We took our basic data grid and took it a step further by customizing the appearance and behavior of the plugin. We learned how to use the jQuery UI ThemeRoller to create a custom theme for our data grid. Then, we learned how to disable searching the table and how to set a default sort for the data grid.

## Pop quiz – building correct tables

Q1. What is the correct order of elements in a table?

1. `thead, tbody, tfoot`.
2. `tbody, thead, tfoot`.
3. `thead, tfoot, tbody`.
4. `tfoot, thead, tbody`.

# Showing graphs and charts

In some cases, a table is the ideal way of presenting a set of data. At other times, it would be more helpful to see that data visualized as a chart or a graph. Unfortunately, charts and graphs can be challenging to present in HTML. Without the help of JavaScript, we are stuck using static images to present graphs, which can then be difficult to update when the data changes.

This is when jQuery comes to the rescue. In this section, we'll take a look at using the Visualize plugin to turn tables of data into graphs and charts. The best part is that site visitors without JavaScript enabled will still have access to the data in the form of an HTML table, so nobody misses out on what we're trying to share. The data also remains accessible for those who visit our page and who might have visual impairment or other disabilities that would prevent them from consuming the data if it were presented in a static image.

## Time for action – showing data in graphs and charts

Perform the following steps to create graphs and charts from HTML tables:

1. We'll get started as usual with our basic HTML file and associated files and folders, just like we did in *Chapter 1, Designer, Meet jQuery*. Inside the `<body>` element of the HTML document, we'll include a heading and a table with some numerical data, as follows:

```
<div class="content">
  <h1>A Mad Tea-Party</h1>
</div>
```

```
<table id="menu">
  <caption>Menu Items</caption>
  <thead>
    <tr>
      <td>Title</td>
      <th scope="col">Total Items</th>
    </tr>
  </thead>
  <tbody>
    <tr>
      <th scope="row">Scones</th>
      <td>23</td>
    </tr>
    <tr>
      <th scope="row">Tea Sandwiches</th>
      <td>18</td>
    </tr>
    <tr>
      <th scope="row">Pastries</th>
      <td>19</td>
    </tr>
    <tr>
      <th scope="row">Tea</th>
      <td>28</td>
    </tr>
  </tbody>
</table>
```

Note that just as with the data table example, we're careful to use the correct markup for our table, wrapping the header row in a `<thead>` element, and the body of the table in a `<tbody>` element. Additionally, we've included the scope attribute on all the `<th>` elements to specify whether they apply to the column or the row in which they are placed. Notice also that we included an id attribute for the table to make it easy to select with jQuery later.

2.  Next, we'll include some CSS to style the table. Open your `styles.css` file and add the following lines of code:

```
table {
  border-collapse: collapse;
  margin: 2.531em 0;
}

td, th {
```

```
    background: white;
    border: 1px solid #ddd;
    color: #444;
    padding: 0.5em 1em;
    text-align: left;
}

thead th, thead td {
    background-color: #a1d36e;
    border-color: #8dc059;
}

caption {
    margin: 0 0 0.5em 0;
}

caption {
    font-size: 1.5em;
}
```

Feel free to adjust these styles to suit your own tastes. Now, if we view the page in a browser, we see a nicely styled table, as shown in the following screenshot:

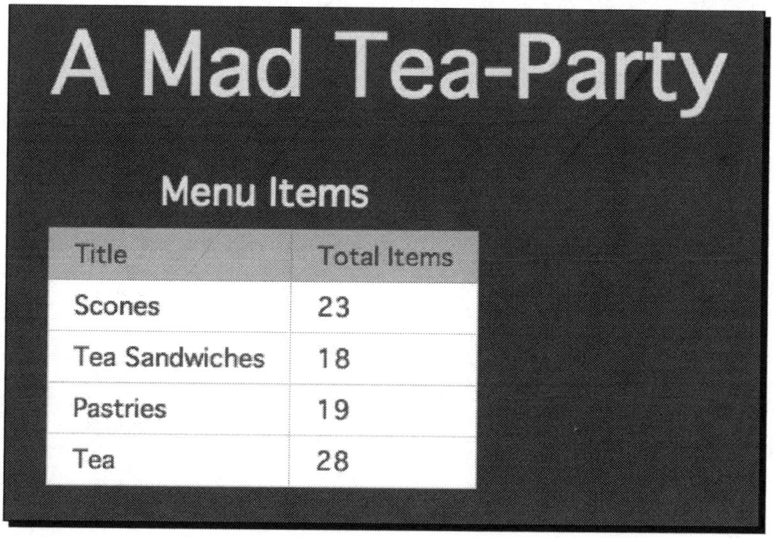

This table effectively communicates our data, and is accessible to anyone who might visit the page, no matter what their abilities or the capabilities of their device and browser are. However, we can progressively enhance the experience.

**3.** The files for the jQuery Visualize plugin itself are available on GitHub at `https://github.com/filamentgroup/jQuery-Visualize`. Click on the **Download ZIP** button to grab a copy of the files.

 While the Visualize plugin and the examples are available for download at GitHub, the documentation for the plugin can be found on the Filament Group's website at `http://filamentgroup.com/lab/update_to_ jquery_visualize_accessible_charts_with_html5_from_ designing_with/`.

**4.** Unzip the downloaded file. Inside, you'll find some example files, images, CSS, and the necessary JavaScript files.

Inside the `js` folder, find the `visualize.jQuery.js` file and copy and paste it to your own `scripts` folder. Inside the `css` folder, find the `visualize.css` file and copy that to your own `styles` folder. In addition to this CSS file, which includes the basic styles needed to display the charts and graphs, you'll also need to choose one of the color scheme files. Visualize comes with both a dark and light color scheme. We'll go with the light color scheme for this example, so also copy `visualize-light.css` to your own `styles` folder.

**5.** In your `index.html` file, attach the `visualize.jQuery.js` file at the bottom after jQuery but before your own `scripts.js` file, as follows:

```
<script src="scripts/jquery.js"></script>
<script src="scripts/visualize.jQuery.js"></script>
<script src="scripts/scripts.js"></script>
</body>
</html>
```

In the `<head>` section of the document, attach the `visualize.css` file as well as our color scheme styles, before your own `styles.css` file, as shown in the following code:

```
<title>Chapter 10: Charts and Graphs</title>
<link rel="stylesheet" href="styles/visualize.css">
<link rel="stylesheet" href="styles/visualize-light.css">
<link rel="stylesheet" href="styles/styles.css">
</head>
```

**6.** Next, open your `scripts.js` file so we can write some JavaScript. Get started by adding the document ready statement, as follows:

```
$(document).ready(function(){
  // Our code will go here
});
```

the table element that contains our data, and call the `visualize()` method:

```
cument).ready(function(){
'#menu').visualize();
```

resh the page in the browser, and you'll see that a graph has been inserted after
table in the document, as shown in the following screenshot:

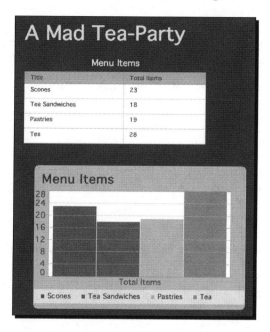

The `<caption>` tag for the table is repurposed as the title of the graph. The text we
included in the table's `<th>` elements are used as labels for the data in the graph.

The chart works and accurately represents our data, but it doesn't fit our design very
well. Let's take a look at how we can customize the appearance of the chart.

8.  Just like several other jQuery plugins we've used so far, the Visualize plugin includes
    several options we can use to customize the charts and graphs it creates. First up,
    we can specify a set `width` and `height` for the graph:

```
$('#menu').visualize({
  width: '460px',
  height: '205px'
});
```

**9.** Next, we can specify what colors should be used for each of the bars in our chart with the colors option. The colors option accepts an array of colors. Remember that an array is just a collection. Specifying an array of colors looks like this:

```
$('#menu').visualize({
  width: '460px',
  height: '205px',
  colors: ['#e75845','#967dd9','#8dc059','#42b0d8']
});
```

We'll wrap the array, or collection of colors, in square brackets [...]. Each color value is wrapped in quotes and a comma separates each color value.

**10.** We can also specify the amount of space between each bar in the chart with the barMargin option. Let's add some extra white space around each bar in the chart, as follows:

```
$('#menu').visualize({
  width: '460px',
  height: '205px',
  colors: ['#e75845','#967dd9','#8dc059','#42b0d8'],
  barMargin: 20
});
```

Now, refresh the page in the browser and you'll see our customizations take effect, as shown in the following screenshot:

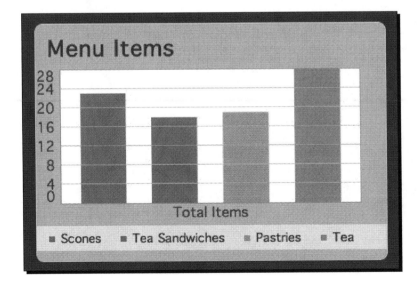

**11.** We can customize our graph even further by modifying the CSS code. In the `<head>` section of `index.html`, remove the `visualize-light.css` file, as follows:

```
<title>Chapter 10: Charts and Graphs</title>
<link rel="stylesheet" href="styles/visualize.css">
<link rel="stylesheet" href="styles/styles.css">
</head>
```

Rather than using the style as provided to us with the plugin, we'll write our own CSS file. This is often an option with jQuery plugins. Just use the provided CSS file as a guide for creating your own.

**12.** Open your `styles.css` file. We'll get started with some general styles for the graph container. Add the following styles:

```
.visualize {
  margin: 3.797em 0;
  padding: 3.797em 2.531em 5.695em;
  background: white;
  -moz-border-radius: 3px;
  -webkit-border-radius: 3px;
  border-radius: 3px;
}


.visualize canvas {
  border: 1px solid #aaa;
  margin: -1px;
  background: #fff;
}
```

**13.** Next up, we'll add some custom styles for the labels that appear on the graph, as follows:

```
.visualize-labels-x,
.visualize-labels-y {
  font-size: 0.75em;
  left: 30px;
  top: 70px;
  z-index: 100;
}


.visualize-pie .visualize-labels {
  left: 40px;
  position: absolute;
  top: 70px;
}
```

```
.visualize-labels-x li span.label,
.visualize-labels-y li span.label {
  color: #444;
  padding-right: 5px;
}
```

**14.** Now, we'll add some styles for the lines, graph information, and the graph title, as follows:

```
.visualize-labels-y li span.line {
  border-style: solid;
  opacity: .7;
}


.visualize .visualize-info {
  background: none;
  border: 0;
  opacity: 1;
  position: static;
}


.visualize .visualize-title {
  color: #333;
  font-size: 1.688em;
  font-weight: bold;
  left: 20px;
  margin-bottom: 0;
  position: absolute;
  right: 20px;
  text-align: center;
  top: 20px;
}
```

**15.** Finally, we'll add some styles for the key:

```
.visualize ul.visualize-key {
  background: #efefef;
  bottom: 1em;
  color: #aaa;
  left: 0;
  padding: 0.75em;
  position: absolute;
  right: 0;
  z-index: 10;
}
```

```
.visualize ul.visualize-key li {
  float: left;
}

.visualize ul.visualize-key .visualize-key-color {
  display: inline-block;
  height: 1em;
  margin: 0 0.25em 0 0;
  position: static;
  vertical-align: baseline;
  width: 1em;
}

.visualize ul.visualize-key .visualize-key-label {
  color: #333;
}
```

Now, refresh the page in the browser, and you'll see that our graph is completely customized and matches the design of our page perfectly. Have a look at the following screenshot:

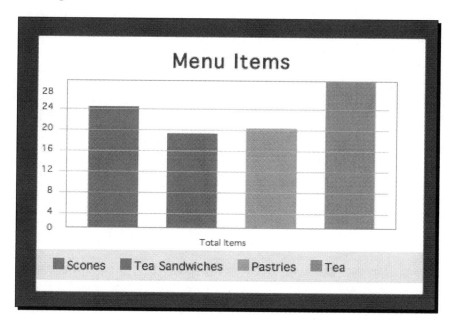

## What just happened?

We used the jQuery Visualize plugin to take data in an HTML table and present it as a graph on the page. The `<caption>` tag for the table is repurposed as the title of the graph, and the table headings that we included in the table's `<th>` elements repurposed for the labels of the data points in the graph. We saw how we could customize various options in the graph and how we could further customize the graph by writing our own CSS code to style the assorted components of the graph. Now, let's take a look at how we can do even more with the charts and graphs generated by the Visualize plugin.

## Creating pie charts

We've already taken a look at some of the options available to us with the jQuery Visualize plugin, but there's even more we can do. In this section, we'll take a look at how we can use the plugin to create pie charts.

## Time for action – creating a pie chart

We'll keep working with the files we set up in the previous section. Perform the following steps to create a pie chart with the Visualize plugin:

1.  Inside the HTML file, add a second HTML table that contains some data, as shown in the following code:

    ```
    <table id="eaten">
      <caption>Who had what?</caption>
      <thead>
        <tr>
          <td> </td>
          <th scope="col">Scones</th>
          <th scope="col">Tea Sandwiches</th>
          <th scope="col">Pastries</th>
          <th scope="col">Tea</th>
        </tr>
      </thead>
      <tbody>
        <tr>
          <th scope="row">Alice</th>
          <td>1</td>
          <td>3</td>
          <td>1</td>
          <td>2</td>
        </tr>
        <tr>
          <th scope="row">Mad Hatter</th>
          <td>0</td>
          <td>6</td>
    ```

```
        <td>3</td>
        <td>1</td>
      </tr>
      <tr>
        <th scope="row">Dormouse</th>
        <td>1</td>
        <td>6</td>
        <td>0</td>
        <td>3</td>
      </tr>
      <tr>
        <th scope="row">March Hare</th>
        <td>2</td>
        <td>3</td>
        <td>2</td>
        <td>1</td>
      </tr>
    </tbody>
</table>
```

Just like last time, we've been careful to use appropriate table markup, and have included `<thead>`, `<tbody>`, and `<th>` elements where appropriate. This time, our dataset is a bit more complex, including multiple columns as well as rows of data. Refresh the page in the browser to view the new table, as shown in the following screenshot:

| Who had what? | | | | |
| --- | --- | --- | --- | --- |
| | Scones | Tea Sandwiches | Pastries | Tea |
| Alice | 1 | 3 | 1 | 2 |
| Mad Hatter | 0 | 6 | 3 | 1 |
| Dormouse | 1 | 6 | 0 | 3 |
| March Hare | 2 | 3 | 2 | 1 |

2. Next, open your `scripts.js` file. Inside the document ready statement, select the new table and call the `visualize()` method, as follows:

```
$(document).ready(function(){
  $('#menu').visualize({
    ...
  });

  $('#eaten').visualize();
});
```

**3.** Now, we'll pass some options to the new chart, as shown in the following code. First up, let's specify that we want to work with a pie chart this time, rather than a bar graph.

```
$('#eaten').visualize({
  type: 'pie'
});
```

The Visualize plugin includes four options for graph and chart types: bar, pie, line, and area.

**4.** We'll set a width and height for the pie chart, and include a set of colors to be used for the segments of the pie, as follows:

```
$('#eaten').visualize({
  type: 'pie',
  width: '460px',
  height: '205px',
  colors: ['#e75845','#967dd9','#8dc059','#42b0d8']
});
```

Refresh the page in the browser, and you'll see our pie chart displayed after the second table, as shown in the following screenshot:

**5.** However, what if we don't want to display both the table and the chart? If our site visitor has JavaScript enabled, then we want to hide the table and display just the chart. Site visitors without JavaScript enabled will just see the table. The following code shows how we can do that:

```
$('#eaten').addClass('accessHide').visualize({
  type: 'pie',
  width: '460px',
  height: '205px',
  colors: ['#e75845','#967dd9','#8dc059','#42b0d8']
});
```

We just add another method to our chain. The CSS file included with the Visualize plugin includes a CSS class called accessHide, which positions our table off the screen. The data included in the table is still accessible to screen readers, but won't be seen within the page. Refresh the page in the browser and you'll see that the table is no longer visible—we just see the pie chart, as shown in the following screenshot:

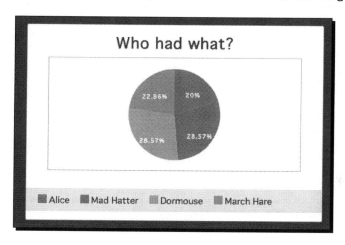

**6.** Our pie chart looks nice, but it's a wee bit on the small side. Let's decrease the white space around the pie chart. We can do that using the pieMargin option, as shown in the following code:

```
$('#eaten').addClass('accessHide').visualize({
  type: 'pie',
  width: '460px',
  height: '205px',
  colors: ['#e75845','#967dd9','#8dc059','#42b0d8'],
  pieMargin: 10
});
```

Now, refresh the page in the browser and you'll see that the white space around the pie chart is reduced. Take a look at the following screenshot:

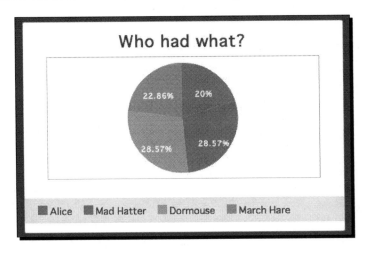

This helps our pie chart to appear a tad bigger. The default setting is 20 pixels, so we've cut that in half by setting it to 10.

7.  So far, we've only placed our chart either directly after or in place of our table. However, we can also move the chart around the page, and display it wherever we wish. Let's add a few paragraphs of text beneath the HTML tables in the `index.html` file:

```
<div class="content">
  <p>
    There was a table set out under a tree in front of
    the house, and the March Hare and the Hatter were
    having tea at it: a Dormouse was sitting between them,
    fast asleep, and the other two were using it as a
    cushion, resting their elbows on it, and talking over
    its head. &lsquo;Very uncomfortable for the
    Dormouse,&rsquo; thought Alice; &lsquo;only,
    as it&apos;s asleep, I suppose it doesn&apos;t mind.&rsquo;
  </p>
  <p>
    The table was a large one, but the three were all crowded
    together at one corner of it: &lsquo;
    No room! No room!&rsquo; they cried out when
    they saw Alice coming. &lsquo;There&apos;s
    PLENTY of room!&rsquo; said Alice indignantly,
    and she sat down in a large
    arm-chair at one end of the table.</p>
  ...
</div>
```

**8.** Somewhere inside the block of text, we'll place a `<div>` element that will act as a placeholder for our chart, as follows:

```
<div class="content">
  <p>
    There was a ...
  </p>
  <div id="pie-container" class="chart left"></div>
  <p>
    The table was ...</p>
  ...
</div>
```

We'd like to display our pie chart inside this `<div>` element. If the `<div>` element has no content, then it collapses to zero width and zero height, taking up no space in our HTML document.

**9.** Next, open your `styles.css` file and add some styles for the newly created `<div>` element, as follows:

```
.chart.left {
  float: left;
  margin: 0 1em 0.5em 0;
}

.chart.right {
  float: right;
  margin: 0 0 0.5em 1em;
}
```

**10.** Now, inside the `scripts.js` file, we'll use jQuery's `appendTo()` method to move the newly generated pie chart to the `<div>` element we just created, as shown in the following code. After moving the chart, we do have to trigger a refresh.

```
$('#eaten').addClass('accessHide').visualize({
  type: 'pie',
  width: '460px',
  height: '205px',
  colors: ['#e75845','#967dd9','#8dc059','#42b0d8'],
  pieMargin: 10
}).appendTo('#pie-container').trigger('visualizeRefresh');
```

We've selected the `id` attribute of the `<div>` element to move our chart there. Then, we used the `trigger()` method and passed it `visualRefresh` to ensure that our chart displays correctly.

Refresh the page in the browser, and you'll see that rather than appearing at the top of the document, the pie chart is now displayed inside our text block, as shown in the following screenshot:

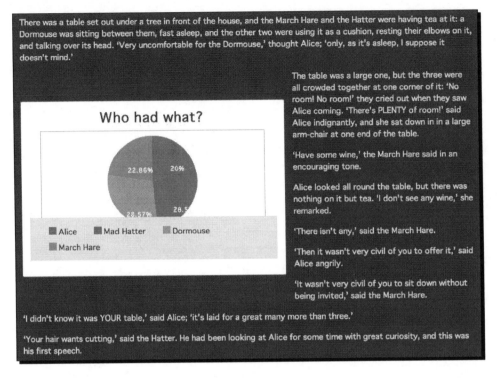

We're getting closer, but our pie chart needs a bit of style adjustment. Now that we're trying to include it inside a text area, the large margins we specified above and below the chart don't work. Also, the style of the key and labels seems a bit off.

**11.** Open up `styles.css`. First, we'll add a bit of CSS to remove those large top and bottom margins if the pie chart appears inside a block of text:

```
.chart .visualize {
  margin: 0;
}
```

**12.** The misalignment of the pie chart's labels and key are because of some styles set for our text block that are interfering with the styles set for the pie chart. Just add a bit of CSS code to override those, as shown in the following code snippet:

```
.chart .visualize ul {
  margin: 0;
}
```

Now, if you refresh the page in the browser, you'll see that the pie chart is displayed as expected, and is seamlessly integrated into our block of text:

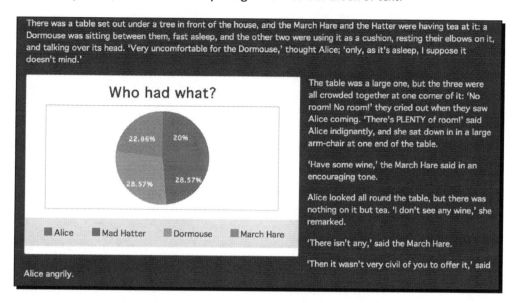

## Using charts and graphs in responsive designs

We've learned how to create charts and graphs to represent tabular data, but if you've tried resizing your browser window, you would have likely noticed that the size of the charts and graphs remains fixed, making them less than ideal for use in responsive designs. While we can't make the charts and graphs completely fluid, we can detect the ideal width and height based on our browser window's width, and adjust accordingly.

## Time for action – calculating the ideal size for charts and graphs

We'll keep working with the files we created in the previous section. Perform the following steps to dynamically set the width and height of our charts and graphs according to the width of the browser window:

1. Open your `scripts.js` file. We'll want to add a few quick calculations. First up, let's set a preferred width for our graphs and charts, as follows:

```
$(document).ready(function(){
    var preferredWidth = 450;
```

```
$('#menu').visualize({
   ...
});

$('#eaten').addClass('accessHide').visualize({
   ...
}).appendTo('#pie-container').trigger('visualizeRefresh');

});
```

We created a variable named `preferredWidth`. Recall that a variable is just a container—in this case, the variable contains the size in pixels that we'd like our charts and graphs to appear by default.

2. Next, we need to get the actual width of the available content area on our page. As our CSS code is fluid, this will change depending on the width of the browser window. The exact element you use to calculate this will change depending on what your HTML markup looks like. In this case, we can use the width of the paragraphs inside the text block, as shown in the following code:

```
$(document).ready(function(){
  var preferredWidth = 450,
    contentWidth = $('.content p:first').width() - 83;


  $('#menu').visualize({
     ...
  });

  $('#eaten').addClass('accessHide').visualize({
     ...
  }).appendTo('#pie-container').trigger('visualizeRefresh');
});
```

We're selecting the first paragraph in the text block, and getting its width. Then, because the graphs have a considerable amount of padding around them, we're subtracting 83 pixels from that width to allow for the padding.

3. Now that we've got both the `preferredWidth` variable and the actual content width, it's just a simple matter of comparing the two to calculate the correct width. Take a look at the following code:

```
$(document).ready(function(){
  var preferredWidth = 450,
    contentWidth = $('.content p:first').width() - 83,
    finalWidth = (preferredWidth > contentWidth) ?
      contentWidth : preferredWidth;
```

```
$('#menu').visualize({
   ...
});

$('#eaten').addClass('accessHide').visualize({
   ...
}).appendTo('#pie-container').trigger('visualizeRefresh');
});
```

We've seen this type of statement before. Recall that this is called a **ternary operator**. First, we're comparing our `preferredWidth` variable with our `contentWidth` variable to see which is wider. If the `preferredWidth` variable is wider, then we want to set the `finalWidth` variable equal to `contentWidth`—as `preferredWidth` is too wide for our page. Otherwise, we can use our `preferredWidth`.

4. Next, we need to calculate the height of the charts and graphs. We'll make it half the width, as follows:

```
$(document).ready(function(){
  var preferredWidth = 450,
    contentWidth = $('.content p:first').width() - 83,
    finalWidth = (preferredWidth > contentWidth) ?
      contentWidth : preferredWidth,
    finalHeight = finalWidth/2 + 'px';


  $('#menu').visualize({
     ...
  });

  $('#eaten').addClass('accessHide').visualize({
     ...
  }).appendTo('#pie-container').trigger('visualizeRefresh');
});
```

5. We just have to add the measurement to the end of the `finalWidth` variable, as follows:

```
$(document).ready(function(){
  var preferredWidth = 450,
    contentWidth = $('.content p:first').width() - 83,
    finalWidth = (preferredWidth > contentWidth) ?
      contentWidth : preferredWidth,
    finalHeight = finalWidth/2 + 'px',
    finalWidth += 'px';
```

```
$('#menu').visualize({
    ...
});

$('#eaten').addClass('accessHide').visualize({
    ...
}).appendTo('#pie-container').trigger('visualizeRefresh');
});
```

6. Now that we've calculated the best possible value for the width and height of our charts, we just have to insert those values as the `width` and `height` options inside each `visualize()` method:

```
$('#menu').visualize({
    width: finalWidth,
    height: finalHeight,
    colors: ['#e75845','#967dd9','#8dc059','#42b0d8'],
    barMargin: 20
});

$('#eaten').addClass('accessHide').visualize({
    type: 'pie',
    width: finalWidth,
    height: finalHeight,
    colors: ['#e75845','#967dd9','#8dc059','#42b0d8'],
    pieMargin: 10
}).appendTo('#pie-container').trigger('visualizeRefresh');
```

7. If you refresh the page in the browser, you'll see that the charts and graphs resize to best fit in the available area, as shown in the following screenshot:

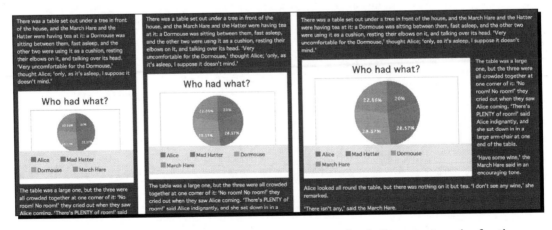

If you resize the browser window, you'll have to refresh the page in order for the charts and graphs to recalculate their sizes. It's not quite as fluid as responsive designs typically are, but it's much nicer than just allowing the charts and graphs to always appear the same size.

## *What just happened?*

While we can't make our charts and graphs as fluid as other elements on the page in a responsive design, we can improve the experience a bit by calculating the best possible size for the charts and graphs when the page is first loaded into the browser. We learned how to compare our preferred width with the actual width available for displaying the charts and graphs and set the correct value for both the width and height accordingly. It's not a perfect solution to displaying charts and graphs in a responsive design, but it's a big improvement over always displaying the charts and graphs at a single fixed size, regardless of the window width.

# Summary

In this chapter, we learned how to turn an ordinary HTML table into an interactive data grid. Our site visitors can now take advantage of sorting different columns of the table to view the data in different ways. Site visitors with JavaScript disabled simply see an ordinary HTML table that contains all of the data. Data grids aren't terribly exciting, but they can make dealing with large amounts of data worlds easier for your site visitors. We also took a look at how to display numerical tabular data in charts and graphs, adding visual interest to our pages. Next up, we'll take a look at using scrolling effects in our pages, including parallax effects.

# 11
# Reacting to Scrolling

*We can create some fun effects by reacting to our site visitors when they scroll up/down through our pages. As they scroll down the page, we can create parallax effects, animate various elements on the page, and trigger other changes on the page as well. This helps our pages to feel dynamic and alive—we can turn the simple act of scrolling through a page to read the content into an interactive one.*

In this chapter, we will:

- Set up an HTML document (page) divided into sections
- Create a parallax effect in one of the sections on the page
- Trigger an animation in one of the sections on the page
- Add and activate navigation for the page that also reacts to scrolling

## Setting up the document

The first step in creating a page with scrolling effects is to plan an HTML page divided into clear sections. In this example, we're going to set up a weather forecast—each day or night will be one block with its own icon, text, and background.

# Time for action – setting up the HTML file

Perform the following steps to set up an HTML document that is ideal for adding the scrolling effects:

**1.** We'll get started as usual with our basic HTML file and associated files and folders, just like we did in *Chapter 1, Designer, Meet jQuery*. Note that because we're going to be creating several full-width sections, the CSS file for this chapter is slightly modified from the starting CSS file we used in the previous chapters. You'll find the correct version of the CSS file in the code samples for the book.

Inside the HTML document, we'll create a series of the `<section>` elements, each of which will contain the day or night, an icon, and a short weather forecast. To do this, take a look at the following code:

```
<section class="scrollblock" id="monday">
  <div class="day">Monday</div>
  <div class="forecast">72&deg; Sunny</div>
  <div class="icon"><img src="images/Sun.svg" alt
    ="Sunny" width="300" height="300"></div>
</section>

<section class="scrollblock" id="moneve">
  <div class="day">Monday evening</div>
  <div class="forecast">62&deg; Clear</div>
  <div class="icon"><img src="images/Moon.svg" alt
    ="Clear" width="300" height="300"></div>
</section>

<section class="scrollblock" id="tueday">
  <div class="day">Tuesday</div>
  <div class="forecast">67&deg; Cloudy</div>
  <div class="icon"><img src="images/Cloud.svg" alt
    ="Cloudy" width="300" height="300"></div>
</section>

<section class="scrollblock" id="tueeve">
  <div class="day">Tuesday evening</div>
  <div class="forecast">58&deg; Rainy</div>
  <div class="icon"><img src
    ="images/Cloud-Drizzle-Moon.svg" alt
    ="Rainy Night" width="300" height="300"></div>
</section>

<section class="scrollblock" id="wedday">
  <div class="day">Wednesday</div>
```

```
    <div class="forecast">69&deg; Windy</div>
    <div class="icon" id="wind"><img src
      ="images/Cloud-Wind.svg" alt
      ="Cloudy Windy" width="300" height="300"></div>
  </section>

  <section class="scrollblock" id="wedeve">
    <div class="day">Wednesday evening</div>
    <div class="forecast">57&deg; Clearing</div>
    <div class="icon"><img src
      ="images/Cloud-Fog-Moon.svg" alt
      ="Clearing" width="300" height="300"></div>
  </section>
```

Note that every `<section>` element has the class `scrollblock`, but every element also has a unique `id` attribute, which will help us to target just the block with either JavaScript or CSS.

The code samples provided with the book use the excellent Climacons from Adam Whitcroft, which are available for download at `http://adamwhitcroft.com/climacons/`. I'm using the `.svg` format in this tutorial—if your browser doesn't yet support SVG images, you'll need to use the source files provided by Adam Whitcroft to create `.png` files.

2. Next, we'll add some styles. Open your `styles.css` file and get started by adding some general styles for the page and for each of our forecast blocks, as follows:

```
html, body {
  height: 100%;
}

.scrollblock {
  left: 0;
  min-height: 28.833em;
  position: relative;
  right: 0;
}

.day {
  font-size: 2.25em;
  left: 1em;
  position: absolute;
  top: 1em;
}
```

```
.forecast {
  bottom: 1em;
  font-size: 2.25em;
  position: absolute;
  right: 1em;
}

.icon {
  left: 50%;
  position: absolute;
  top: 50%;
}

.icon img {
  margin: -50% 0 0 -50%;
}
```

These styles set up a minimum height for each block, then position the day, icon, and forecast within each block. If you look at our page in the browser, you'll see that the elements are in place, as shown in the following screenshot:

The page is shaping up, but we don't have any visual divide between the different sections on the page. Let's take care of that in the next steps.

3.  In `styles.css`, let's add a different background color to each section of the forecast, as follows:

```
#monday {
  background: #7ec0ee;
}

#moneve {
  background: #003366;
}
```

```
#tueday {
  background: #999;
}

#tueeve {
  background: #333;
}

#wedday {
  background: #6a93b1;
}

#wedeve {
  background: #003366;
}
```

Now, it's easier to see the separation between the blocks as you scroll down through the page.

**4.** In addition to the background colors, let's also add background images to some of the blocks, as follows:

```
#moneve {
  background: #003366 url(../images/starrysky.jpg)
    50% 50% / cover fixed no-repeat;
}

#tueday {
  background: #999 url(../images/cloudysky.jpg)
    50% 50% / cover fixed no-repeat;
}

#wedeve {
  background: #003366 url(../images/sunset.jpg)
    50% 50% / cover fixed no-repeat;
}
```

We're using the shorthand for backgrounds here. Recall that writing out all the background values on one line is just a shorthand way of writing them out individually, as shown in the following code snippet:

```
#moneve {
  background-color: #003366;
  background-image: url(../images/starrysky.jpg);
  background-position: 50% 50%;
  background-size: cover;
```

```
    background-attachment: fixed;
    background-repeat: no-repeat;
}
```

There is one new property that you might not recognize: `background-size`. This is a newly-provided background property introduced by CSS3. We can specify either a fixed size for our background image, such as `100px`, or we can use `cover` to indicate that the background image should cover the entire area. You can read up on the new `background-size` property at CSS3.info (`http://www.css3.info/preview/background-size/`).

If you refresh the page in the browser, you'll see that every section is nicely separated from the others by its background color or image, and the images have a nice effect as we scroll down the page—thanks to the combination of `background-size: cover` with `background-attachment: fixed`.

## What just happened?

We set up our HTML document and got it ready to add some snazzy scrolling effects. We added a different background color or image to each block of our weather forecast and used the new CSS `background-size: cover` property along with `background-attachment: fixed` to create a nice background scrolling effect even for those site visitors who have JavaScript disabled. Next, we'll look at adding a parallax scrolling effect to one of the sections on the page.

## Setting up HTML for scrolling animations

Now that we have our HTML set up, it's time to start getting things ready to add animations. We'll be using the Scrollorama plugin from John Polacek. We just have some preliminary work to do before we get ready to add in our fancy effects.

## Time for action – setting up HTML for Scrollorama

Perform the following steps to get the page set up to add scrolling animations:

1. Head over to `http://johnpolacek.github.io/scrollorama/`. You'll find a link to download a ZIP file right near the top of the page, but feel free to take a moment to scroll down the page to see demos of the different types of animations that are possible. When you're done, go ahead and download the file and unzip it.

   Inside, you'll find a couple of sample CSS style sheets, a sample `index.html` file, a README file, a `.json` file, and some JavaScripts. The JavaScripts include jQuery itself, the Scrollorama plugin, and the Lettering.js plugin. Yep, this is the same Lettering.js plugin that we used in *Chapter 9*, *Improving Typography*. In this case, the plugin's author, John Polacek, used it to create animations on individual letters in the samples provided with the plugin.

   The only file we'll need here is `jquery.scrollorama.js`. Go ahead and copy it to your own `scripts` folder.

2. Next, at the bottom of your HTML file, attach the Scrollorama plugin after jQuery but before your own `scripts.js` file, as follows:

   ```
   <script src="scripts/jquery.js"></script>
   <script src="scripts/jquery.scrollorama.js"></script>
   <script src="scripts/scripts.js"></script>
   ```

3. We'll implement our reliable class-switching trick to apply different CSS to the page, whether or not JavaScript is enabled. In the HTML file, add a `class` attribute of `jsOff` to the `<html>` element, as shown in the following code:

   ```
   <!DOCTYPE html>
   <html class="jsOff">
   <head>
   ```

4. Then, in your `scripts.js` file, add the document ready statement:

```
$(document).ready(function() {
  // Our code goes here
});
```

5. Inside the document ready statement, remove the `jsOff` class and add a `jsOn` class instead, as follows:

```
$(document).ready(function() {

  /* CSS classes for JS state */
  $('html').removeClass('jsOff').addClass('jsOn');

});
```

   Notice that we've included a comment before the line of text we just added. Our JavaScript file will ultimately contain quite a bit of code, so we need to write little notes to ourselves or to any other developer who might work on this file about what each bit of the code does.

6. Next, we'll make each block of our weather forecast the same height as the window. If our site visitor has a large screen, we should take advantage of it to really showcase our animations. If they have a smaller screen, we'll want to adjust to ensure that the forecast fits nicely without a lot of extra scrolling required. First, we have to calculate the height of the window. Later on, we'll also need the width of the window, so we'll go ahead and measure it now, as shown in the following code:

```
  /* CSS classes for JS state */
  $('html').removeClass('jsOff').addClass('jsOn');

  /* Vars that we'll need */
  var win = $(window),
    winHeight = win.height(),
    winWidth = win.width();
```

   If we're setting up more than one variable, then we can just separate them with commas, and we don't have to keep typing `var` repeatedly.

   First, we set up a variable for the window since we're using it twice—once to get the width and once to get the height. Next, we use jQuery's `height()` method to quickly grab the window's height and jQuery's `width()` method to grab the width. Now, we have these values safely stored away for easy use later on in our code.

**7.** We'll select each block of our weather forecast and set its height to the height of the window, as follows:

```
/* Vars that we'll need */
var win = $(window),
  winHeight = win.height(),
  winWidth = win.width();

/* Set each block to window height */
$('.scrollblock').css('height', winHeight);
```

Each block has a class of `scrollblock`, so we use this to select the all the blocks. Then, we use jQuery's `css()` method to set the height of each block.

## What just happened?

We downloaded the Scrollorama plugin and attached it to our page. Then, we did some initial setting up of our document and JavaScript in order to get ready to add animation effects. We used our handy class-switching trick to enable us to style the page with different CSS, depending on whether or not JavaScript is enabled. Then, we selected each block of our weather forecast and set the height to the height of the window. If you scroll through the page now, you'll see that each block is equal to the height of the window.

## Adding a parallax effect

If you look out of the window while riding in a car or a train, you'll notice that the grass and trees that are closer to you seem to go by much faster than the trees or mountains that are further away from you. There's a complex body of geometry that explains this effect, but luckily, we don't have to dig into that in great detail to be able to recreate this effect on our web pages.

As we scroll down the page, the elements on the page will go by at the speed that our site visitor is scrolling. We can then react to that scrolling action to make other elements on the page appear to go by faster or slower than the page elements that are simply moving with the scroll.

This sounds complicated, but it's as simple as shifting the vertical position of elements within their container while scrolling. For example, if an element starts at the top of its container and then moves towards the bottom of the container while I scroll by, it will appear to be moving more slowly than the other elements on the page. Vice versa, if it moves from near the bottom to near the top, it will appear to go by more quickly than the other elements on the page.

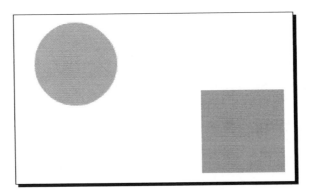

The circle will move with the page when it's scrolled as expected. The square will be animated towards the top of the page.

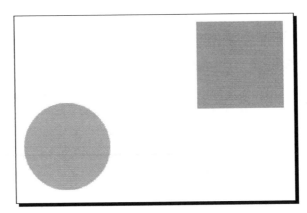

As we scroll by, we'll animate the position of the square so that it moves towards the top of the page. The square appears to move more quickly than the circle as we scroll.

We'll take advantage of this optical illusion to create three layers of clouds that will move by at different speeds as we scroll past our cloudy weather forecast on Tuesday. We'll reuse the same cloud icon that we used in the forecast—our site visitors will already have that asset loaded into their browser cache, so there's no extra download. Also, since we're using SVG, we can easily resize the icon to any size and it will remain crisp and clear.

# Time for action – creating a parallax effect

Perform the following steps to add a parallax effect to the cloudy weather forecast:

1. We'll get started by adding the layer of clouds that will appear to be furthest away. Inside the section of the cloudy forecast, add a `<div>` element and place several cloud icons inside it, as shown in the following code:

```
<section class="scrollblock" id="tueday">
  <div class="day">Tuesday</div>
  <div class="forecast">67&deg; Cloudy</div>
  <div class="icon"><img src="images/Cloud.svg" alt
    ="Cloudy" width="300" height="300"></div>

  <div class="cloud-layer" id="cloud-layer-back">
    <img src="images/Cloud.svg" alt="Cloudy" width
      ="100" height="100" id="bcloud1">
    <img src="images/Cloud.svg" alt="Cloudy" width
      ="150" height="150" id="bcloud2">
    <img src="images/Cloud.svg" alt="Cloudy" width
      ="125" height="125" id="bcloud3">
    <img src="images/Cloud.svg" alt="Cloudy" width
      ="112" height="112" id="bcloud4">
    <img src="images/Cloud.svg" alt="Cloudy" width
      ="75" height="75" id="bcloud5">
    <img src="images/Cloud.svg" alt="Cloudy" width
      ="140" height="140" id="bcloud6">
  </div>

</section>
```

2. In `styles.css`, add some styles to position the clouds so that they're scattered over the forecast block, as follows:

```
.cloud-layer {
  height: 100%;
  left: 0;
  position: absolute;
  top: 0;
  width: 100%;
}

.cloud-layer img {
  position: absolute;
}
```

```
#cloud-layer-back { opacity: .1; }
  #bcloud1 { top: 98%;  left: 10%; }
  #bcloud2 { top: 40%;  left: 85%; }
  #bcloud3 { top: 60%;  left: 30%; }
  #bcloud4 { top: 0%;   left: 45%; }
  #bcloud5 { top: 15%;  left: 5%; }
  #bcloud6 { top: 5%;   left: 65%; }
```

First, we absolutely position the `.cloud-layer` class and make it the same width and height as that of its parent. Next, we absolutely position all the images. Then, we select the entire back cloud layer and set the `opacity` to `.1`. Since these clouds are furthest away, it makes sense that they would be the smallest and faintest. Then, we specify percentage positions for each of the clouds inside the layer. We're using percentages because we're keeping responsive design in mind.

If you refresh the page in the browser, you'll see several faint and small cloud icons scattered over the forecast block, as shown in the following screenshot:

3.  Next, we'll add a middle layer. To do this, first add the block of HTML to add several cloud icons inside the cloudy forecast block, as follows:

```
<section class="scrollblock" id="tueday">
  <div class="day">Tuesday</div>
  <div class="forecast">67&deg; Cloudy</div>
  <div class="icon"><img src="images/Cloud.svg" alt="Cloudy"
width="300" height="300"></div>

  <div class="cloud-layer" id="cloud-layer-back">
    ...
  </div>

  <div class="cloud-layer" id="cloud-layer-mid">
```

```
<img src="images/Cloud.svg" alt="Cloudy" width
  ="150" height="150" id="mcloud1">
<img src="images/Cloud.svg" alt="Cloudy" width
  ="225" height="225" id="mcloud2">
<img src="images/Cloud.svg" alt="Cloudy" width
  ="188" height="188" id="mcloud3">
<img src="images/Cloud.svg" alt="Cloudy" width
  ="169" height="169" id="mcloud4">
<img src="images/Cloud.svg" alt="Cloudy" width
  ="113" height="113" id="mcloud5">
<img src="images/Cloud.svg" alt="Cloudy" width
  ="207" height="207" id="mcloud6">
</div>

</section>
```

Note that we're making these cloud icons just a bit bigger than the back layer. Since they're a bit closer, it makes sense that they'd appear to be a little larger.

**4.** Next, open up `styles.css` and add the styles to position these cloud icons:

```
#cloud-layer-mid { opacity: .5; }
  #mcloud1 { top: 2%;   left: 15%; }
  #mcloud2 { top: 60%;  left: 35%; }
  #mcloud3 { top: 40%;  left: 70%; }
  #mcloud4 { top: 90%;  left: 65%; }
  #mcloud5 { top: 80%;  left: 80%; }
  #mcloud6 { top: 40%;  left: 5%; }
```

We're setting the opacity of this layer to `.5` so that these clouds appear a bit brighter than the back layer. If you refresh the page in the browser, you'll see this new layer of clouds appear over the one we placed previously, as shown in the following screenshot:

Even though we haven't introduced any animation yet, you can still see how displaying the icons at different sizes and opacities lend a visual effect of depth.

5. Now, we'll add the final layer, the front layer of clouds. Add a block of HTML to your `index.html` file to display another set of cloud icons, as shown in the following code:

```
<section class="scrollblock" id="tueday">
  <div class="day">Tuesday</div>
  <div class="forecast">67&deg; Cloudy</div>
  <div class="icon"><img src="images/Cloud.svg" alt
    ="Cloudy" width="300" height="300"></div>

  <div class="cloud-layer" id="cloud-layer-back">
   ...
  </div>

  <div class="cloud-layer" id="cloud-layer-mid">
   ...
  </div>

  <div class="cloud-layer" id="cloud-layer-front">
    <img src="images/Cloud.svg" alt="Cloudy" width
      ="200" height="200" id="fcloud1">
    <img src="images/Cloud.svg" alt="Cloudy" width
      ="300" height="300" id="fcloud2">
    <img src="images/Cloud.svg" alt="Cloudy" width
      ="250" height="250" id="fcloud3">
    <img src="images/Cloud.svg" alt="Cloudy" width
      ="225" height="225" id="fcloud4">
    <img src="images/Cloud.svg" alt="Cloudy" width
      ="150" height="150" id="fcloud5">
    <img src="images/Cloud.svg" alt="Cloudy" width
      ="275" height="275" id="fcloud6">
  </div>
</section>
```

As this layer of clouds will appear to be closest, we've made these even larger than the middle layer.

6. Next, open `styles.css` and position the cloud icons on this layer, as follows:

```
#cloud-layer-front { opacity: .9; }
  #fcloud1 { top: 50%;  left: 60%; }
  #fcloud2 { top: 10%;  left: 5%; }
  #fcloud3 { top: 0;    left: 85%; }
```

```
#fcloud4 { top: 5%;    left: 30%; }
#fcloud5 { top: 60%;   left: 20%; }
#fcloud6 { top: 90%;   left: 40%; }
```

As these clouds are closest, we've set the `opacity` to `.9` to make these the brightest clouds. Refresh the page in the browser to see the effect of all three layers of clouds, as shown in the following screenshot:

Now that we've got a very nice cloud effect that has a visual depth to it, let's make those clouds move.

7.  Open your `scripts.js` file. First, we have to tell Scrollorama that we want to use it and what our blocks of content are called. Inside the document ready statement, after the code we've added so far, add the following bit of code:

```
$(document).ready(function() {
  ...

  /* Scrollorama setup */
  var weather = $.scrollorama({
    blocks:'.scrollblock'
  });

});
```

First, we create a new variable and call it `weather` as we're presenting a weather forecast. Then, we call the `scrollorama()` method. We pass the `scrollorama()` method the selector for our blocks of content. As each block has a class of `scrollblock`, this is the selector we pass.

Now, Scrollorama is all set up and ready for us to use. Let's take a look at how to animate the movement of our cloud layers.

**8.** Now that we've got Scrollorama set up, we can use that weather variable to tell Scrollorama what to animate. The following code shows how we animate the back layer of clouds:

```
/* Scrollorama setup */
var weather = $.scrollorama({
  blocks:'.scrollblock'
});


/* Parallax cloud animation */
weather
  .animate('#cloud-layer-back', {
    duration:  1000,
    property:  'top',
    start:     100,
    end:       -100
  });
```

Let's take a moment to step through this. We've broken this out onto separate lines to make it easier to read and understand, but this is all actually one line of code. We start with `weather`, then we call the `animate()` method. We want to animate this layer of clouds with the scroll, so that makes sense.

Next, we pass in a selector of what we want to animate. We gave that back layer of clouds an `id` attribute of `cloud-layer-back`, so we can use that now to select this layer for animation.

Then, we tell Scrollorama exactly how that animation should work by passing in a set of key/value pairs. We use the `duration` key to specify how many pixels of scrolling the animation should last. Here, we've set up a long animation—we'll see the clouds moving for 1000 pixels of scrolling.

We use the `property` key to tell Scrollorama which CSS property to animate. Just like with regular old jQuery animations, we can select any numeric CSS property. We've selected `top` since we want to move the entire cloud layer up and down.

We use the start key to specify what the starting value for the selected property should be. Here, we're working with `top`. So at the start of our animation, it will be like assigning this CSS style to the back cloud layer:

```
#cloud-layer-back { top: 100px; }
```

That's where our cloud layer will start off as we scroll by. We use the end key to specify where the cloud layer will end up after the animation completes. It's like assigning this CSS style to the back cloud layer:

```
#cloud-layer-back { top: -100px; }
```

We're moving the cloud layer 200 pixels in total, from 100 pixels to -100 pixels. This will make it appear to move just a bit faster than the rest of the content going by as we scroll.

9. If you refresh the page in the browser at this point, you'll notice that the back cloud layer moves when you scroll up and down past the cloudy weather forecast. However, specifying the duration, start, and end values in pixels can be problematic in responsive designs. With so many different screen sizes, how can we possibly know or set exact pixel values for the cloud animation? We might want those to move only 50 pixels on smaller screens, but we might want them to move 400 pixels or more on larger screens to make the parallax effect really work.

   However, Scrollorama doesn't accept percentage values. We can't tell Scrollorama to move the cloud layer from 10 percent to -10 percent. So we have to get a little more resourceful.

   Luckily, JavaScript is really good at doing math. Remember how we grabbed the width and height of the browser window earlier? We can now use those values to calculate pixel values for the duration, start, and end, based on the size of the browser window. Here's how we can do that. Go back to the code we added in step 8 and edit it so that it looks like the following code:

```
/* Parallax cloud animation */
weather
  .animate('#cloud-layer-back', {
    duration:  winHeight * 2,
    property:     'top',
    start:     winHeight * .1,
    end:       -winHeight * .1
  });
```

   Now, we're letting JavaScript do all the hard work of calculating the values for us, based on our site visitor's screen size. For example, if our site visitor's browser window is 400 pixels tall, the duration of the animation will be 800 pixels, and the clouds will start at 40 pixels and move to -40 pixels.

   If, on the other hand, our site visitor's screen is 1,600 pixels tall, then the duration will be 3200 pixels, with the clouds moving from 160 pixels to -160 pixels. Just like magic, our animation adjusts to our site visitor's browser window size.

10. Now that we've got animating a cloud layer all figured out, let's go ahead and add the code to animate the middle and front cloud layers to `scripts.js` as follows:

```
weather
  .animate('#cloud-layer-back', {
    duration:  winHeight * 2,
    property:  'top',
```

```
        start:      winHeight * .1,
        end:        -winHeight * .1
    })
    .animate('#cloud-layer-mid', {
        duration:   winHeight * 2,
        property:   'top',
        start:      winHeight * .25,
        end:        -winHeight * .25
    })
    .animate('#cloud-layer-front', {
        duration:   winHeight * 2,
        property:   'top',
        start:      winHeight * .5,
        end:        -winHeight * .5
    });
```

First up, notice that we're taking advantage of jQuery's chaining feature—this is just one line of code! But that would not be very easy to read, so we've broken it up to make it easier for us to read, understand, and edit. Also, be very careful with the placement of semicolons—because this is all one line, we don't need to place a semicolon until the very end of the statement

Next, notice that we're increasing the position for the animation for each layer. For the first layer, we just moved the clouds from 10 percent to -10 percent. However, for the middle layer, we're moving from 25 percent to -25 percent, and for the top-most layer, we're moving from 50 percent to -50 percent. The clouds that appear closer will move much more quickly as we scroll past. Refresh the page in the browser and scroll past the cloudy weather forecast a few times to see the effect of the moving clouds. Nice, right?

## What just happened?

We created three layers of clouds and then animated them at different speeds to give the illusion of depth. As we scroll by the cloudy weather forecast, the clouds move by at different speeds, all moving faster than the rest of the content as we scroll.

While the Scrollorama plugin is limited to accepting pixel values, we were able to use the magic of JavaScript to dynamically calculate the values for our animation, which allows our design and animation to adjust better to different screen sizes, making it ideal for use in responsive designs.

## Creating other animations

Parallax scrolling effects are nice, but we can also create other types of animations with the Scrollorama plugin. Let's take a look at how we can emphasize the windy weather forecast by animating the cloud that is blowing across the screen as we scroll by.

# Time for action – creating a horizontal animation

Perform the following steps to create a horizontal animation in the windy weather forecast.

**1.** Inside `index.html`, the only change we'll make is to add an `id` attribute of `wind` to the `<div>` element that contains the weather icon, as follows:

```
<section class="scrollblock" id="wedday">
  <div class="day">Wednesday</div>
  <div class="forecast">69&deg; Windy</div>
  <div class="icon" id="wind"><img src
    ="images/Cloud-Wind.svg" alt="Cloudy Windy" width
    ="300" height="300"></div>
</section>
```

Technically, this isn't strictly necessary as we have other available ways to select that item for animation, but selecting an item by `id` is the quickest and most efficient way. By working directly with `id`, we can get a little performance boost from our code.

**2.** Next, we can open up `scripts.js` and add the details of the animation we'd like to create. Add the following code just below the animation block we added to create the parallax animations, still inside the document ready statement:

```
/* Animate wind */
weather
  .animate('#wind', {
    duration:  winHeight * 1.7,
    property: 'left',
    start:    winWidth * .7,
    end:      winWidth * .3
  });
```

This should look pretty familiar. We're using the same `winHeight` and `winWidth` values we calculated back at the beginning of the chapter. In this case, we want the animation to last 170 percent of the window height—I arrived at that value through experimentation. I just tried out different values until I found one that looked the way I wanted.

Since we're animating the cloud horizontally rather than vertically, we're using `winWidth` rather than `winHeight` to calculate the values. We'll move the cloud from a `left` value of 70 percent to a `left` value of 30 percent.

Also note that we could have just chained this function onto the functions we wrote to create the parallax cloud animations we coded in the section *Adding a parallax effect*. It would have worked just fine, but in this case, I decided to make my code just a bit longer in the interest of keeping it readable.

Refresh the page in the browser window and scroll past the windy forecast. You'll see the cloud blow across the screen as you scroll by.

## What just happened?

We used Scrollorama to create a horizontal animation as we scroll by. We can animate any numeric CSS property. This leaves a lot of possibilities open: we can move items horizontally, vertically, and diagonally; we can adjust the opacity to fade items in and out; and we can adjust the font size, width, height, padding, margins, border width, rotation, and so on.

## Have a go hero – add custom animations

The only limit to what you can animate with the Scrollorama plugin is your imagination. Take a look through the weather forecasts and see what else you might like to animate. Can you fade in the day of the week headers in each block? Can you add animations to the other weather icons?

## Adding navigation

Now, let's make it easier both to navigate through the weather forecast days and to understand where we are on the page. We'll use JavaScript to dynamically create a navigation bar. Our site visitors will be able to use the navigation bar to move directly to the different days in the forecast. Additionally, as our site visitor scrolls down the page through the different days in the forecast, we'll update the highlighted item in the navigation to show them where they are.

## Time for action – adding navigation to sections of the page

Perform the following steps to add navigation to our weather forecast:

1. Open up `scripts.js`. The first thing we want to do is create an unordered list to hold our navigation. After the animation code we wrote earlier, but still inside the document ready statement, add the following bit of code:

   ```
   var dotnav = $('<ul id="dotnav"></ul>');
   ```

First, we create a variable, `dotnav`. Recall that a variable is just a container. Inside this container, we're going to create a jQuery object that holds an unordered list with the `id` attribute of `dotnav`.

2. Now that we've got our unordered list, the next thing we'll do is add it to our document. That's easy enough, just one short line of code:

```
var dotnav = $('<ul id="dotnav"></ul>');
$('body').append(dotnav);
```

We're selecting the `<body>` element of the document and appending our navigation to the end of the body using jQuery's `append()` method.

3. Next, we need to fill the navigation with links to the various parts of the document. We know that each block of our weather forecast is wrapped in a `<section>` element with the class `scrollblock`. We can use those sections to create just the right links in our navigation as follows:

```
var dotnav = $('<ul id="dotnav"></ul>');
$('body').append(dotnav);
$('.scrollblock').each(function(){
  var id = this.id;
  dotnav.append('<li><a href="#' + id + '"></a></li>');
});
```

Let's step through that to make sure we understand. First, we select all the `<section>` elements with a class of `scrollblock`. Then, we use jQuery's `each()` method to loop through each block, one at a time.

Inside the `each()` method, we write a function. The function first gets the `id` attribute of the current section and stores it in a variable.

Finally, we get our navigation, which we've stored in the variable called `dotnav`, and append a new list item and link. We add an `href` attribute that points us to the `id` attribute for each section. For example, for the Monday forecast, this bit of code will add a list item and a link that looks like this:

```
<li><a href="#monday"></a></li>
```

That's pretty easy to understand. If we had created the navigation in HTML, that's how we would have linked to the different sections on the page. If you refresh the page in the browser, you won't see anything new on the page—without CSS, our new element is invisible. However, if you use the web developer tools to take a look at the code on the page, you'll see the new navigation element at the end of the document, as shown in the following screenshot:

4. Now, let's use a bit of CSS to style our navigation. Open up `styles.css` and add the following styles for the navigation:

```css
#dotnav {
  position: fixed;
  right: 1em;
  top: 50%;
}

#dotnav li {
  background: rgba(255,255,255,0.8);
  box-shadow: 0 0 5px rgba(0,0,0,0.2);
  border-radius: 50%;
```

```
    display: block;
    height: 0.8em;
    margin: 0.333em 0;
    padding: 0.2em;
    width: 0.8em;
}

#dotnav a {
    background: transparent;
    border-radius: 50%;
    display: block;
    height: 0.8em;
    transition: background 200ms;
    width: 0.8em;
}
```

Now, if you refresh the page in the browser, you'll see the navigation appear vertically along the right-hand side of the page, as shown in the following screenshot:

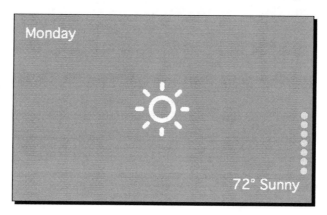

5. We're making progress, but the navigation is a bit too low. Let's use our trusted `winHeight` measurement to bump that up into the right position. In `scripts.js`, add the following bit of code:

```
var dotnav = $('<ul id="dotnav"></ul>');
$('body').append(dotnav);
$('.scrollblock').each(function(){
    ...
});
var navHeight = dotnav.height();
dotnav.css('top', (winHeight/2 - navHeight/2));
```

First, we get the height of our navigation bar itself, and store it in a variable named `navHeight`. Next, we need to calculate what the appropriate top value of the navigation should be. We divide the `winHeight` value in half, then subtract the `navHeight` value divided in half to get the proper value for the top of the navigation bar. We use jQuery's `css()` method to set that value and position the navigation right in the middle of the screen.

Refresh the page in the browser and you'll see that the navigation is now positioned correctly, as shown in the following screenshot:

6. If you click on the dots in the navigation, you'll see that they work—the page jumps to the different days in the weather forecast. However, it jumps so quickly that we don't get to see our fancy animations. Let's modify the jumping so we can appreciate all the hard work we've done so far. First, we need to select the elements we want to work with—the links inside the navigation bar—and attach a click event, as follows:

```
dotnav.css('top', (winHeight/2 - navHeight/2));

dotnav.find('a').on('click', function(e){
  // Our code will go here
});
```

In plain English, the highlighted code says "Get all the links inside the navigation and do something special when they're clicked on." Now, we have to write the code to say what should happen.

7. The first thing we want to do inside this function is to stop the immediate jumping to each section of the page. We can do this as follows:

```
dotnav.find('a').on('click', function(e){
  e.preventDefault();
});
```

We use the `preventDefault()` method to stop the default action. By default, the browser jumps immediately to a section. We don't want that to happen, so we prevent it with this bit of code. If you refresh the page in the browser and try clicking on the navigation, you'll see that nothing happens. We canceled the default action, but we haven't said what to do instead.

8. When we click on one of the navigation links, we want to animate scrolling for that section. To animate scrolling, we'll animate the `<html>` and `<body>` elements. Let's select those elements and call jQuery's `animate()` method, as follows:

```
dotnav.find('a').on('click', function(e){
  e.preventDefault();
  $('html, body').animate();
});
```

Now that we're ready to animate the scrolling, we just have to tell the `animate()` method what to animate.

9. The first thing the `animate()` method needs to know is what property we want to animate. Since we're animating the scrolling, the property we'll be working with is `scrollTop`. Thus, add it to the `scripts.js` file as shown in the following code:

```
dotnav.find('a').on('click', function(e){
  e.preventDefault();
  $('html, body').animate({
    scrollTop:
  });
});
```

10. We want to scroll to the top of the block of the weather forecast that we're navigating to, but the `animate()` method is expecting a pixel value—how many pixels down the page should we scroll? Luckily, it's pretty easy to calculate how many pixels down the page each of our weather forecast blocks are using jQuery's `offset()` method. Let's say we wanted to find out how far down the page the Tuesday evening weather forecast was. We'd find out as follows:

```
$('#tueeve').offset().top;
```

We'd just select the element, then call the `offset()` method. After that, we can get either the top or the left properties.

That seems easy enough, but in this case, we're clicking on a link and we want to scroll to the matching weather forecast. How do we select the right forecast? We set up our links to point at the right sections. All the information we need is stored right in the `href` attribute of each link. We can select the right forecast block as follows:

```
$(this.hash);
```

The following code shows how this all looks in our function that handles what happens when we click on a navigation link:

```
dotnav.find('a').on('click', function(e){
  e.preventDefault();
  $('html, body').animate({
    scrollTop: $(this.hash).offset().top + 1
  });
});
```

In this case, we're adding one more pixel to the value to make sure the navigation interacts nicely with Scrollorama.

If you refresh the page in the browser, you'll see that clicking on the navigation links now scrolls you smoothly to each weather forecast block. However, the page sure does go by quickly. We don't even get a chance to enjoy the animations going by.

**11.** By default, any animations we set up with jQuery's `animate()` method happen in 400 milliseconds—less than half a second. That's really fast. Let's slow that down a bit maybe to a full second:

```
dotnav.find('a').on('click', function(e){
  e.preventDefault();
  $('html, body').animate({
    scrollTop: $(this.hash).offset().top + 1
  }, 1000);
});
```

We just pass in a second value to the `animate()` method—the number of milliseconds the animation should take to complete.

If you refresh the page in the browser now and try clicking on the navigation links, you'll see the scrolling is much slower. You might want to experiment with different values. Where can you best see the animations going by without delaying the site visitors from reaching their destination too much?

**12.** Now that we've got the navigation and animation working, wouldn't it be nice if we could see exactly where we were on the page by highlighting the current weather forecast block in the navigation?

We could add some code to our `click` function to just add a class to each link that is clicked. But what about the times that our site visitors just scroll down the page and don't click on the links at all? We still want to show them how far down the page they are and how many sections are left.

Luckily, Scrollorama gives us a way to detect when we're seeing a new block of our page and to trigger other changes on the page. Let's take a look at how we can highlight the right item in the navigation depending on how far down the page we've scrolled. We can do that with the `onBlockChange()` method.

But first, let's set up the `.active` style for the navigation links in `styles.css`, as follows:

```
#dotnav a.active {
  background: #e75845;
}
```

We'll change the background color of the link to a bright orange color when it's the current link.

**13.** Now, we'll jump back into `scripts.js` and set up a function that will run each time we scroll to a new block. After the `click` function that we wrote, but still inside the document ready method, add the following lines to set up our new function:

```
/* Update dotnav while scrolling */
weather.onBlockChange(function() {
  // Our code will go here
});
```

We're still leaving little notes for ourselves or for any other developer who comes along to work on our code about what each bit of code does. We select our weather variable and then call the `onBlockChange()` method. We pass an empty function to the method.

**14.** The first thing we need to do inside that function is figure out which block we can see in the window. Scrollorama makes that easy for us with the `blockIndex` property, as shown in the following code:

```
weather.onBlockChange(function() {
  var i = weather.blockIndex;
});
```

Now, the `i` variable contains the index of the current block. When we're looking at the first block, `i` will be equal to `0`—don't forget that JavaScript starts counting at `0` and not at `1`.

**15.** Now that we know which block is currently visible, we just have to select the matching link in the navigation. That's easy enough—if we're on the second block, we'll just select the second link. The following code shows how we can do that:

```
weather.onBlockChange(function() {
  var i = weather.blockIndex;
  dotnav.find('a').eq(i);
});
```

Here, we get our `dotnav` variable, which contains the navigation, and then we find all the links. Then, we use jQuery's `eq()` method to select the link that matches the currently visible block.

**16.** Now, we just have to add the `active` CSS class to the link:

```
weather.onBlockChange(function() {
  var i = weather.blockIndex;
  dotnav.find('a').eq(i).addClass('active');
});
```

That's easy enough, right? However, scroll down through the page and you'll see that very quickly every link in the navigation is highlighted. This is handy if we just want to keep track of where we've been, but not very handy for telling us where we currently are.

**17.** After a block isn't visible any more, we need to remove the `active` class from its matching link. We can do that pretty easily by just removing the `active` class from all the links before we add it to the matching one, as follows:

```
weather.onBlockChange(function() {
  var i = weather.blockIndex;
  dotnav.find('a').removeClass('active')
    .eq(i).addClass('active');
});
```

Now, if you refresh the page in the browser, and scroll down, you'll see that the navigation changes to reflect your current position on the page. The navigation also updates if you click on the links—since those links scroll the page, the `onBlockChange()` event is still fired. We don't have to write separate code to highlight the links while clicking on them and highlighting the links while scrolling. Just one bit of code handles both nicely.

## What just happened?

We used jQuery to create a navigation bar for our blocks of weather forecast. Then, we animated the scroll to each of those blocks when the navigation links were clicked. Finally, we used the `onBlockChange()` method provided by Scrollorama to change the CSS classes on the links to make it obvious where we were on the page.

## Pop quiz – using Scrollorama in responsive design

Q1. How can we use Scrollorama effectively in responsive designs?

1. Use percentage values for animation duration, animation start, and animation stop.

2. There's no need to do anything special—Scrollorama is responsive by default.

3. Use JavaScript to calculate appropriate values based on the current screen size.

4. Scrollorama cannot be used in responsive design.

# Summary

In this chapter, we looked at a few different ways of reacting to our site visitors who scroll down the page. We created a parallax effect by animating the position of layers of content at different speeds as we scroll down the page. We created a horizontal animation that reacts to scrolling. Finally, we created a navigation bar that not only updates as we scroll down the page but also allows us to easily move to the different areas of the page. Not too shabby. Next up, we'll look at some ways to make forms nicer-looking as well as easier for our site visitors to work with.

# 12
# Improving Forms

*If you've ever tried to work with web forms, you know how complex they can be. Luckily, the authors of HTML5 are working hard to ensure that the experience improves for designers, developers, and web site visitors alike. Browser support for the new HTML5 form elements and attributes is coming along really nicely, and even in browsers that don't have support, the new elements and attributes are backward compatible.*

In this chapter, you'll learn:

◆ How to mark up a form with some of the new HTML5 attributes

◆ How to place the cursor in the first form field automatically

◆ How to validate your site visitors' form entries

◆ How to style stubborn form elements such as file uploads and select dropdowns

## An HTML5 web form

We'll get started by taking advantage of some of the new attributes made available to us in HTML5. The great thing about these additions is that they are completely backward compatible—browsers that don't know how to handle them will either ignore them or default to a simple text input, and our site visitors on older browsers will be able to use our forms without even knowing what they're missing.

First, a word of caution about web forms. A **web form** doesn't work by itself—it needs to have some fancy backend programming on a server somewhere to collect the form entries and process them, which could mean writing fields to the database or sending the form information via an e-mail. Because of this, the forms we build in this chapter won't actually function—nothing will happen after clicking on the Submit button on the form. If you want to add a functioning web form to a project, you have a few options, which are as follows:

- You can learn to do server-side programming to handle your form, but server-side programming is well beyond the scope of this book.

- You can use a CMS that will most likely include form handling either in its core functionality or as an add-on. Good candidates include Drupal, WordPress, and Joomla.

- You can hire a server-side developer to get your form working, or befriend one and barter your design skills for their coding skills.

- You can use a web form service to handle all the server-side processing of your form. My personal favorite is WuFoo (`http://wufoo.com`), which I have used for years without a single hiccup.

Any of these methods will help you create a working web form to be included in your project. However, let's take a look at how we can make the frontend of our form the best it can be.

## Time for action – setting up an HTML5 web form

Perform the following steps to set up a form using the new HTML5 elements and attributes:

*1.* We'll get started with a simple HTML document and the associated files and folders, just like we set up in *Chapter 1, Designer, Meet jQuery*. Inside the `<body>` tag, open up a `<form>` tag as shown in the following code:

```
<form action="#" id="account-form">
</form>
```

The form tag needs an `action` attribute in order to appear correctly on our page. Since our forms are just dummy forms used for scripting and styling purposes, we'll just use # as the value for this attribute. The value of the `action` attribute is usually a URL—the place on the server where we're going to send our form data for processing. We also added an `id` attribute to make it easy to select the form for CSS and JavaScript purposes later.

**2.** Next up, we'll create a section for our site visitor to create the **Username** and **Password** fields. We'll wrap these two fields in a `<fieldset>` element with a `<legend>` element to group them together, as follows:

```
<form action="#" id="account-form">
  <fieldset>
    <legend>My Account</legend>
    <p>
      <label for="username">Username</label>
      <input type="text" name="username" id
        ="username" placeholder="Choose a username&hellip;">
    </p>
    <p>
      <label for="password">Password</label>
      <input type="text" name="password" id
        ="password" placeholder="Choose a secure
        password&hellip;">
    </p>
  </fieldset>
</form>
```

Here, we've wrapped each field and its associated label in a paragraph tag (`<p>`). There is a world of opinions out there on the best tags to use to mark up your form fields. Some developers swear by simple `<div>` elements, while others like to make the form a list (`<ul>`) with each field a list item (`<li>`). Some others like to use a definition list (`<dl>`) and place the labels inside the `<dt>` tags and the form fields inside the `<dd>` tags. Pragmatically speaking, any of these will do just fine and your form will work as expected for your site visitors. Use the tags that you personally prefer.

Look carefully at the HTML markup we've written so far for our form. There are a few important things to note, which are as follows:

- Each `<input>` tag has a `type` attribute that is relevant to its purpose. The username field has a `text` type, and the password field has a `password` type.

- Each `<input>` tag has a unique `id` attribute. Remember that each `id` must to be unique on the page, so select the `id` attributes of your form inputs carefully.

- Each `<input>` tag has a `name` attribute. This is passed to the code that is handling your form on the server side. It's a common practice to use the same value for the `name` and `id` attributes of a form element, but it's not compulsory. You can easily select a different value for the `id` value anytime you like, but if you'd like to change the `name` value, you should first check with your server-side developer to ensure that the code they have written will continue to work.

❏ Each `<input>` tag has a `placeholder` attribute. This new attribute, introduced in HTML5, currently has very good browser support. The value of this attribute is displayed as grayed-out text in each field until the site visitor starts typing. It can be useful to give additional instructions for a field or to give an example of the type of information the site visitor should enter.

❏ Each `<label>` tag has a `for` attribute that associates it with a particular form element. The value in the `for` attribute is equal to the `id` value of the form element with which it is associated (not the `name` attribute). This makes some nice functionality available to our site visitors—clicking on a label will bring focus to the associated form element. This behavior is especially useful for checkbox and radio button inputs, which are small and can be difficult to click.

Each browser has its own default way of styling form elements. For example, with no CSS attached to the preceding HTML markup, the following screenshot shows what the form element looks like in Google Chrome on Mac OS X:

Note that the default CSS code we use with the example code in this book removes (or resets) most of these default styles. The following screenshot shows how the form appears after attaching our CSS file:

**3.** Next up, we'll create an **About Me** section for our form, as follows:

```
<fieldset>
  <legend>About Me</legend>
  <p>
    <label for="name">Name</label>
    <input type="text" id="name" name="name" placeholder
      ="First Last">
  </p>
```

```
  <p>
    <label for="email">Email address</label>
    <input type="email" id="email" name="email" placeholder
      ="you@example.com">
  </p>
  <p>
    <label for="website">Website</label>
    <input type="url" id="website" name="website" placeholder
      ="Don't forget the http://&hellip;">
  </p>
  <p>
    <label for="birthdate">Birth date</label>
    <input type="date" id="birthdate" name="birthdate">
  </p>
</fieldset>
```

Again, the `text` type was used for the **Name** field, as names are strings. However, take a look at the `type` attribute for the **Email address**, **Website**, and **Birth date** fields. We're using the new HTML5 input types here. In browsers where these input types are not supported, these fields will look and work just like inputs with a `type` attribute of `text`. However, in browsers where these input types are recognized, they'll behave in a slightly different way. The browser will automatically validate the user input. For example, if a site visitor types an invalid e-mail address into an input with the type `email`, the browser will warn them that they've entered an invalid e-mail address. Also, on devices with soft keyboards, the keyboard keys will be altered to reflect the characters necessary for entering that data type. For example, an input with a type of `email` will open a keyboard with the . key and the @ key showing on an iPhone or an iPad, making it easier for your site visitors on these devices to complete the required information.

4.  The next section in the form will be a section about beverage preferences. We want the site visitor to select their favorite beverages from a list and then answer a question about how many days per year they drink a beverage. The following code is a sample of what the list looks like:

```
<fieldset>
  <legend>Beverage Info</legend>
  <fieldset>
```

```
    <legend>Select your favorite beverage(s)</legend>
    <p>Please select at least three but no more than
      six beverages.</p>
    <ul>
      <li>
        <input type="checkbox" name="favorites[]" id
          ="bev-water" value="bev-water">
        <label for="bev-water">Water</label>
      </li>
      <li>
        <input type="checkbox" name="favorites[]" id
          ="bev-juice" value="bev-juice">
        <label for="bev-juice">Juice</label>
      </li>
      ...
    </ul>
  </fieldset>
  <p>
    <label for="days">How many days of the year do you
      drink a beverage?</label>
    <input type="number" id="days" name="days" placeholder
      ="How many days?">
  </p>
</fieldset>
```

Now, when you refresh the page, you'll see the list as shown in the following screenshot:

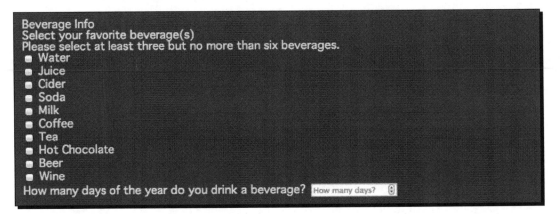

A few new things to note about the HTML that we've used to mark up this section:

- ☐ Fieldsets can be nested. A **fieldset** is an excellent way to group a set of checkboxes or radio buttons together, and we can use the `legend` tag of the `fieldset` element to create a header for our radio or checkbox group.

- ☐ A set of checkboxes are identified as such because they will all share the same name. Because a site visitor can select more than one item in a set of checkboxes, we add square brackets ( `[]` ) at the end of the name so that the server will collect all of the answers into an array.

- ☐ Each checkbox in the set has its own unique `id` and `value` attributes. The `id` and `value` attributes do not necessarily have to match, but it's often easy to make them the same.

- ☐ Finally, the number of days per year is given an input type `number`, as only a number would be acceptable here. Be careful with this input type. It is very strict and will not accept any nonnumeric characters. Some bits of data appear to be numbers but are actually strings, for example, telephone numbers and credit card numbers. If you wouldn't do some sort of math with your number, then it shouldn't be the `number` input type.

5. The next section we'll add to our form is a payment information section, which is shown in the following code:

```
<fieldset>
  <legend>Payment Info</legend>
  <fieldset>
    <legend>Credit Card Type</legend>
    <ul>
      <li>
        <input type="radio" name="cc-type" id
          ="cc-visa" value="cc-visa">
        <label for="cc-visa">Visa</label>
      </li>
      <li>
        <input type="radio" name="cc-type" id
          ="cc-mastercard" value="cc-mastercard">
        <label for="cc-mastercard">Mastercard</label>
      </li>
      <li>
        <input type="radio" name="cc-type" id
          ="cc-amex" value="cc-amex">
        <label for="cc-amex">American Express</label>
      </li>
```

```
      <li>
        <input type="radio" name="cc-type" id
          ="cc-discover" value="cc-discover">
        <label for="cc-discover">Discover</label>
      </li>
    </ul>
  </fieldset>
  <p>
    <label for="cc-number">Credit card number</label>
    <input type="text" name="cc-number" id
      ="cc-number" placeholder="xxxx xxxx xxxx xxxx">
  </p>
</fieldset>
```

Much like the checkboxes, we've grouped a set of radio controls inside a fieldset with the `legend` tag acting as the header for this section. Just like checkboxes, all the radio buttons in the set of radio buttons share the same name, but each has its own unique `id` and `value` attributes. However, in the case of radio buttons, only one can be selected at a time, so there is no need to mark them as an array.

We've also added a field for collecting our site visitor's credit card number. Note that we've assigned an input type of `text` to this field. Even though a credit card number appears to be a number, we want to store it just as it is, and won't ever be performing calculations with this number. The following screenshot shows the payment information section:

6.  Finally, we'll add a checkbox for our site visitor to accept our terms of service, and a **Submit** button for them to submit the form information to us, as follows:

```
<fieldset>
  <ul>
    <li>
      <input type="checkbox" name="tos" id="tos" value="tos"/>
      <label for="tos">Click here to accept our terms
        of service</label>
    </li>
  </ul>
```

```
<p>
  <input type="submit" value="Sign me up!"/>
</p>
</fieldset>
```

The only new thing here is the **Submit** button. By default, the `input` tag with a `type` attribute of `submit` will read **Submit**. We can change the text by adding a `value` attribute with the text we'd like to display on the button. The following screenshot shows the text that we used; in our case, it is **Sign me up!**:

7. The only thing left to do is to style our form with a bit of CSS. The following code shows the CSS used for this simple form in the sample code for the book:

```
fieldset {
  background: white;
  border-radius: 5px;
  color: #656d78;
  margin: 1em 0;
  padding: 1em;
  width: 80%;
}

legend {
  background: #fa6f57;
  border-radius: 5px;
  color: white;
  font-size: 1.125em;
  padding: 0.333em 1em;
}

fieldset fieldset legend {
  background: transparent;
  color: #42b0d8;
  padding: 0;
}
```

```
fieldset p {
  line-height: 1.5em;
  margin: 1em 0;
}

fieldset label {
  display: inline-block;
  width: 20%;
}

fieldset li {
  line-height: 1.5;
  margin: 0.5em 0;
}

fieldset ul label {
  display: inline;
  width: auto;
}

input[type='text'],
input[type='password'],
input[type='email'],
input[type='url'],
input[type='email'],
input[type='date'],
input[type='number'] {
  border: 1px solid #ccd1d9;
  border-radius: 5px;
  color: #656d78;
  font-family: inherit;
  font-size: inherit;
  padding: 0.222em;
  transition: border 300ms;
}

input[type='text']:focus,
input[type='password']:focus,
input[type='email']:focus,
input[type='url']:focus,
input[type='email']:focus,
input[type='date']:focus,
input[type='number']:focus {
  border-color: #656d78;
  outline: none;
}
```

Note that the `type` attribute of our inputs can be used to select them for styling. In this case, we've styled them all identically, but it would also be possible to give each one its own set of styles if desired.

The following screenshot shows how the form looks with this CSS. Feel free to get creative and write your own styles for the form.

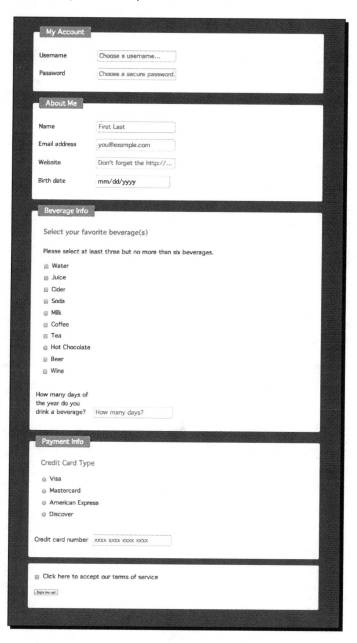

## What just happened?

We took a look at some of the new HTML5 input types and how to use them properly to put together a web form. We saw how to use the `fieldset` and `legend` tags to group fields together under a heading and how to associate labels with form elements. We learned the proper use of the `text`, `password`, `email`, `url`, `date`, `checkbox`, `radio`, and `number` input types.

### Pop quiz – working with HTML5 form elements

Q1. HTML5 provides several new types of `<input>` elements for us to work with (`url`, `email`, `number`, and so on). What happens to these form elements in older browsers that don't have explicit support for them?

1. They appear and function as though they were of type text.

2. They aren't visible on the page.

3. They appear as checkboxes.

4. They cause an error and render the form unusable.

# Setting focus

If you head over to `http://google.com`, you'll see that they've made it really easy for you to conduct a web search—as soon as the page is loaded in the browser, the cursor is blinking in the search field. There are other sites on the Web that behave this way too, making it quick and easy to get started with filling in a form.

Any time you have a page where the site visitor's main task will be to complete a form, you can make things easy for your site visitor by placing the cursor into the first form field so they can just start typing. And it's wicked easy with jQuery. Here's how to do it.

### Time for action – setting focus to the first field

We'll keep working with the sample form we set up in the previous example. Perform the following steps to set the focus to the first field in the form.

*1.* Open up your empty `scripts.js` file and add a document ready statement, as follows:

```
$(document).ready(function(){
  // Our code goes here
});
```

**2.** Next up, we want to select the first field in our form. There are many different ways to go about this. While we could use the `id` attribute of the first field, this is not very flexible. If we update our form later to add a new field at the beginning, we'd also have to remember to update our JavaScript. Instead, let's just find the first input element, as follows:

```
$(document).ready(function(){
  $('input').first();
});
```

This works pretty well, but there are several cases where we would not like to set the focus on the first input element, for example, if the first element is disabled, or if it's a button, a checkbox, or a radio button. Let's add a filter to remove these, as follows:

```
$('input').first().not(':radio,:checkbox,:button,
  :disabled,:file,:image,:reset,:submit');
```

We won't bother setting the focus to radio buttons, checkboxes, buttons, disabled form elements, file inputs, image inputs, reset buttons, or submit buttons.

**3.** All that's left to do is to call the `focus()` method for the selected element, as follows:

```
$('input').first().not(':radio,:checkbox,:button,
  :disabled,:file,:image,:reset,:submit').focus();
```

Now, if you refresh the page in the browser, you'll see that the cursor is blinking in the **Username** field of the form—the very first field.

## What just happened?

We used a couple of lines of jQuery to move the focus to the first field in our form to make it easy for our site visitors to jump right in to completing our form. It was as simple as selecting the first form element and then calling the `focus()` method for that element.

# Validating site visitor entry

Sometimes, it can feel frustrating for a site visitor when they have to submit a form several times over, correcting errors that they've made while filling it out. Without JavaScript, the only way to validate the information that the site visitor has entered is to wait for them to submit the form, then identify the issues on the server, and send back a page that contains the form along with any error messages that might help the site visitor correct the problem.

Showing errors as soon as they occur goes a long way towards making your form feel snappy and responsive and helping your site visitors submit the form correctly on the first try. In this section, we'll learn how to use the Validation plugin from Jörn Zaefferer. This plugin is powerful and flexible and can handle validation in several different ways. We'll take a look at the most straightforward way of adding client-side validation to your form.

## Time for action – validating form values on the fly

We'll continue working with the form we've been creating through the last three sections. Perform the following steps to validate user entry into the form:

1.  The first thing we'll do is download the Validation plugin and get it attached to our page.

    Head over to `http://jqueryvalidation.org/` and click on the **Download** button in the **Files** section to download a ZIP file.

2.  Open up the ZIP file and take a look at what we've got.

    There's a lot going on here—there are several different JavaScript files, some demos, a change log, and so on. Remember how I said this plugin is powerful and can handle lots of different approaches to validation? That's what all this is for—handling form validation in just about any old crazy situation you might find yourself in.

    Luckily, though, our situation is pretty simple, so we don't have to do anything complicated.

3.  Inside the `dist` folder, find `jquery.validate.min.js` and copy it to your own `scripts` folder. Then, attach it to your HTML page, as follows:

    ```
    <script src="scripts/jquery.js"></script>
    <script src="scripts/jquery.validate.min.js"></script>
    <script src="scripts/scripts.js"></script>
    ```

4.  Next, we're going to go back to our form and add some information that the Validation plugin will use. Let's start with the **Username** field:

    ```
    <p>
      <label for="username">Username</label>
      <input type="text" name="username" id="username" placeholder
        ="At least 5 characters long" minlength="5" maxlength
        ="20" required/>
    </p>
    ```

This is a required field—any site visitor who completes this form must select a username, so we'll simply add an attribute called `required`. This attribute is for form validation purposes, but we could also use it to create a special style in our CSS for the required fields in the form.

All usernames must be between five and 20 characters long. So we've added the `minlength` and `maxlength` attributes.

5. Next up is the **Password** field, which is also a required field. So let's add the `required` attribute, as follows:

```
<p>
  <label for="password">Password</label>
  <input type="password" name="password" id
    ="password" required placeholder
    ="Choose a secure password"/>
</p>
```

While we're at it, let's add the `required` attribute to the e-mail field too:

```
<p>
  <label for="email">Email address</label>
  <input type="email" name="email" id="email" placeholder
    ="you@example.com" required/>
</p>
```

6. Next, let's take a look at that list of favorite beverages. Remember we included a note in the fieldset to indicate that the site visitor was to select at least three but not more than six beverages? We can actually enforce that with the Validation plugin. Go to the first checkbox in the series and add the `minlength` and `maxlength` attributes as follows:

```
<li>
  <input type="checkbox" name="favorites[]" id
    ="bev-water" value="bev-water" maxlength="6" minlength
    ="3" required/>
  <label for="bev-water">Water</label>
</li>
```

We only have to add this on the first checkbox and not on all of them. Validation is smart enough to figure out that we're referring to the entire set of checkboxes.

7. Now, let's take a look at the field where we ask the site visitor how many days per year they drink a beverage. Obviously, as there are only 365 days in a year, it's the highest number they could enter in this field. So we'll add a `max` attribute to specify the highest possible number:

```
<p>
  <label for="days">How many days per year do you
    drink a beverage?</label>
  <input type="number" name="days" id="days" max="365"/>
</p>
```

8. This brings us to the payment section. Whatever we're selling, it's not free, so we're going to require both the credit card type and credit card number. To require entry for radio buttons, we just have to add the `required` attribute to the first radio button in the set, as follows:

```
<li>
  <input type="radio" name="cc-type" id="cc-visa" value
  ="cc-visa" required/>
  <label for="cc-visa">Visa</label>
</li>
```

We don't have to make any other changes to the radio button series.

9. Now, let's handle the credit card number itself. We need to add the `required` attribute, as shown in the following code. We also need to add a `creditcard` class to validate that the number entered is, in fact, a valid credit card number:

```
<p>
  <label for="cc-number">Credit card number</label>
  <input type="text" name="cc-number" id
  ="cc-number" placeholder="xxxxxxxxxxxxxxxx" class
  ="creditcard" required/>
</p>
```

10. At the bottom of our form, we have a checkbox to accept the terms of service. This is required too, so we'll add the `required` attribute, as follows:

```
<li>
  <input type="checkbox" name="tos" id
  ="tos" required value="tos"/>
  <label for="tos">Click here to accept our
    terms of service</label>
</li>
```

11. Now, we just need to call the `validate()` method that Validation makes available to us. In `scripts.js`, inside the document ready statement, select the form and call the `validate()` method, as shown in the following code:

```
$(document).ready(function(){
  $('input').first().not(':radio,:checkbox,:button,:disabled,
    :file,:image,:reset,:submit').focus();

  $('#account-form').validate();

});
```

**12.** Now, if you refresh the page in the browser, you'll see that you can't submit the form without filling anything in—the required fields will be marked with an error message that says the field is required. If you try to type an invalid URL or e-mail address into the **Website** or **Email address** fields, you'll get an error message that will let you know there's a problem to be corrected. However, those error messages are in a weird place for our checkboxes and radio buttons, as shown in the following screenshot:

This doesn't really help people understand exactly what's going on. Luckily, Validation allows us to add our own error messages to the page wherever we'd like them to display.

We're going to add an error message before the list of credit card type radio buttons:

```
<fieldset>
  <legend>Payment Info</legend>
  <fieldset>
    <legend>Credit Card Type</legend>
    <label for="cc-type" class="error"></label>
    <ul>
      ...
    </ul>
  </fieldset>
  ...
</fieldset>
```

We'll add a `<label>` element to the document where we'd like the error message to show. The `for` attribute will refer to the name of the field—in this case, all the radio buttons share the `cc-type` name. We'll add a `class` attribute of `error`.

In this case, the `for` attribute of our label is referring to the `name` attribute of the field rather than the `id` attribute. This is a special case created by the Validation plugin. If you're not using custom error messages with the Validation plugin, then your label's `for` attribute should always reference the `id` attribute of the form element.

13. Next, we don't want any error messages showing up on the page unless they're needed. We'd also like them to display in red so that they stick out and are easy to find. Open your `styles.css` file and add some styles for the error messages, as shown in the following code:

```
fieldset label.error {
  color: #e75845;
  display: none;
  margin-left: 0.5em;
  width: auto;
}
```

We're adding a `width` value as we've set the other labels to a width of 20 percent. We're also adding a little margin for some space between the error message and the field it's referring to.

Now, if you refresh the browser and try to submit the form without selecting a credit card type, you'll get the error message in a much better place, as shown in the following screenshot:

14. Next, we need to do the same thing for our favorite beverages and our **Terms of Service** checkbox. The following code shows what we'll add as our favorite beverages:

```
<fieldset>
  <legend>Beverage Info</legend>
  <fieldset>
    <legend>Select your favorite beverage(s)</legend>
```

```
    <p>Please select at least three but no more
      than six beverages.</p>
    <label for="favorites[]" class="error"></label>
    <ul>
      ...
    </ul>
  </fieldset>
  ...
</fieldset>
```

The following code is what we'll add to the terms of service checkbox:

```
<fieldset>
  <ul>
    ...
  </ul>
  <label for="tos" class="error"></label>
  ...
</fieldset>
```

Now, if you refresh the page in the browser and try to submit the form without completing the required fields or try to enter invalid information in the form, you'll get error messages in the appropriate places.

**15.** While our error messages are now showing up in better spots on the page, they're not always very helpful. For example, if we only select two beverages, the error message reads **Please enter at least 3 characters**.

The default error messages work in many cases, but not in all cases. Luckily, it's easy to customize the error messages. All we have to do is add a `title` attribute to the form element with the error message we'd like to show. Add this `title` attribute to the first `<input>` element in beverages, as shown in the following code:

```
<input type="checkbox" name="favorites[]" id
  ="bev-water" value="bev-water" minlength="3" maxlength
  ="6" required title="You must select at least three but
  not more than six beverages">
```

Now, the error message makes more sense for our site visitors. You can add a `title` attribute that contains an error message specific to that field to any of the form elements in the form.

## What just happened?

We used the Validation plugin to add some simple client-side validation to our form. The simplest way to use the Validation plugin is to simply add some class names and attributes to your form elements. Validation will take care of the rest—it's smart enough to recognize the HTML5 input types and validate them, and it offers some other useful validation rules such as required fields, a maximum number value, minimum and maximum lengths, and credit card numbers. We dropped in a bit of CSS to style the error messages the way we wanted.

# Improving the appearance

If you've tried styling web forms with CSS, then you've probably discovered that some form elements, such as text inputs and buttons, are pretty easy to style. There are a few quirks, but once you get those figured out, you can get those form elements to look just about any way you'd like. Other form elements, however, are much more stubborn and don't respond much, if at all, to CSS styles. It's so frustrating to design a lovely form only to realize that it's technically impossible.

These troublesome form elements are as follows:

- `<select>`
- `<input type="file">`
- `<input type="checkbox">`
- `<input type="radio">`

Not only are these four form elements impossible to style with CSS, but they also look radically different in different browsers and operating systems, leaving us with little control over the appearance of our form. Let's see how Lutrasoft's Fancyform plugin can help us out.

## Time for action – improving form appearance

Perform the following steps to take advantage of the styling options made possible by the Fancyform plugin:

1. We'll get started with a basic HTML file and associated files and folders, just like we set up in *Chapter 1, Designer, Meet jQuery*. We'll work with a new HTML file, but let's keep using the styles we set up for the earlier forms. Open your `styles.css` file and paste in the styles we used for our forms in the previous sections.

2. For this example, in the body of the HTML document, we're going to set up a simple form with examples of each type of hard-to-style form element. Get started with a `<form>` tag, as follows:

```
<form id="pretty-form" action="#">
</form>
```

**3.** Then, inside our form, we'll add our form elements. We'll start off with a `select` drop-down option, as follows:

```
<fieldset>
  <legend>Select your favorite juice</legend>
  <p>
    <label for="juice">Favorite Juice</label>
    <select id="juice" name="juice">
      <option>Select one</option>
      <option value="orange">Orange Juice</option>
      <option value="grape">Grape Juice</option>
      <option value="grapefruit">Grapefruit Juice</option>
      <option value="cranberry">Cranberry Juice</option>
      <option value="tomato">Tomato Juice</option>
      <option value="pineapple">Pineapple Juice</option>
      <option value="apple">Apple Juice</option>
    </select>
  </p>
</fieldset>
```

We're following the same rules we followed for the previous form, making sure the form works properly and is accessible.

Exactly what this `<select>` element looks like will depend on your browser and operating system, but the following screenshot shows how mine looks in Google Chrome on Mac OS X:

**4.** Next, we'll add a file input, as shown in the following code:

```
<fieldset>
  <legend>Fruit Picture</legend>
  <p>
    <label for="fruit-photo">Upload a photo of your
      favorite fruit</label>
    <input type="file" id="fruit-photo" name="fruit-photo"/>
  </p>
</fieldset>
```

It's hard to believe that this innocent-looking little tag could be the source of so much styling headache, but there you are. The following screenshot shows how it looks in Google Chrome on Mac OS X:

5. Next up, let's add a few checkboxes, as follows:

```
<fieldset>
  <legend>Which hot beverages do you enjoy?</legend>
  <ul>
    <li>
      <input type="checkbox" name="hot-bevs[]" id="hot-coffee">
      <label for="hot-coffee">Coffee</label>
    </li>
    <li>
      <input type="checkbox" name="hot-bevs[]" id
        ="hot-chocolate">
      <label for="hot-chocolate">Hot Chocolate</label>
    </li>
    <li>
      <input type="checkbox" name="hot-bevs[]" id="hot-tea">
      <label for="hot-tea">Tea</label>
    </li>
  </ul>
</fieldset>
```

If you refresh the page in the browser, the checkboxes will appear as shown in the following screenshot:

6. Then, let's add some radio buttons, as follows:

```
<fieldset>
  <legend>Select your favorite soft drink</legend>
  <ul>
    <li>
      <input type="radio" name="soft-drinks" id="soda"/>
      <label for="soda">Soda</label>
    </li>
```

```
      <li>
        <input type="radio" name="soft-drinks" id
          ="sparkling-water"/>
        <label for="sparkling-water">Sparkling water</label>
      </li>
      <li>
        <input type="radio" name="soft-drinks" id="iced-tea"/>
        <label for="iced-tea">Iced Tea</label>
      </li>
      <li>
        <input type="radio" name="soft-drinks" id="lemonade"/>
        <label for="lemonade">Lemonade</label>
      </li>
    </ul>
</fieldset>
```

If you refresh the page in the browser, the radio buttons will appear as shown in the following screenshot:

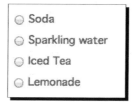

**7.** Finally, the last thing that we'll do is add a few elements to our form that are easy to style, so that we can learn how to style these to match our custom styles:

```
<fieldset>
  <legend>Some other stuff about me</legend>
  <p>
    <label for="name">My name</label>
    <input type="text" id="name" name="name"/>
  </p>
  <p>
    <label for="about-me">About me</label>
    <textarea rows="10" cols="40" id="about-me" name
      ="about-me"></textarea>
  </p>
</fieldset>
```

```
<p class="buttons">
  <input type="submit"/>
  <input type="reset"/>
</p>
```

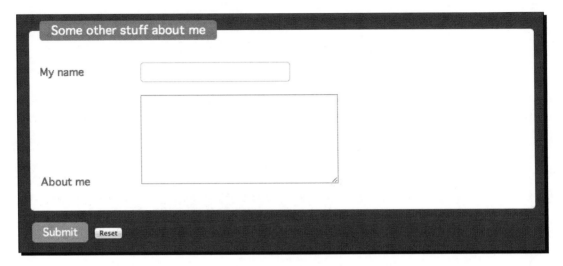

We've already written CSS to style the fieldset, legend, text input, and submit input. We haven't yet styled the text area or the reset input. We'll tackle these in a bit.

## What just happened?

Now, we've got our unstyled form set up. Exactly what our form looks like will depend on your browser and operating system. We followed all the rules established earlier in this chapter for setting up a correct and accessible form. Except that this time, we've included some difficult-to-style form elements. Let's take a look now at how we can use the Fancyform plugin to get our form to look better and uniform across as many browsers as possible.

## Styling the unstyleable

If you want to take a little time out and try writing some CSS to style these form elements, you'll see that there's not much that touches them. Some of them don't seem to be affected by CSS at all, and when they are, it's not always in the way that you'd expect. No wonder these form fields give everyone so much trouble. This is when jQuery comes to the rescue.

# Time for action – adding Fancyform to style the unstyleable

Perform the following steps to use the Fancyform plugin to gain styling control over your form elements:

1. Let's get the Fancyform plugin and take a look at how it works. Head over to `https://github.com/Lutrasoft/Fancyform` and click on the **Download ZIP** button.

2. Unzip the file and take a look inside the folder.

   This is pretty straightforward, right? We've got a demo folder, a README file, the Fancyform JavaScript, and some other associated scripts—we've seen this all before. We also see a V2 folder—the developer is starting on the next version of the plugin. If you read the notes in GitHub carefully, you'll see that V2 isn't quite ready for prime time yet, so we'll just ignore that for now.

3. Next, we need to add the Fancyform script to our own project and attach it to our HTML page. Copy `jquery.fancyform.js` to your own `scripts` folder and attach the Fancyform script between jQuery and your own `scripts.js` file, as follows:

```
<script src="scripts/jquery.js"></script>
<script src="scripts/jquery.fancyform.js"></script>
<script src="scripts/scripts.js"></script>
</body>
</html>
```

4. Open your `scripts.js` file and add the document ready statement, as follows:

```
$(document).ready(function(){
  // Our code will go here
});
```

5. Next, select all the `<select>` elements and call the `transformSelect()` method, as follows:

```
$(document).ready(function(){
  $('select').transformSelect();
});
```

If you refresh the page in the browser now, you'll see that the `<select>` element is replaced by a bit of text. Clicking on the text opens up a list of options. Then, clicking on one of the options changes the bit of text to the option we clicked. The following screenshot shows what happens:

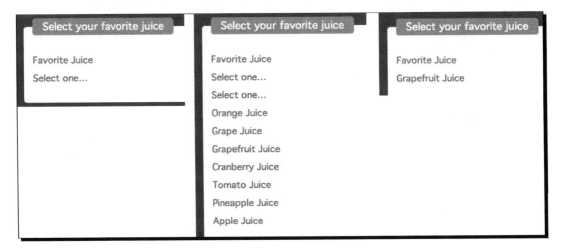

The basic functionality is present; we just have to style everything with CSS to look the way we'd like.

6. Let's get started with the styles by styling the select box itself. Open your `styles.css` file and add the following styles:

```css
.transformSelect {
  display: inline-block;
  vertical-align: middle;
  width: 200px;
}

.transformSelect li {
  margin: 0;
  position: relative;
}

.transformSelect > li > span {
  background: white;
  border: 1px solid #ccd1d9;
  border-radius: 5px;
  color: #656d78;
  cursor: pointer;
  display: block;
  left: 0;
```

```
    line-height: 20px;
    margin: 0;
    overflow: hidden;
    padding: 3px 5px;
    text-overflow: ellipsis;
    top: 0;
    white-space: nowrap;
}
```

Refresh the page in the browser and you'll see that the select box is placed correctly and has a border and border radius that match the styles we've created so far for our forms.

**7.** Now, we'll create the arrow on the right-hand side of the drop-down box:

```
.transformSelect > li > span:before {
    border-left: 1px solid #ccd1d9;
    bottom: 4px;
    content: '';
    position: absolute;
    right: 2em;
    top: 4px;
}

.transformSelect > li > span:after {
    border-left: 7px solid transparent;
    border-right: 7px solid transparent;
    border-top: 10px solid #ccd1d9;
    content: '';
    height: 0;
    margin-top: -4px;
    position: absolute;
    right: 10px;
    top: 50%;
    width: 0;
}
```

This is the CSS triangle technique we've used many times already. Refresh the page in the browser and you'll see that our select box is looking pretty good, as shown in the following screenshot:

8.  Now, let's tackle the list of options that appears after we click on our styled select drop-down menu, as follows:

```
.transformSelect li.open > span {
  border-radius: 5px 5px 0 0;
}

.transformSelectDropdown {
  background: white;
  border: 1px solid #ccd1d9;
  border-radius: 0 0 5px 5px;
  border-top: 0;
  box-shadow: 5px 5px 10px rgba(0,0,0,0.2);
  position: absolute;
  width: 198px;
}

.transformSelectDropdown span {
  cursor: pointer;
  display: block;
  padding: 0.222em 0.5em;
}

.transformSelectDropdown span:hover {
  background: #ccecf8;
}

.transformSelectDropdown li:last-child span {
  border-radius: 0 0 5px 5px;
}
```

This is all pretty straightforward—no magic tricks here. Refresh the page in the browser and you'll see that we've got a perfectly styled drop-down form element, as shown in the following screenshot:

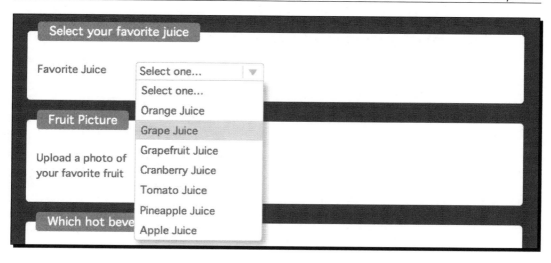

9. Next up, let's tackle that file input. This is one of the toughest elements to style as it looks wildly different in different browsers. In your `scripts.js` file, select all file inputs and call the `transformFile()` method, as follows:

```
$(document).ready(function(){
    $('select').transformSelect();
    $(':file').transformFile();
});
```

What does `:file` mean? That's one of the shortcut selectors that jQuery makes available for us. Using the `:file` selector is the same as using the following line of code:

```
input[type='file']
```

However, it requires a lot less typing.

Refresh the page in the browser, and you'll see that the file input is now replaced by a bit of text, as shown in the following screenshot:

Clicking on the text opens up your system file dialog to allow you to browse and find a file to upload. Just like with the select drop-down box, we've got the functionality down; we just have to write some CSS to make it look the way we'd like.

10. First, we'll style the wrapper element that contains our styleable version of the file input. Add the following lines to `styles.css`:

```
.customInput {
  cursor: pointer;
  display: inline-block;
  vertical-align: middle;
}

.customInput:after {
  clear: both;
  content: '';
  display: table;
}
```

See how we've styled the `:after` pseudoclass? This is just a way of clearing floats—we're going to be floating the elements inside this container, and we want to make sure they are cleared.

11. Next, we'll style the element that will show the path to the file we've selected. In `styles.css`, add the following lines:

```
.inputPath {
  border: 1px solid #ccd1d9;
  border-right: 0 none;
  border-radius: 5px 0 0 5px;
  color: #656d78;
  cursor: pointer;
  display: block;
  float: left;
  padding: 0.222em;
  width: 188px;
}

.customInputMouseOver .inputPath {
  border-color: #addf7a;
}
```

Refresh the page in the browser and you'll see that we're getting there—our file input looks half-styled, as shown in the following screenshot:

**12.** Now, we'll style the button part of the element. Add the following lines to
`styles.css`:

```css
.inputButton {
  background: #a1d36e;
  border: 1px solid #a1d36e;
  border-radius: 0 5px 5px 0;
  color: white;
  cursor: pointer;
  display: block;
  float: left;
  padding: 0.222em 0.75em;
  -webkit-transition: background 300ms;
  -moz-transition: background 300ms;
  -ms-transition: background 300ms;
  -o-transition: background 300ms;
  transition: background 300ms;
}

.custonInputMouseOver .inputButton {
  background: #addf7a;
}
```

Now, if you refresh the page in the browser, you'll see that our file input is styled
consistently with our other form elements, and even better, has a consistent style
when viewed in different browsers.

That wasn't so hard, right? Let's keep going.

**13.** Let's take a look at the checkboxes. Just like with the other elements, our first step in customizing their appearance is to open up our `scripts.js` file, select the elements we want to work with, and call the right transform method. Inside the document ready statement, add the following bit of code:

```
$(':checkbox').transformCheckbox({
  base: 'class',
  trigger: 'parent'
});
```

Once again, we've used jQuery's shortcut selector (`:checkbox`) to select all the checkboxes on the page. Then, we called the `transformCheckbox()` method, but this time, we passed a few options to the method.

First, the `transformCheckbox()` method requires us to specify a `base` option. This option has two possible values: `class` or `image`. If we choose the `class` option, then the Fancyform plugin adds a `<span>` element with a class to our document, and we can style that with CSS to our heart's content. If we choose the `image` option, then Fancyform will replace our checkboxes with an image. We'd then have to set a few more options—one for the image path for a checked checkbox and one for an unchecked checkbox.

The `image` option is a lot less flexible, and it requires loading up at least two additional resources on our page. With the power of CSS3 on our side, there's not much we can't accomplish if we choose the `class` option.

Second, the `trigger` option also has two possible values: `self` or `parent`. With the `self` option, clicking only on the checkbox itself will result in the checkbox being checked. With the `parent` option, clicking anywhere on the parent element will check the checkbox. That's a lot easier for our site visitors, so we'll go with the `parent` option.

If you refresh the page in the browser, you'll see that the checkboxes have simply disappeared, as shown in the following screenshot:

While not visible, our checkboxes have been replaced by `<span>` elements. Now, we just have to write a bit of CSS to style them.

**14.** In `styles.css`, add the following lines to style the `<span>` elements:

```
.trans-element-checkbox {
  border: 1px solid #ccd1d9;
  border-radius: 3px;
  display: inline-block;
  height: 1em;
  margin: 0 0.5em 0 0;
  position: relative;
  vertical-align: text-bottom;
  width: 1em;
}

.trans-element-checkbox.checked {
  background-color: #ccecf8;
  border-color: #55c1e7;
}
```

Refresh the page in the browser, and you'll see our empty checkboxes appear. Click on the checkbox or the text next to it, and you'll see that the box turns blue with a blue border, as shown in the following screenshot:

At least it's an indicator that a box has been clicked, but our site visitors will no doubt be accustomed to seeing a tick mark appear in the checkboxes.

**15.** We'll use a well-known icon font, Font Awesome, to create the tick marks in our checkboxes. Head over to `http://fortawesome.github.io/Font-Awesome/` and click on the **Download** button to grab a ZIP file.

Unzip the file. Copy the `fonts` folder to your own project file, where it will sit alongside your `styles` and `scripts` folders. Then, open the `css` folder and copy `font-awesome.css` to your own `styles` folder. Now, your project files should look like those shown in the following screenshot:

16. In the head section of the HTML document, add the Font Awesome style sheet, before your own `styles.css` file:

```html
<head>
    <title>Chapter 12: jQuery for Designers</title>
    <link rel="stylesheet" href="styles/font-awesome.css">
    <link rel="stylesheet" href="styles/styles.css">
</head>
```

Now, the Font Awesome icon font is all loaded up on our page and ready to use.

17. Now, head back into `styles.css` and we'll add a bit of code to show tick marks in the checkboxes, as follows:

```css
.trans-element-checkbox.checked:before {
    content: '\f00c';
    font-family: 'FontAwesome';
    height: 1em;
    left: 50%;
    margin: -0.7em 0 0 -0.5em;
    position: absolute;
    top: 50%;
    width: 1em;
}
```

Now, if you refresh the page in the browser, you'll see that clicking on the checkboxes turns them blue and shows a tick mark, as shown in the following screenshot:

Perfect! Just what our site visitors will expect. The good news is that as we're using CSS and an icon font to create our checkboxes, we can make them any size, and they'll appear on the page crisp and clear, even on retina displays.

18. Now, let's tackle those radio buttons. They function and are styled very similarly to the checkboxes. First, in the `scripts.js` file, add the following bit of code inside the document ready statement to replace the radio buttons with spans that we can style:

```
$(':radio').transformRadio({
  base: 'class',
  trigger: 'parent'
});
```

This is very similar to the code we used for checkboxes.

19. Next, let's add some styles for the radio buttons. In `styles.css`, add the following lines of code:

```
.trans-element-radio {
  border: 1px solid #ccd1d9;
  border-radius: 50%;
  display: inline-block;
  height: 1em;
  margin: 0 0.5em 0 0;
  position: relative;
  vertical-align: text-bottom;
  width: 1em;
}

.trans-element-radio.checked {
  border-color: #55c1e7;
}
```

```
.trans-element-radio.checked:before {
  color: #55c1e7;
  content: '\f111';
  font-family: 'FontAwesome';
  font-size: 0.8em;
  height: 1em;
  left: 50%;
  line-height: 1;
  margin: -0.45em 0 0 -0.5em;
  position: absolute;
  text-align: center;
  top: 50%;
  width: 1em;
}
```

Once again, there are a lot of similarities between this CSS code and the CSS we used for checkboxes. We used a 50 percent border radius for the radio buttons as they are usually circular rather than squared. We also used a different icon from Font Awesome for the checked state of the radio buttons. Refresh the page in the browser, and you'll see that the radio buttons behave as expected when we click on them, as shown in the following screenshot:

Just like with the checkboxes, we can easily resize the radio buttons to any size we might like. We are also free to experiment with border colors, sizes or colors, background colors or gradients, box shadows, and so on to get just the appearance we need for our design, and the design will appear consistently across different browsers.

**20.** Now, the only thing left to style is the text area and the reset button that weren't styled earlier. Inside `styles.css`, add the following lines to style these elements:

```
textarea {
  border: 1px solid #ccd1d9;
  border-radius: 5px;
  color: #656d78;
  font-family: inherit;
  font-size: inherit;
  padding: 0.333em;
  transition: border 300ms;
}

textarea:focus {
  border-color: #656d78;
  outline: none;
}

input[type='reset'] {
  background: #ccd1d9;
  border: 0 none;
  border-radius: 5px;
  color: white;
  cursor: pointer;
  font-family: inherit;
  font-size: inherit;
  padding: 0.333em 1em;
  transition: background 300ms;
}

input[type='reset']:hover {
  background: #a5aebc;
}
```

Now, if you refresh the page in the browser, you'll see that all of our form elements are styled consistently and appear the same across browsers, as shown in the following screenshot. Great work!

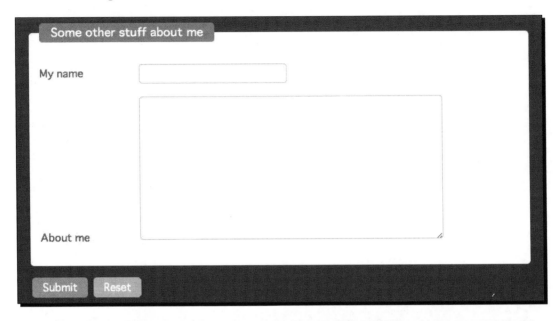

## Have a go hero – a fully custom form

Combine what you've learned about form validation with the Validation plugin and what you've learned about customizing form elements with the Fancyform plugin to create a new form. Design a custom style for all elements in the form (be sure to use some of the unstyleable form elements) and also make custom validation rules for the fields in the form.

# Summary

Well, this wraps up the chapter on forms. We learned how to properly use the new HTML5 form elements to create a form that functions perfectly and is accessible to boot. We learned how to focus the first field in the form, validate our site visitor's form input, and style those stubborn and notoriously unstyleable form elements. Now, you've got an arsenal of tools on your side to create gorgeous-looking forms that enhance your site visitors' experience on your site. And the best of all, they all degrade gracefully for users with JavaScript disabled as we approached our forms with the progressive enhancement mindset—by first building a working form, and then layering in enhancements for site visitors whose browsers support them.

I know that JavaScript can be a scary subject for designers. Kudos to you for sticking with me to the end of the book! I hope that you now have a basic understanding of jQuery and feel sure that you'll be able to tackle your next JavaScript challenge with confidence. You know how to put the jQuery library to good use to enhance your sites. You know how to find good plugins to make coding interactions quick and easy. You know how CSS and JavaScript can work together to enhance the site visitor's experience on your site. You also know that there is no shortage of online tutorials, resources, help forums, articles, and discussions to help you along if you get stuck.

For its part, jQuery gets better with every release—sleeker, faster, and more capable. The jQuery team is careful to keep the documentation updated, so you'll always be able to figure out just how to use each method. The jQuery team is smart and quick, and new jQuery updates are being announced on a regular schedule. All of this points to a lively and useful library that will only continue to grow in popularity across the Web. It's a favorite of many coders, from experienced hackers to beginners like you.

I hope that you've enjoyed this book and that it's given you many new ideas to design and build interactive elements for your sites. Be sure to stay connected to the jQuery community—it will be your best resource moving forward while further improving and growing your JavaScript skills.

# Pop Quiz Answers

## Chapter 1, Designer, Meet jQuery

### Pop quiz – setting up a new project

| | |
|---|---|
| Q1 | 1 |

## Chapter 2, Enhancing Links

### Pop quiz – working with events

| | |
|---|---|
| Q1 | 5 |
| Q2 | 2 |

## Chapter 4, Building an Interactive Navigation Menu

### Pop quiz – understanding the cascade in CSS

| | |
|---|---|
| Q1 | 4 |

## Chapter 5, Showing Content in Lightboxes

**Pop quiz – loading content into Colorbox**

| Q1 | 1 |
|----|---|

## Chapter 6, Creating Slideshows and Sliders

**Pop quiz – working with jQuery chaining**

| Q1 | 3 |
|----|---|

## Chapter 7, Working with Responsive Designs

**Pop quiz – choosing breakpoints for responsive design**

| Q1 | 3 |
|----|---|

## Chapter 8, Getting the Most from Images

**Pop quiz – building accessible pages**

| Q1 | 5 |
|----|---|

## Chapter 9, Improving Typography

**Pop quiz – sizing text in responsive designs**

| Q1 | 3 |
|----|---|

# Chapter 10, Displaying Data Beautifully

## Pop quiz – building correct tables

| Q1 | 3 |
|----|---|

# Chapter 11, Reacting to Scrolling

## Pop quiz – using Scrollorama in responsive design

| Q1 | 3 |
|----|---|

# Chapter 12, Improving Forms

## Pop quiz – working with HTML5 form elements

| Q1 | 1 |
|----|---|

# Index

fitText() method  245, 246
fitText option  265
FitVids
   URL  190
   used, for fitting videos in responsive
      designs  186-192
fitVids() method  192
fixed size
   setting, for Colorbox  106
focus() method  343
Font Awesome
   URL  363
for attribute  334, 347
form
   first field, selecting  342, 343
   user entry, validating  343-350
form appearance
   Fancyform plugin, using  354-368
   improving  350-354
form elements  350
Frequently Asked Questions. *See* **FAQ page**
fullscreen background image
   challenges  233
   creating  233-238
fullscreen slideshow
   creating  239-241
function, JavaScript  14

## G

GitHub
   URL  41
graceful degradation, JavaScript  10
graphs
   creating, from HTML tables  279-288
   height, setting  295-298
   width, setting  295-298

## H

hamburger  193
headlines
   sizing, to screen width  244-247
horizontal animation
   creating, in windy weather forecast  319, 320
horizontal drop-down menu
   about  78
   creating  78-85

hoverIntent plugin  94, 95
HTML
   setting up, for Scrollorama  307-309
HTML5 specs
   URL  66
HTML5 web form
   about  331, 332
   pop quiz  342
   setting up  332-342
HTML document
   setting up, for scrolling effect addition  301-307
HTML file, FAQ page
   setting up  64-66
HTML tables
   charts, creating from  279-287
   graphs, creating from  279-287

## I

id attribute  332
ImageOptim
   URL  234
image option  362
images
   fullscreen backgrounds, using  233
   lazy loading images  219
   transition, modifying between  105
   zoomable images, creating  226
initialHeight setting  107
initialWidth setting  107
innerHeight setting  106
innerWidth setting  106
Internet Explorer (IE)  17
itemSelector option  213

## J

JavaScript
   about  12
   basics  10
   function  14
   moving, from one element to other  67-69
   objects  12, 13
   variables  12
JavaScript basics
   graceful degradation  10
   progressive enhancement  10
   web pages, behavior  11

# Thank you for buying
# jQuery for Designers Beginner's Guide
## *Second Edition*

## About Packt Publishing

Packt, pronounced 'packed', published its first book "*Mastering phpMyAdmin for Effective MySQL Management*" in April 2004 and subsequently continued to specialize in publishing highly focused books on specific technologies and solutions.

Our books and publications share the experiences of your fellow IT professionals in adapting and customizing today's systems, applications, and frameworks. Our solution based books give you the knowledge and power to customize the software and technologies you're using to get the job done. Packt books are more specific and less general than the IT books you have seen in the past. Our unique business model allows us to bring you more focused information, giving you more of what you need to know, and less of what you don't.

Packt is a modern, yet unique publishing company, which focuses on producing quality, cutting-edge books for communities of developers, administrators, and newbies alike. For more information, please visit our website: www.packtpub.com.

## About Packt Open Source

In 2010, Packt launched two new brands, Packt Open Source and Packt Enterprise, in order to continue its focus on specialization. This book is part of the Packt Open Source brand, home to books published on software built around Open Source licenses, and offering information to anybody from advanced developers to budding web designers. The Open Source brand also runs Packt's Open Source Royalty Scheme, by which Packt gives a royalty to each Open Source project about whose software a book is sold.

## Writing for Packt

We welcome all inquiries from people who are interested in authoring. Book proposals should be sent to author@packtpub.com. If your book idea is still at an early stage and you would like to discuss it first before writing a formal book proposal, contact us; one of our commissioning editors will get in touch with you.

We're not just looking for published authors; if you have strong technical skills but no writing experience, our experienced editors can help you develop a writing career, or simply get some additional reward for your expertise.

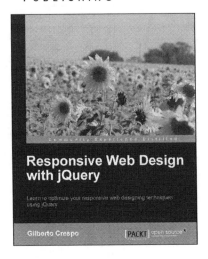

## Responsive Web Design with jQuery

ISBN: 978-1-78216-360-2      Paperback: 256 pages

Learn to optimize your responsive web designing techniques using jQuery

1. Learn to swiftly design responsive websites by harnessing the power of jQuery.

2. Get your responsive site ready to meet the device-agnostic world.

3. Display highlighted content in a carousel and implement touch gestures to control them.

4. Understand the mobile-first philosophy and put its concept into practice.

## jQuery UI Cookbook

ISBN: 978-1-78216-218-6      Paperback: 290 pages

70 recipes to create responsive and engaging user interfaces in jQuery

1. Packed with recipes showing UI developers how to get the most out of their jQuery UI widgets.

2. Solutions to real-world development issues distilled down in a reader-friendly approach.

3. Code examples written in a concise and elegant format making it easy for the reader to adapt to their own style.

Please check **www.PacktPub.com** for information on our titles

## Learning jQuery
### Fourth Edition

ISBN: 978-1-78216-314-5       Paperback: 444 pages

Better interaction, design, and web development
with simple JavaScript techniques

1.  An introduction to jQuery that requires minimal
    programming experience.

2.  Detailed solutions to specific client-side problems.

3.  Revised and updated version of this popular
    jQuery book.

## jQuery Hotshot

ISBN: 978-1-84951-910-6       Paperback: 296 pages

Ten practical projects that exercise your skill, build
your confidence, and help you master jQuery

1.  See how many of jQuery's methods and properties
    are used in real situations. Covers jQuery 1.9.

2.  Learn to build jQuery from source files, write jQuery
    plugins, and use jQuery UI and jQuery Mobile.

3.  Familiarize yourself with the latest related
    technologies such as HTML5 and CSS3 and
    frameworks such as Knockout.js.

Please check **www.PacktPub.com** for information on our titles

Made in the USA
San Bernardino, CA
14 March 2016